Morning Bird

Songs
Daily Words from Heaven!

by

Herticine Goree

Copyright © 2022 Herticine Goree

All rights reserved. No part of this publication may be reproduced, distributed, or transmitted in any form or by any means, including photocopying, recording, or other electronic or mechanical methods, without the prior written permission of the publisher, except in the case of brief quotations embodied in critical reviews and certain other noncommercial uses permitted by copyright law.

ISBN-978-1-951300-67-8

Liberation's Publishing LLC
West Point - Mississippi

Morning Bird

Songs
Daily Words from Heaven!

Morning Bird Songs – *Daily words from heaven!*

Table of Content

Introduction 1

Songbirds in the Garden.. 3

The Voices of the Morning.. 6

Memories in the Wind... 8

Webbed In Lies... 10

Learning to Trust.. 13

Awakening.. 15

Morning Mysteries.. 17

Because of Love... 19

Learning... 20

Picture of Life in Jesus' Hands..................................... 22

When Sin Sleeps with You 24

Silly to Man 25

The Eyes of Heaven 27

Guilty Party 29

Jesus Lives... 31

The Enemy in Your House.. 33

Sin Bites 35

Never Satisfied... 38

Trusting 40

Good Morning... 42

A Different World	44
Gifts Are to Be Used	45
Listening	47
Crying	49
God Is Not Blind	51
My Redeemer	54
Always Amazed	56
I'm Sorry Lord	58
My Rock	60
Hidden Gifts	61
Rejoicing	62
Forgiven	64
Set Apart	65
Not Abandoned	67
Heart of Tears	69
Visiting	72
Word of Encouragement	74
Rescue Me	76
You Are Good	78
Pages of Life	80
Only God's Voice	82
Lazy Day Breeze	84
96 and 1	86

Standing in Truth	88
Who God Says I am	90
My Own Faith	91
Walk With Me Lord	93
Heavenly Confession	95
New Morning	97
All Around Me I See Jesus	100
Jesus' Love	102
Somebody's Child	105
Hugs of The Morning	107
One Road Leads to Jesus	110
Promises Without Holes	113
The Aroma of Love	115
Unquenchable	116
Through The Eyes of a Child	118
Words of Harm	120
Playing Church	122
Why I Do What I do	124
Crooked Steps	126
Booster Club for Christ	128
What Do I Want for Mother's Day	130
But What If ... But What	131
Elm Tree	132

Portrait of Heaven	134
Ballroom Dance	136
Walking In Forgiveness	138
Jesus Is Worthy of My Boasting	141
The Reason I Sing	143
Hearing God	146
Old Saying	148
Song In the Wind	150
Seeking	152
Singing	154
Two Cities	156
Two Cities Part 2	158
Lord Is My Light	159
Eyes On Man	162
Song of the Morning	163
Testimony	165
Sunrise of Promise	167
If I Would Have	169
Wisdom	172
Confidence	174
Passover	175
Praise The Lord	176
Love Never Fails	179

God Sees	181
Attention Please	183
Same Tree	184
Early Morning Sunrise	186
Morning Praise	188
Memories of Love	190
Songs of the Night	191
Hello Morning	192
Words Make a Difference	194
Laughter	196
The Spirit of the Lord	198
God Hears	199
Awaken	201
Journey to Freedom	203
Written Pages	205
Feeding Fear	206
Morning Paradise	208
Song of the Morning	210
Welcome	212
Walking with God	214
Stillness	216
Wanderer	218
Humble	220

Testimonies 222

Guidance 224

Student 226

Tears In a Bottle 228

Rooted 229

Shelter 231

Words 232

Conjugal 234

Enemy Is Loud 236

Times of Troubles 237

Fishing 239

Kind Words 241

Fear Fades with Praise 242

Judge Ye Not 244

Servant's Heart 246

Rewards 247

No Retirement 248

Too Often 249

Home 251

Bowing Down 252

Kindness 253

Hidden Gifts 255

Hope 257

Traps of the World	259
Sweet Aroma	261
Victory In Jesus	263
Compassion	265
Memories	267
Lemon Day	269
Taking A Break	270
No More Putting Jesus in a Box	272
Praise Songs	274
Call Unto Me	276
Friendship	278
Staying with the Familiar	280
Rainbow Promises	282
He Is Mine	283
In God's Presence	285
Love Affair	286
Guard My Lips	287
Word Fulfilled	288
Planted in God's Soil	289
Listening	291
Winds of the Morning	292
Only God's Way	294
Sounds of Trouble	296

Blot Them Out Lord 298

Plans For My Life...300

Not 303

Remembering 305

Surrounded By Love..307

Unfailing Promises 310

Look Lord 311

Foolishness Blinds..312

No Other God..314

My Prayer 317

Feelings 319

Lost 321

A Word of Encouragement in Times of Weariness 323

Sadden 325

Your Gifts 326

Who Am I 327

Introduction

God knew us before time began. He knew when He wanted each of us to be born. He knew what He was creating us to be, and the time we would fulfill our destiny in this life. As a child, I always walked among the grass on the meadow, and sat among the grass to  see the butterfly move gracefully from blossom to blossom on flowers and weeds. Their wings spread wide with the most amazing colors. Man cannot create the paint to paint the butterfly's beauty on canvas.

Hearing the birds sing before dawn and the bugs singing me to sleep at night are in my memories of yesterday's walk with God in nature. God touched me with joy and peace as I heard the wind singing through the chimes, the trees waltzing with the breeze, the birds singing with the tone of the wind. The sun rays are like light on a ballroom floor as it directs each step-in time with Jesus' heartbeat of love. This is why I desire to share the *Morning Bird Song Daily Word from Heaven* with others.

God speaks and shows Himself through His creation surrounding us. Take a moment each day to hear God speak to you through His creations, He shows His love through each song of the bird.

"Yahweh your God is among you, warrior who saves. He will rejoice over you with gladness. He will bring you quietness with His

love. He will delight in you with shouts of joy." Zephaniah 3:17

Songbirds in the Garden

"Look at the birds of the air; they do not sow or reap or store away in barns, and yet your heavenly Father feeds them. Are you not much more valuable than they?" Matthew 6:26 KJV

In Jesus' Garden of wonders is where I spent my childhood not even knowing Jesus was teaching me to love the beauty of His handiwork. Being in the school of Jesus is where I learned to hear His acceptance of me instead of the remarks of man concerning who I was as a child compared to others. The Joy of His beauty kept me company while I climbed the hills in the green meadow where the cricket danced. Assurance of His love kept me safe. Within myself were negative words that were not allowed to grow roots of inferiority.

Roaming the hills and valleys of the family's land each day brought revelations I took for granted. Mainly, I thought everyone had visions, and dreamed dreams of heavenly things. Dreams of the wonders around me rather than faraway lands of city lights fill my days. Loneliness was never a part of my days because Jesus entertained me with wonders all around me from grass with butterfly swaying like a swing in the breeze, to vines of maypops climbing the tree as the summer worms ate their leaves. I thought if I dreamed beautiful dreams everyone did. If I saw beauty in a butterfly, everyone did. If I enjoyed an onion from the garden everyone did.

The apple trees on the hill where we chopped cotton called to me to sit and taste the sweetness of God's apple planted as a seed becoming a harvest. Maypops row by row made a path of popcorn sounds in the summer months as we walked to the fields, and mushroom softness in the fall as we returned to gather the crops. Seeing a seed planted as one and then bringing a harvest to feed a hungry crew of children, was a wow factor to me.

The worm wrapped in a cocoon during the summer crops then turning into a butterfly to fold and die to live again in springtime. God prepared it to survive the coming winter. The ants moving across my feet and biting my hand as I wiped them from the sweet tea jar left in the hot field bag showed me little things hurt too. The grasshoppers standing one legged on the stall of cotton as the cool fall wind pushed back and forward, what a showoff! Bees buzzing on the red coves occasionally stung the ones not wearing shoes. My safety pinned flip flop kept my feet from harm until the safety pin pooped open and the pin stung. What amazing walk-in times of yesteryears.

A journey to the crawdad hole when fish were hiding from the morning heat, and the crawdad were looking for something to hang on to come from the noonday water...were my playmates of the day. But my they could bite...

Each adventure of the day carried me to the seeking fountain. I was thirsty for more of God's 'beautiful show' of His wonders to beheld. Eyes of wonderments, ears of amazements, heart of repertory longing for what I did not know I was longing for. As the sun dance beautifully over the morning, to noonday shadow so I could place my feet on my head, to the eastern sky where everything during the day is longing for a nighttime rest. And even me from my busy day.

My heart wasn't satisfied because I knew that there was more, I needed to see...But what? As night closed around me and suppertime calling, I took my time coming to supper trying to count the stars which were too many to count. My body going round and around trying to see what I missed, even to thinking I was seeing a man in the moon... Oh the fascinated fantasies of a child's mind of undiscovered wonders.

The Morning bird's Song has called me from sleep since the time I can remember. The birds of all kinds flying through the sky during the day, singing a nighttime song at night, and the bats awakening from a day's rest to clean up the day's mess left behind.

Amazingly, the birds' songs of the morning woke my seeking heart to hear and see heaven singing a wake-up song to my sleeping spirit. God was speaking to my heart, but I didn't know it was Him. My eyes were touched with the loveliness of the morning sun looking through the horizon to see who was seeking the beauty of a new day. I didn't know it was Him.

The birds in the barnyard danced a twirling gig through the hay as playing children play during the day. The crows peaking at the warm dropped cow dungs was a nasty sight to me. The morning bugs flying over the misty water as I waited to see if a fish would jump up to receive its morning meal. The worms crawling in and out from damp soil of morning to be caught for the fishing pole later on before the hot noonday sun. No ticks to buy poison to kill the many chickens ate each one for their morning meal.

The birds sang songs smoothing to the weary soul until it was time to walk a mile to work in the fields under the hills. Never afraid to walk the pasture and the 'look out mountains' because the train dog took care of us children. Even more so, Jesus walked with me as He was teaching me to see Him as I made my daily rounds of seeking to see beauty from the grass to the dry hay. The chick pushed through the shell bringing life to save life from hunger since I loved eggs rather than meat; even to the snake eggs I wanted to kill with my safety pin flip flop...

From safety pin flip flop to visions of sheep in the pasture Jesus chose me as a child to see Him in the midst of His beautiful creations. This is the reason I'm rejoicing over the morning bird song...

The Voices of the Morning

Sing a new song to the LORD; sing to the LORD, all the earth. Psalm 96:1
Sing a new song to the LORD, for He has performed wonders; His right hand and holy arm have won Him victory. Psalm 98:1

Good morning, sunrise welcoming me to a new day of song, of heaven. Songs no man can write. Songs no man can play or sing. Songs of the morning singing a new song greeting me as I walk joyfully into a new day of wonders ahead of me. Only God knows what lies ahead. Good morning, wonderful day the Lord has created and prepared for me to rejoice in. He knows what lies before me and have held back the plans of the enemy, because I am His and He is mine. Thank you, Holy Spirit, for the morning song of the birds, the songs only they can sing and rejoice in.

Good morning, my people! Have you heard the robin song this morning? Did you hear the chickadee singing through the night. Did you hear and see the red cardinal singing a song as its feed his young? Good morning, trees housing the goldfinch and letting your leaves lift them in ballerina pirouette in harmony with the songs of the wind. Good morning grosbeak sing with the wind beneath your wings.

Good morning, hawks flying high in the sky... Can you see God from your lofty height? You trust God because you are soaring with the wind. Good morning beautiful martins swirling in the new sunlight of the morning, in lovely dance. Sing your praises to God, but may I sing with you the new song of the morning? Dance praises before the Lord this lovely morning sun rays on the tree leaves. Blossom sweet fragrances as the morning dew bathe you with a heavenly bath of God's aroma. Soar above the clouds beautiful hawk. God sees your morning praises and see your lovely dance in the wind.

Have you even seen a bird dance in the water after a rain? Have you ever seen a dove' eye follow you as walk nearby? Have the even seen the noonday birds play shadow games in the grass? Have you ever wondered why the birds sing as you frown in worries? Have you ever wondered why the birds don't have a doctor's office and why the lilies don't go shopping? God have and He is singing over us to give you peace and clothes us in His love. The birds have no worries because Jesus said so, worries bring doctor visits. The lilies trust God in the wind, and He clothes them beautifully. The birds have food to eat because Jesus feeds them. The lilies have clothes to wear because Jesus clothes them. The birds have a house and shelter in the storm. Jesus shelters and protects them, and He sees when a sparrow falls.

Are you not more than the birds? In weariness God sends a love song of comfort through the birds, they are His mouthpiece... Have you listened to the song Jesus wants you to hear so you can trust Him as the birds? Have you heard the whip-poor-will? Jesus is singing His peace over you when you turn to fear and worrying during the night, the whip-poor-will song breaks chases row enemy. Listen and hear the Savior speaking, don't you hear Him? Listen to the whip-poor-will, God is singing a song of love and rest. The nightingales are singing to calm you from the stress the enemy have pour over you. Sing nightingale the song from the storehouse of God's peace in heaven. Sing the joy song to quietening weary souls.

Mockingbirds sing the song of midnight so sleep will stay when it is trying to escape into the bedroom of comfort and peace. God created everything we need in times of pleasures and sorrow. Everything around us speaks of His glory. The birds are one of the creation God created to bring joy and peace as we walk through the life of ups and downs. Singing bring joy. Jesus sang with His disciples, and they were only in fear and worrying when they couldn't see Jesus face to face. Only when Jesus out the disciple's sight did they fall into despair.

Each day, the Holy Spirit lets us know He is near. Paul wrote God did not give us the spirit of fear. Why should my heart be troubled with when there is no place, I can go that Jesus isn't there. Psalm 139 gives a very good picture of us never walking alone. The morning bird song is a clear example of Jesus' promises for each of us... *"I will never leave you or forsake you."* The birds are our example to follow Jesus. He is the song of peace in the valley of the shadow of death...He wants us to sing as we walk through weary time and the enemy will be defeated as they were when Jehoshaphat sang in 2 Chronicles 20.

Memories in the Wind

"Be strong and courageous. Do not be afraid or terrified because of them, for the LORD your God goes with you, he will never leave you nor forsake you."
Deuteronomy 31:6

The wind sings the memories of my walks with God. My mind is reminiscing the Wednesday, December 14, 2011, the sixty-third year of my birth...I allowed the Holy Spirit to take me on a quiet walk with Him. However, there were communications between He and nature relayed to me. He showed me clearly there will be storms in this life...however; it is up to each of us how we will carry/walk through each. Nevertheless, we will surely go through them...but how will we go through the storm? That is the question.

Standing in faith that God's Word is true...He will never leave me...nor forsake me. Or allow the storm to bend us over in doubts and fears...that God's promises are not true? But rest assure, the storm will not fade if you are in faith or fear until it is over.

On this walk, the Holy Spirit took me to the pond...the water was clear, and the sun rays were dancing on the windy waves. The ducks were floating freely and lovely on ripple...so it seemed. Wherever the waves moved... the duck flowed with them...the beauty of obedience was amazing and peaceful to look upon. The ducks were submitting themselves to the will of their Creator. They were trusting Him on the windy waves...they were trusting Him to be their Guide and Provider...they were trusting in Him because He was their compass in the wind...as He is also ours.

Then I heard once again, this sweet whisper of reassurance. "No matter the battle...no matter the struggle... no matter the pain...no matter the many disappointments... no matter the storm you are in...I Am the Compass which guides you in each storm." So, on this sixty- third year of my birth...I allowed God to carry me on the windy waves of this day...because I know my arms are too weak... although, God's is not too short...to go against the wind. Moreover, God's arms can calm each ripple on the water. How will I go through the storms of life? I choose to go standing in faith.... because bending over in the battles of life causes pain to the back.

Happy sixty-third Birthday to me, and Thank You, God My Father for keeping and holding me these many years! I know also what heaven began in me the devil can't stop.

Listen carefully, some of you are lying in bed in a darkened room of pity because of troubles of the past storm. Guess what? God is there with you, just look up because He is the Light that lights the darken places so you can see your way out! He is the Guild in the valley, He is the sight in the grown grass, He is the hoe which removes the weeds from the path, He is the Force the wind cannot come through, He is all and all because with All nothing can be added.

Also, some of you think you are climbing an upward battle hill that you will never get it over. Guess what? God didn't say to go over the valley, He said He would carry you through the valley. Reach out your hand from the locked cell you are in right now and God will unlock each one, because heaven's plans for your life must take place. Remember, the devil is under God's authority don't be afraid.

Webbed In Lies

No. No! You will not die," the serpent said to the woman. Genesis 3:5

A Spider spins a web each night in the place where it was swept down the day before. Satan's web of doubts and lies are spun daily to keep many blinded to God's blessings and truths. So, right now, do you actually know how blessed you are? You have food on your table when your neighbor can't buy milk. You have three cars, when your neighbor is walking to work. You have a hundred pairs of shoes, when your neighbor has one pair with a pin holding them together. Your knees get sore after your daily walk, when your neighbor's feet are too swollen to walk. You are healed from walking pneumonia when your neighbor is dying of bronchitis.

You frown on a couple who chose to have an abundance of children, when your neighbor can't have done (any). You buy an outfit for each special occasion, when your neighbor is not invited and if he was, he would have nothing to wear. So, do you know how actually blessed you are? With each new day God allows you to choose Him if you haven't. And be thankful because you are blessed with another day to make a choice to follow Jesus!

Time is short, but Satan has blinded too many that they can wait another day to come to Jesus, "you have time" he says. Each heartbeat is a blessing, but the next one isn't promised. Don't try to count your blessings one by one because it will take you a lifetime. But do thank God for the things He has done for you by your walk, talk, and actions. Life is not a movie which has reruns, life is your young todays turning into old tomorrows. We die once and judgment is made Hebrews 9:27 states, "Life is beautiful because God is our Life Source."

So, tell me why are so many listening to Baal's lies that an unborn baby is better off dead? Every person wanting to pull life from the womb before the baby is allowed to say hello to the world. This is a web of lies from the enemy and God's truth have been thrown aside. The birds sing a new song each morning giving praise to their Creator for another chance to fly high into the sky

Rejoicing in life given, the bird's egg is not aborted. Man will catch an egg from bird's nest and keep it warm until the baby come, is the bird more important than a human baby? Yet, man takes a knife and cutaway the life of a child as if it will be a heartache to the world. Heaven sends life from above, yet man hears and obeys the voice of the one below. Weep for the babies as the mourning dove weep over the loss of its mate. Heaven sends songs from above for us to sing. Don't you think heaven cry tears for the lack of love for a life sent from above? Spiders web webs to catch its prey. Jesus held love in His hand on the cross to set mankind free of the lies of the enemy. Forgive us Father for believing the webbed lie against the innocent babies You created, but man's webbed mind wants to do it his way. I am sorry Lord. Amen.

Learning to Trust

Look, I am coming like a thief. The one who is alert and remains clothed so that he may not go around naked, and people see his shame is blessed. Revelation 16:15

Good morning daylight, the birds are singing an early morning prelude to your arrival. Good morning blue sky the clouds passed over for the sunlight to come forth. Good morning, green grass not growing back by man's hands. Good morning shadows on the barn door made by sunlight reflecting through the trees. Hello, breath from God and thank You for Your guiding light. Good morning Heavenly Father and thank You for Your reminder of Revelation 16:15 "Blessed is he that watcheth". But do I watch? Help me to be watchful and mindful of...

Good morning people with eyes not seeing, heart not believing, ears not hearing the Word that Jesus is coming. The birds of the air know Jesus is coming because they listen. The ants know He is coming because they are preparing. The clouds know He is coming because they carry Him. Jesus speaks and the clouds obey, and the thunder of His voice speaks to the storehouse of the lightning, and it moves across the horizon. The sun didn't forget to rise, and the moon didn't forget to fade to give the sun glory.

However, Jesus knew many faithful servants would forget to do the things He left for us to do...1 Corinthians 11:24 Jesus said to take communion as often in remembrance of Him. The reminders from heaven who gives life are constantly before us, but we fail to see, hear, feel, smell, and taste the goodness of God. Yet with His loving kindness Jesus reminds us to remember Him. Creation is God's gifts to each one who believes or don't believe because rain rains on the just as well as the unjust.

The birds wake me each morning with singing, unless there is danger from a storm. Then they remain silent. They hear God. Birds join together in a choir made-up of the obedient fowls of the air singing praise, praise to the Lord on high. The human choir is made up of four-part harmony, so is the bird choir. However, I believe there are more parts in a bird choir because there are so many sounds of the musical birds. The chorus singing, the just as well as the unjust. When I was in Israel during the month of the bird migration, which comes through Jerusalem. I have never seen so many different colors and kind of birds in my whole life. Songbirds and birds, I did not know existed were there in the trees, bushes, flowers, sidewalk, parking lots innumerous in numbers. Only God directs the birds to migrate through a place He has chosen as the New Heaven.

One day we, who follow Jesus will migrate from this place called earth to the New Jerusalem our final home. I see God as the sun rest on the top of the tree in mid-day, but more so, I see the smile of God as some of the tree sway with the breeze as the other nearby stand motionless...they hear God. Who can do such a wondrous thing other than God! I know I'm loved as the gentle breeze sweeps my skin like a sweet perfume as I seek God's presence in the coolness of the day. I look around and see the grass cut a few days before grown back for the bumblebee to feed from the nectar of the coves. I look and see one side of my flower leaning toward the sunlight while the other side fail to keep up with its growing. God is calling. Will we answer? Creation does.

God is speaking! Will we listen? God is watching! Do we see Him? God is singing with the wind! Are you receiving His gift of love? God is knocks but He doesn't enter where He is not welcome. Just like the sun makes shadows on the doors and roofs of my garage but it can't make a shadow on the cars if I don't open the doors to allow the sunlight to come in.

Years ago, darkness was my company from hurts and disappointments of the past, but I decided to open the door to my heart when Jesus was knocking to come in. The light didn't receive the darkness, the light made darkness fade. The shadows of false hope were dispelled when the light was welcome in. Yes, I see Jesus in everything around me because He opened my eyes as I prayed Ephesians 1:18 and my life haven't been the same. I see my spirit awaken through the song of the birds that sing the morning songs.

The birds follow where the sun goes each day. The birds listen when God calls for their migration of the year. They follow the voice of the Lord to Jerusalem each year when Jesus calls. Learn from the ways of the birds, when you listen and look closely, they will teach you to trust Jesus as your Guide.

Awakening

My love calls to me: arise, my darling. Come away, my beautiful one. For now, the winter is past; the rain has ended and gone away. Song of Song 2:10-11

Good morning sunrise as the crows sang songs calling forth the dawn. Good morning springtime as the winter sleeps and the spring awakes with aromas of praise. Good afternoon thunder bringing forth springtime showers. Goodbye winter as you take a long spring nap.

Hello new leaves on the tree. Welcome spring seeds bringing forth the joy of new birth. Fragrant flowers rejoice with beauty to a new season of God's love as God calls each bulb from its rest. "Rise up, my love, my fair one, and come away." Song of Song 2:10. God's love calls me from slumber to awaken me to the sweet fragrance of Jesus' calling me to blossom in His favor from the desires of my yesterdays.

I bathe in Jesus' wondrous sights of the morning; I'm carried back to the harvest fields of my upbringing. Crows were the predator of the planted seeds of the spring, summer, and fall crops of my father's fields, as scarecrows graced the fields dressed in clothes worn out through the years. The seeds called to the crows as my father called for the gun to scare them away. Planted seeds with poison covering were used to kill off the crows invading the fields planted with seeds of the spring...and scarecrows were planted in the fields that grew the fruits and vegetables. However, strange but true, the scarecrows scared me more than the crows, and they gave a hiding place to the ones sneaking in the vegetables fields to steal before my father arose to walk to the barn and check on the fields.

Times store memories of good and bad, the memories of good outweighs the bad. How is this? When the hand of God reaches down to lead us through the day is a good day. Thinking back over the years about crows and scarecrow God is speaking. Man sought to control the crows by planting seeds coated with poison. Not only did it rear the field of crows but many other birds. Morning after morning the songbirds and all types of birds would sing in the tree, barn, grass, on the fence during the day. The bats which flew at dust began to fade. The flying squirrels stop coming during dust of the early lite night. The owls stopped peeking through the trees they hoot was gone. No more did I hear the nightingales or whippoorwills; the frogs fail to croak because someone told man to kill the crows. The scarecrows left the fields that scared me rather than the crows. Then the Holy Spirit said, "Man's plans killed the crows, but I will restore their voices again." As I think of the scarecrow, I'm reminded that God did not give us the spirit of fear. Fear is false hope appearing real. The scarecrow couldn't talk, couldn't walk, couldn't move its hand so the crows sat on its head. Fearing what appears to be real can't harm or run us down. We can sit on fear's head because it's false hope created by man that the enemy have more power than Jesus had in His hands. Lies will be sat on by truth.

Morning Mysteries

I thought about my ways and turned my steps back to Your decrees. Psalm 119:59

Another good morning, this windy cloud laden sky as the birds sings as if waving the clouds to pass by. The flowers stems are pointing to the sky as each one is asking the clouds to stay and pour on them the gentle rain. The Corinthian bells sang as if singing in choir duet praises to the Lord beyond the clouds. Yes, this is a morning of God's many mysteries to come forth in praise of His grace. Each day amazes me with different sights I have not seen before. As I sit watching my disobedient dog, Sugar rejecting my call to come back from the road, a beautiful yellow and black bumblebee flew by seeking the holly tree nectar.

Then I recalled the joy of serving God, but there was a time I rejected His call like my wayward dog does each morning. I once was in a foreign land of sin and a lost heart filled with bitterness like the lemon tree bears bitter lemons, but God can use even bitter lemons. The bumblebee was my reminder of God taking what man treats as if there is no hope and make lemonade out of the bitterness to show the world that it can taste and see that He is good. After service today, I sat on my south side bench watching the clouds when a man walking on the road talking to himself decided he wanted a person he could see walked in my yard. With a bag in his hand and a long saber knife tired around his leg all the way to his knee as the top was hooked on his belt around his waist. He talked for a while then he began to curse as he talked about Jesus. I politely said, "Don't curse." "Oh, I'm sorry my queen." He was like the bumblebee, thinking he was a misfit because society told him so. He looked across my yard and said a few more things I didn't understand just before he left talking again to an invisible man. Darkness filled a place in his mind where light should be. Rejection has become his companion, as he felt grace and mercy had no place in his heart. As the cloud passed over and the sunlight is dancing and comforting the ground, I'm praying a warm word from my heart spoken to this man will come a part of his memory as he goes through this day and the ones to come. Also, a prayer is prayed for this hurting soul confused from war of mind, raging in uncertainties to be renewed with a mind knowing Jesus' love for him. Not despising himself because a war poured in his heart of hurts and pains of life, he didn't ask to have.

When I think of Jesus' love, I hear His parable of the lost sheep and coin in Luke 15. No one is forgotten by God. He runs us down with His love and sing over us. The prodigal son's father ran to meet him, which is usual for an elderly man in the Middle East. He kissed his son even with him smelling like the pigpen. Physical filth doesn't matter to God, it's the spiritual filth God frowns on. This wondering soul isn't hopeless, nothing is hopeless in God.

The bumblebee went into hiding in the holly bush, but it will return when it finishes its job. Sadly, a broken spirit and a hurting soul find rest in isolation and imaginary friends. Despair is a friend to the hurting. Weariness is a companion to the rejected. Wars always have casualties be it physical or spiritual lives are changed; God have the answer and He teaches our hand to war and our fingers to battle (Psalm 144) the only gear needed is trust partnering with faith...

Father, thank You for the opportunity to say a prayer for a weary soul. Thank You for helping me to look beyond his faults to see his needs, as you do for each of us when we stumble on the hopeless path, you pull us back when we repent. Amen.

Because of Love

Love does no wrong to a neighbor. Love, therefore, is the fulfillment of the law.
Romans 13:10

Good morning, this Passover day the birds are rejoicing with song, the clouds are forming with the voice of thunder and vision of lightning, the leaves on the trees are motionless, the windmills aren't moving, the grass grew taller overnight, these things are respecting the presence of the Lord.

Being a recipient of Jesus' love this Passover day I rejoice in excitement because of Calvary and the love of the Passover Lamb, Jesus. His love speaking through the ages because the birds never stopped singing, the sun never stopped rising, the dew never stopped watering, the rain never stopped coming, the rainbow never stopped forming to remind God of His promises and each of us of God's love even when we are in darkness. Jesus' love to wait until we are saved and serving Him before He comes for His Church. His Word never returns to Him void, as Jesus' love and faithfulness never fails.

Jesus' love which defeated doubts and fears, He did at Calvary. His love which took the keys of death from Satan, was done at Calvary. His love which gives the sinner new life was conquered and received at Calvary hill where Satan screamed "what have I done?" I rejoice with love for my fellowman because of the Passover Lamb slang for man's sins. Food for today: C. S. Lewis wrote, "Do not waste your time bothering whether you 'love' your neighbor; act as if you did. As soon as we do this, we find one of the great secrets. When you are behaving as if you loved someone, you would presently come to love him."

Jesus didn't talk of love, He lived it, died for it, rose for it, ascended into heaven for it, and interceding in heaven for His love for us... He who loves much, does much more than talk about. Passover day is a 'love's day' because my sins were cleansed on the day 'sin' thought Jesus was passing away forever, but faith knew He would rise again on the third day as the victorious Passover Lamb that took my sins away.

Learning

Love must be without hypocrisy. Detest evil; cling to what is good. Romans 12:9

Learning to confess our sins and forgiving ourselves is a huge tool Satan will use against us if we don't. Can I get an Amen to this realization!!!!

Unconfessed sins make you hide in the room of weariness, as the voice of the enemy screams, "You will be hated and rejected if your sin is found out!" The enemy speaks loudly in the darkness because he has your emotion, but if we listen closely, we will be able to hear the Holy Spirit whispering, "Come to the Light of forgiveness. You are loved!" However, the question is, who do you believe Jesus that unforgiveness holds you hostage, or Satan that jail is fun?

For instance, there's a story about a little boy and his sister who went to visit their grandparents on the farm. The boy was given a slingshot, so he went out to practice, but he couldn't hit anything. He turned and came back to the yard, and he saw his grandmother's pet duck, and he decided to take a practice shot. He hit the duck killing it. He hid the dead duck under a pile of wood thinking no one saw him. However, his sister was standing in the window watching. When it was time for her to wash dishes, she whispered in the boy's ear, "I saw the duck." So, the boy washed the dishes. Then it was time for her to help in the garden, "I saw what you did to the duck!" Finally, the boy grew tired of her using him to do her chores, so he told his grandmother what he did to the duck. His grandmother told him she was waiting on him to tell her, because she was standing in the window and saw what he did. "I forgive you for killing the duck, but you didn't know you were forgiven because you hadn't asked."

The devil will remind you of your mistakes and sins as long as you try to hide them, but God already knows and forgiven you. He's just waiting for you to ask. David prayed Psalm 51 when Nathan the prophet went to David after he had gone into Bathsheba's bed. David thought he was hiding his sins until he was confronted. In his brokenness, David discovered the only effective way to deal with sin is to face it, confess it, and be forgiven.

David recognized that his worst offense was against a Holy God. When we sin, it is God whose standards we violate. While people look to others for comfort, God alone forgives sins. Mark 2:7 "Why does this Man speak blasphemies like this? Who can forgive sins but God alone?"

The Bible never shows up prefect people for us to admire and put on a pedestal. It fully discloses the failings of real people, giving hope and insight to all who struggle with sin, imperfection, and doubt.

God helped David learn from his mistakes, and He wants to help us as well. Our restoration, like David's begins with realization and confession of our many failures as stumbling in this life's journey. God restores the broken hearts and sinking faith of people who call out to Him. He is faithful way to reach down and pull us from the valley of despair and troubling hearts in need of repair of the wounds of yesterdays and todays mistakes.

David prayed that God would not remove the Holy Spirit from him (51:11). We must do the same.

Picture of Life in Jesus' Hands

See, I have engraved you on the palms of My hands; your walls are ever before me. Isaiah 49:16

Last week, I saw a video of a duck with her many ducklings; however, one was caught in a thick patch of broken limbs and nets. Two men walking by saw the trapped little duck, so one pulled his shoes off and went into shallow covered water rocks to help release the duckling. But each time the man reached down to free the duckling the mother duck would rush back to protect her duckling from the man. She would fly up at the man in protective mode... When the man would reach down to free the duckling again the duck would fly up at him to make him leave her ducking along. The mama duck couldn't get her duckling free, so she floated on with her other ducklings leaving the trapped one behind to help itself.

The world will leave us behind when it sees no hope for us, but Jesus left the ninety-nine safe sheep and searched for the lost one (Luke 15:1-7). After a while, she (duck) sadly had to leave her baby duckling behind because she couldn't get it out. However, her baby wasn't alone because the man waited until the mother duck and her other babies were a long way away before he and his friend cut the duckling free. As soon as the duckling was free it rushed to join its family. The mother duck and the other ducklings turned around to greet its return to the family... just like the demonic man with the legion of demons in (Mark 5:1-20) he went home to his family after he was set free by Jesus. I wonder if there are grandmother ducks who celebrated the freedom of their grand-baby duckling?

As I looked at the video, I thought about my daughter and son-in-law leaving their youngest child behind at Jackson State University Last Fall. It was hard on each of them; even though, this is the third child they have trusted God to take care of...and He did! But this one was different because he's the youngest, and their house was emptied of their children. But like the baby duckling, God put people in his path to be a close hand of help...to encourage him to do his best, and he did. He even had grandparents help and from grandparents' friends and church family praying. There's one thing we are assured of God is faithful to take care of His own, not only are parents and grandparents seeking a wonderful four years for him, aunts, cousins, and even neighbors are stepping in to be a watchful eye. I call this favor...

My daughter cried, my son teased, but his two children are not that many years away from their first college day. His brother dropped him off to start a new page in this new book of life. However, he left behind his words of college wisdom... Oh, I can't tell you what they were because it was a brother-to-brother secret.

We are like the duckling lost in the cleft of the rock without God's watchful eyes over us. We are never alone when we honor God, just look at Joseph in his many ups and downs in life, but he stays steadfast not to bow before any man or other gods...he chose prison over a defiled bed with Potiphar' wife, Genesis 37:36, 39, & 31.

Remember this day, you are never alone when you serve God, and trust Him to take care of the ones out of your reach and eyesight. God knows how to keep our little ones from the nets which are waiting to trap. Psalm 34:17. There are traps waiting to ensnare each of us, but God has given each of His servant's authority to ask Him to turn the traps around so our enemies can fall into them themselves. Remember, when the trap of life tries to entrap us. God's ears are not too dull to hear us, or His arms too short to reach us. We are just a touch away from God.

Blessings

When Sin Sleeps with You

They are like a loin eager to tear, like young loin lurking in ambush. Psalm 17:12

Snakes don't stay babies, and their baby teeth are poisonous to the bite when they sleep with you. Alligators hatch from eggs but love you as meat when you allow them to hatch and grow in your house. A rat is not a pet by itself because it has other rats with no regards for what they like to eat.

Animals are created by God, and they are satisfied until they get hungry then you could become the meal. When sin is allowed to creep into our lives, one way or another it will affect the lives of the ones around us, mainly our children. Sin has no respecter of person who it eats for a meal.

Today, is a good day to choose what you will allow in your house and life. A forest of undergrowth of weeds can be prevented from becoming a forest if the weeded seeds are thrown away first. Matter of fact, burned with fire because the wind can bring each back to take root. However, it is too late and virtually impossible to pick a forest of weeds up to throw it away, but not the seeds when we are watchful if it is a weed or a tree.

This is the same with the sins we allow to creep in our lives...get rid of them before they take root and become a forest of snakes that hide and bit. Alligators that swallow and eat later... Lions that hide in ambush.... And rats that run fast when the lights come on but return when the lights go out. Sin keeps the light of God turned away from the sinner. Obedience turns it back to light a pathway of righteousness. Today, right now is the time to decide whom you will serve in your heart rather than your mouth, God or the man! Remember, Jesus said you can't serve two masters because you will hate one and serve the other... God is calling for true believer not word talker, but God doer in love and deeds. Make your decision before it's too late to say, "Yes, Jesus, I will serve You!"

Daily Word... Man has a choice to choose the plans of God or the ways of the world. Each has a reward of regrets or rejoicing.

Silly to Man

The one enthroned in heaven laughs; the Lord ridicules them. Psalm 2:4

I laugh because God laughs. I'm thankful God made me with joy and laughter in my heart. I have laughed at the silly things since I can remember. In church, I would get in trouble because the silly things to others were funny to me. My mother had me to sit next to her in service because as sure as I was not next to her, I was going to laugh about something and get in trouble. The Holy Spirit reveals what is wrong in our lives, it's left up to us to correct it. So, I choose joy over bitterness with a sense of humor added to it.

A little sin is like a fly in a bowl of soup, it spoils the whole bowl. Doubt is like a bedbug; it hatches many brothers and sisters to make you itch. Laziness is like a cricket; it wants to become a family member in your home when it gets cold outside. Worrying is like a bad apple, it affects everything around it. Ignoring the directions of the Holy Spirit, you will walk into a fire ant mound without ant repellent.

Have you ever just wanted to scream when you have done all you can and it seems as if no one notices or cares, they just want more and more from you? Well, welcome to the God Club... God screamed out to Moses in Exodus time after time, "What else do these people want from Me, I feed them the best of food, I sweeten the water, I keep their clothes from wearing out, I supply all their needs, yet they are never satisfied? What more do they want?" Are you one of them God is talking about who is taking Him for granted? Well, Proverbs 30:16 says sinful desires are like the grave, it's never satisfied. What are you seeking? Hopefully, God's love...

Life's journey builds many bridges...

The bridge of belief that leads to trust...

The bridge of hope that leads to the promises...

The bridge of faith that leads to victory over sin...

The bridge of promises that never fails...

The scenery bridge that reveals all of God's goodness...

Then the bridges of doubts that causes detours...

The bridge of disappointments that opens passages for the ships that

carries the cargo of doubts and failures to enter through.
Finally, the bridge that leads to joy that never ends or misery forever more. Decide this day the bridge you will dismantle. Wow! I don't see a billfold or credit card, yet the birds are eating, and the flowers are clothed in beauty. Sorry Lord for failing to trust You completely.
Faithful pray, God answers
Complain He looks over
Worry He comforts
Doubt He proves
Fear He hugs
Lack of faith He shows hope
Stumbling He catches
Weakness He strengthen
Heavy laden He lightens
Weeping He bottles the tears
Sickness He heals
Tiredness He gives rest
Sadness He gives peace
Sin He forgives
Unworthy He give grace and mercy. At death He receives the ones who walked by faith and not by sight.

Amen

The Eyes of Heaven

Lord, listen to my voice; let your ears be attentive to my cry for help. Psalm 130:2.

My friends, do you realize that God is watching us from His throne room! Job says God test us each moment. How are you standing in faith during this moment in time? Which side of the fence are you standing on? You know it's only one side that God approves of, and that's the right side where He stands. Do you know there's no excuses for siding with wrongs no matter who it is you are standing with if it's against the Word of God.

Snatch yourself from the fire if you are siding with wrongs. God is watching from heaven to see whose standing for Him. I'm crying because I want to be found worthy of my calling. Worthy to be called a child of the King. Worthy to be a voice God can use to cry out for others in the wilderness of despair. God is watching! Remember this, God is watching even if you think you can hide, God sees everything hidden and revealed! Know what's ironic? When a person has been diagnosed with a terminal illness people will say, "Well, he has time to get himself together before he leaves here!" Guess what, in that case, we all have terminal illnesses called "sin and death", and each of us have time to get ourselves together before death comes, each of us will die as the Word tell us so!

We believe Jesus loves us because the Bible tells us so. Easy to believe the good things that are pleasing to our ears, but when the Word says we must repent and be born again, we only choose the path of a Born Again Christian if it meets what pleasing to the ego. We know not the time Jesus is coming, so repent. The birds follow the sun through the day, they sing toward the eastern sky in the morning and in the afternoon, they follow the going down of the sun in the western sky. If the birds follow the light of the sun, are we not wiser than the birds? I don't think so because man want to follow his only path and leave Jesus off of it until the storms began to rage. Then they cry out... "Lord have mercy!" Does Jesus know the voice of the one who never call out to Him? Have a daily, moment-to-moment conversation with Him? Death will come if we are ready or not to gather us home...be it heaven or hell! Yes, the birds sing of

God glory, man sings of God's failures in their lives, this is called the blame game I times of trouble, me game in time of calm from the storm. Oh, what a tangled web we weave. The total truth, God never fails...

Guilty Party

Every word of God is pure; He is a shield to those who take refuge in Him. Proverbs 30:5

How many of us are guilty of putting our eyes and hope on man and in man? Many will say, "Not I!" like the barnyard animals and friends of *Little Red Hen* when she found the grains of corn. They kept their eyes on what they didn't want to do until the harvest came in and the meals prepared for the cold winter's months. As the Little Red Hen ate in warmth her 'missing in action friends 'in a time of planting and harvesting were standing in the cold hungry and unprepared for the long cold winter months.

This is what too many of us have done, left Jesus out in the cold while we looked to man for the answers to our problems. We are unprepared for the troubles lurking in the clod darken valleys of despair and hard tines of weariness.

How can man solve our problem when he is the problem? As the troubles rage around us, who are you seeking and keeping your eyes on man or God? Don't you think it's time to invite Jesus in from the cold where He should have never been in the first place? Man is only loved perfectly by Jesus, and we used by God to get His plan done, because man will fade away like dew on the grass, but God's plans never fade.

Decide right now the ones who's weary and feeling hopeless whom you will keep your eyes of faith on in these troubling times. Remember, "You ain't got no problem, all you need is faith in God!" On December 26, 2020, God showed me this vision of His glory, hopefully it will strengthen you as it did me...

Sometimes it seems that the mountains have gotten higher and too steep to climb. This morning as I awoke, I felt heaviness all around. I began to thank the Holy Spirit for another day, then I got up, got my Bible to hear the Spirit of the Lord speak to me. The phone rang shortly after I finished talking to God. A man from Kentucky who heard me on the radio said hello. He spoke with a pleasant voice and spoke his name, and began playing the harp from his keyboard... "Do you know this song?" He asked. Then he began singing... "There is no secret what God can do."

He called for prayer, but he didn't realize God sent him my way not for me to pray a prayer of hope for him...but to use him first for (God)to speak to me. "There is no secret what I can do." Thank You, Father for never leaving me when the mountains seem too steep for me, you make them anthills.

Jesus Lives

I am the resurrection and the life. The one who believes in Me, even if he dies, will live. John 11:25

Christmas Day, December 25, 2020, is a day of God seeking me as I arose from a warm and safe night's sleep. The children and grands calling to wish me a Merry Christmas, as the sunlight shines through the windowpane as the shadows of the wheel of the windmill dances on the wall directed by the Christmas morning breeze. "Merry Christmas, Jesus! No, Happy Birthday. No, still not the right phrase. Thank You Jesus for coming!" Were the words from my mouth, and love from my heart. The sun pushing the blinds open, so it seemed with its brightness, beckoning me to see its presence this Christmas morn to proclaim our Savior was born and lives, and wanting to be welcome in my heart... Then to my amazing surprise as I opened the blinds, the sun proclaimed in many rays of colors "Jesus is not in the manger but lives in heaven and still gives gifts to man."

Jesus is letting me know He lives so the world will not fall into sorrow and fears during the time the enemy is trying to capture the hearts of believes in fear. Fear, itself was frightened when the birth of Jesus was announced. Fear had Herod to send the solders out to kill the boy babies because the King of kings was born to set a soul free of the grips of the enemy.

Jesus speaks in ways we cannot any imagine. But as I looked at the sunlight making amazing colors of Jesus' gift this Christmas morning, I became ashamed, disappointed, and embarrassed looking at people not even celebrating Jesus' gift of birth because of man-made lies that a virus was mightier than Jesus Christ Himself. His gift of death on the cross was rejected for the lie of man. People too afraid to have a family meal together, and to receive the hand bearing gifts, because of fear pouring more fear, because man's eyes are off of Jesus' birth but on fear. Masks worn rather than a song of joyous celebration that Jesus lives, Jesus was born, Jesus died on the cross, Jesus rose from the grave, Jesus defeated the enemy, Jesus overcame the world, Jesus is alive in heaven. Yet too many hid away in dark gloom of fear because man said so.

Yes, I understand Jesus was speaking to me through the sound of the wind and the turning of the windmill, but more so, through the gift of the Sun's colors through the leafless trees.

"I live!" Is what I saw and heard. "Death could not keep Me in the tomb. Kings could not stop Me from coming. Evil cannot keep Me from blessing My 'chosen one'. I'm seeking the ones hearts not in fear of man's lies to celebrate Me, the own Son of God."

During the Christmas of 2020, many were waiting for a shot to protect them, but they forgot the THE HEALER and hid in darken rooms of fear even though, Jesus lives. Many refuse to have guest for the celebration of the Risen Savior, but they didn't forget the fear wrapped in pretty packages with bows stopping the Guest from coming through the door. Fear is the biggest wrap gift under the tree, the tree the Risen Savior created, but yet fear ruled the hearts. They didn't forget the mask which guarded the mouth from eating the sweet honey of the Born Savior, but fear tasted batter because it had found a home. They rejected the praising and celebrating the Savior born among us and to save us, yet they picked up the lies which imprisoned them in perpetual fear that was growing fatter.

Fear knows Jesus lives, doubts know Jesus conquered the grave, lack of faith rejoices because man rejected the Deliverer, and chose the defeated foe. Sadly, but true the enemy knows Jesus better than the one who calls Him father when fear allows them to do so. Have you ever thought about Jesus has a heart too, and heaven inhabit our praise. Why celebrate the Birth of Jesus when fear is ruling as your god on Christmas Day and all the day the Lord gives us?

Morning Bird Songs - *Daily words from heaven!*

The Enemy in Your House

The leech has two daughters: "Give, Give!" Three things are never satisfied; four never say, "Enough!": Sheol; a childless womb; part, which is never satisfied with water; and fire, which never says, "Enough!" Proverbs 30:15-16

 We live in a Blame-Game Society...

A student gets a failing grade...the teacher is blamed...even though the student used his time playing games rather than studying.

A husband is caught with another woman...the woman is blamed and talked about...even though the husband wasn't held at gunpoint, and it takes two to tango.

A pastor calls a person in to repentance...he is called too righteous.... even though you know sin leads to eternal torment.

A police officer gives you a ticket for running a red light...he is picking on me...even though you know it's wrong to go on red....

A police officer takes you to jail for a DUI...Jack drives the same way...Jack just hit a mother and her three children...

A bill collector calls because your bill is two months late...you call the collector low-down and he's wrong for calling...but you are enjoying what the company trusted you to get and pay for.

Earthly laws carry consequences...just as God's laws. When we are faced with our wrongs many times, we want to cast blame on others to make ourselves feel batter. But remember this one thing...wrong is wrong, and right is right! Facing our wrongs on this side of life with repentance will guarantee a seat at the banquet table when this journey is over. Adam blamed Eve for giving him the fruit to eat, but God didn't excuse the wrong...just like He will not excuse mine and yours... Blame is a fog machine turned on when we want to make wrong right and right wrong. But Jesus said this time would come.

Good morning, foggy morning the Lord awoke me to see. The birds were still in bed when I walked out on the porch, but the spiderwebs weren't hiding; matter of fact, they couldn't hide because the morning fog covered each one, and they were visible with the morning dew. The tree limbs without leaves were webbed, and even some parts of the grass were too. Then the Holy Spirit began to reveal how Satan have invisible webs waiting to catch each of us in it. I mentioned about the webs of stealing yesterday's hope with blame game, and how easily it is to steal and think there is nothing wrong with it.

I'm guilty of walking out the store without telling the cashier the wrong price was rung up, I blame the store rather than doing the right thing. We complain if we are over charged but call it a blessing if we are under charged. Each morning for the last two weeks I have asked the Holy Spirit to shower me in Jesus' blood. I ask Him to wash my mind to think as He wants me to think; my eyes to see as He would have me to see; my ears to hear as He would have me to hear; then my hands to do as He would have them to do....and etc.

Well, next week, I'm returning money to a store that charged me twenty cents less for some bubble bath I had gotten, and I didn't tell the cashier the price was wrong in my favor. I'm returning a dollar because it's not mine to keep. I'm pulling my hand out of Satan's web so he can't accuse be before God. I'm a servant of God the web Breaker not a servant of the web maker. Being covered in Jesus' blood reveals the spiritual webs like the morning fog reveals the natural ones. I am rejoicing in this foggy morning because God revealed the plans of the enemy to me again so I will not be accused of playing the blame game in the games of destruction. Today, this blame game has one less player, and I thank the birds for sleeping later so God could speak to me as I walked in the foggy morning.

There are enemies in each of our houses when we rather do it our way than God's way. Remember, wrongs are hungry and never gets enough...

Sin Bites

They feed on the sin of My people; they have an appetite for their transgressions.
Hosea 4:8

Listen carefully, snake eggs will hatch in the slum as well as the king's palace. They will crawl on dirt as well as diamond carpet. They hiss at the president as well as the factory worker. They bit the queen as well as the prostitute. They live wherever there is food to eat; they have no friends among themselves; even the babies' mama doesn't care if they survive.

So, have you allowed or invited any snakes to have space in your house? They don't care if you are kind, loving, giving, old or young, they even bite the ones who feed them. Remember, snakes only stay where they can find food, this is one of the reasons the snake could stay in the Garden of Eve so long… Adam and Eve were feeding it with their unadvisable attention to his lie of them being like God. You don't have to be a gossiper in order for the enemy to stay in your house…all he needs is for you to listen attentively to his lie and not rebuke him.

Inviting a snake to live with you will ruin your household and life…Adam and Eve found this out the hard way. A snake has no compassion…no love…no beauty…no family…only deception. With every kiss, is venom. With every squeeze is death. With every tongue thrust its counting your size to attack. Why is a snake's conversation poisonous? Because the snake in the Garden of Eve con Adam and Eve to receive the venom of death when its lie led them to eat the fruit of the tree of good and evil…Genesis 3:1-6

Lying is venom that leads to death. From the moment Adam ate the fruit death entered this world, and blood sacrifices from the lamb was needed to cover man's sins…Genesis 3:21. From the snake's conning Adam, God had to make the first prophecy in Genesis 3:15 "I will put enmity between you and the woman, and between your offspring and her offspring; he will bruise your head, and you will bruise his heel."

From man's first stumble Satan has sought to destroy the Promised Seed that will destroy him…starting with the first murder in Genesis 4:6 "Sin is crouching at the door. It desires to dominate you, but you must rule over it." Cain allowed the snake to take room in his heart...he killed his brother, Abel. Abel, the first prophet silent to keep the voice of the Lord.

Lack of peace is like a slithering snake...that causes you not to be satisfied. Lamech how took two wives in Genesis 4:19... starting the absentee father. People accepting the poisonous venom of a snake brings more hatred and jealousy...Joseph's brother sold him. To stop the dream from being fulfilled.

Satan hated the first prophecy of God so badly that he used Pharaoh in Exodus 2 to kill all the Hebrews boys two years old and younger to keep the prophecy from being fulfilled. It didn't work...Moses was born and the promised fulfilled to let the children of Israel go.

Herod in Matthew 2:16-17 killed all the male children in Bethlehem two years old and under to stop the prophecy. It didn't work, Jesus was born, healed, delivered, taught, made disciples, crucified, died, rose, went to heaven and the enemy was defeated, not is defeated but was defeated!

Paul ran down the born-again Jews to keep down the population of heaven. It didn't work, he was saved, and more born-again believers added to heaven's roll.

Stephen was stoned to death to keep new believers away....it didn't work...more were saved, and Paul preached the Gospel.

Hitler killed millions of Jews so the apples of God's eye would be not more, and the seeds to His heart would die....it didn't work, more came to the faith, and lived to talk about it.

Snake goes where there is food...the spiritual snake feeds on the food of hatred, anger, bitterness, unforgiveness, half trues, gossip, and all the things God's Word tells us not to do. Lock the snake out by sealing every negative hole in your life.

Today, know this mighty truth...there is a repellent for all snakes, and there is a place they can't enter.
"A highway shall be there, a roadway, and it shall be called the Highway of Holiness. The unclean shall be for the wayfaring men, and fools shall not wander on it. No lion shall be there, nor any ravenous beast shall go up on it; these shall not be found there, but the redeemed shall walk there, and the ransomed of the LORD shall return and come to Zion with songs and everlasting joy upon

their heads. They shall obtain joy and gladness, and sorrow and sighing shall flee away" (Isaiah 35:8-10).

So let not your heart be trouble...Jesus defeated the snake (Satan) at the cross. And even with the snake crawling in dark places...God even saved the snake from the flood...He let him slither on the Ark. Meaning, your sins are forgiven... God's covenant with its people

Never Satisfied

Bring up, well sing to it! The princes dug the well; the nobles of the people hollowed it out with a scepter and with their staffs. They went from the wilderness to Mattana. Numbers 21:17-18

God always have a way of showing us ourselves when we trust and allow Him to do so. I wake each morning as the birds welcome the new day and I smile with joy. But then as the sun peeks through the trees I know I have another long day ahead of me. I began thinking some days how much I must do, and I began to remember the days of yesterday. How I depended on someone else to make sure the blinds were opened correctly, and the dog allowed to use the potty rather than being rushed back into the house. I remember the garden green and pretty with vegetables and the figs brought in by the five-gallon buckets.

As I look toward the window with the sun anew and it is dancing through the tree leaves, I apologize to the Holy Spirit for weariness. As the Corinthian Bells sing with the wind, I apologize again. As the Holy Spirit comforts, me with the early morning bird song, I become ashamed of myself for ever worrying, no, forever whining over the burdens of what doesn't belong to me. Do I do what I do for show or because of love for the hurting? This is the question I should be asking myself.

Then, I am reminded that Jesus did it all of me, yet I want to do it my way. However, Jesus let me know over the years that He is always with me; He is my Rock that I cannot sink through; He is the River I cannot drown in, only my sorrows; He is the Song in the cool breeze of the morning running me down to calm me; He is the Strength in the wind on my skin which helps me to stand when I feel alone; He is the Reminder He is the Son of God in the sun rays dancing through the tree leaves; He is the Forgiver of my shortcoming as I watch a butterfly fluttering gracefully in colorful beauty; He shows me I cannot be taken from His hand as I see the mighty Oak tree uprooted by the storm but the roots still attached to the soil; He reminds me His eyes are on me when I see the sparrows feeding from the fresh morning grass; He shows me He is my Shelter through the night as I see the flowers reaching toward the sunlight.

As the Holy Spirit shows me my many blessings from the time the birds begin singing in the morning the song of victory and praise, I ask for forgiveness. Forgiveness for not allowing Him to do it His way. Forgiveness for the lack of trust. Forgiveness for sinning with doubts, I refused to think I even had, but trying to do it my way is saying God isn't able... This is doubt.

Yet, I am guilty as the heat of the sun warms the day, and I see what I think is a burden only desiring the TV rather than what he have worked for many years. The reminders through the song of the birds shows how He sees my needs, and He takes care of each one until I pull them back to myself. I'm carrying a cross not fitted for me, a cross, Jesus carried on Cavalry but yet I want to redo what He have already done.

As the Holy Spirit speaks to me through the morning bird song, I burst out in song because the well of faith arises in me as the sun arises to dance through the tree the dance of love and faithfulness.

There's message in the morning's dawn for each person who feels burden because a loved one is sick, or a loved one have passed from this life. Jesus looked at the one casting lots for His clothes and said to the Father in heaven, "Forgive them, they know not what they do." In foolish and selfish ways wanting to have it our way, we cast lots for God's patient because we do not know what we are doing when we choose burdens of the world over Jesus' comfort from the cross. The Israelites sang a song when the water came from the well in Numbers 21:17-18 because they were so happy to have water. But then they forgot what God did for them and complained. We say we would never do what the Israelites did. But we do keep our promises to trust God in the storms and raging waves of life?

This is my prayer and I ask the Holy Spirit to help me because I cannot do it alone. Help, God! Psalm 12:1 this is the best place to be when needs come, in Jesus' care. He can help us, go from the wilderness of weariness to the promises of peace in the storm.

Help me Father to keep my eyes on You when the winds are raging, and the waves are high. Amen.

Trusting

O house of Jacob, come and let us walk in the light of the LORD. Isaiah 2:5

When we follow what God puts in our spirit we never go wrong. November 2005, a vision of a porch with rocking chairs kept coming until I said yes. I already had a small porch, but this vision was of a porch the full measure of my house. After a month or so, I got in touch with a builder and told him what I needed. Within a few days the project began... the brick mason came to lay the foundation, and the trees near the house removed and replanted in another place. Then the builder came with his workers. I had no idea how much the porch would cost or where I would get the money. I just knew a porch had to be built. Each week a $1000.00 check was written for payment to the builder not counting the cost of the lumber. I had no idea where the money would come from each week, but on Saturday afternoon the money was in the bank. After the porch was finished a total of near $17,000.00 was paid out for the porch. As the years passed God have used the porch to harvest souls. The year of 2020 many people have come to just sit on the porch to find a place of peace in the presence of the Lord. And Bible study and prayer gatherings have taken place on the porch, especially the summer of 2020. Still as the years passed this porch have been a haven of many who's seeking a place of comfort. Even atheists have found peace on this porch. One atheist who installed my generator spoke of blessings as he worked and even called and told his supervisor how he enjoyed being in the yard.

Wednesday night I bowed before God in thankfulness and humble submission when a stranger came to meet me because a friend of his told him how he was led back to Christ when he came to my porch during the summer. This man said, "I never pat a person on the back for what they do for God. But he (his friend) told me that I needed to meet you and come to this porch. And my brother told me there is something special about you, I just wanted you to tell you." Tears welled in my heart and eyes thinking how I take for granted how God have used the porch for many years as a place people come to be in the presence of the Lord.

So, my friends, when God gives you a vision to do something for the kingdom, He will make it possible to get it done. There is no earthly price for a soul but our obedience to move when God tells us to do so. I'm glad I trusted God for the finances to build a place prayers are prayed for the sick; videos are recorded for the weary and downtrodden...where God's voice is heard through the whistling of the wind through the chimes; where a vision of God's love is seen through the feeding of the birds; where God's breath is felt as the wind touches my skin; where the fragrance of God's presence is smelled as the rain waters the dry grass. A lady messaged me to ask where she could find the music that plays on the daily videos...if it was on YouTube. My answer, "This is the sounds of the wind singing through the Corinthian Bells/chimes from God's heavenly musical storehouse." Today, I'm thankful to be a part of God's kingdom assignment more now than ever before. God needs willing vessels to hear and do His will so the ones once lost can be found... A little boy came with his mother one Tuesday because he didn't feel well. As we sat in the rocking chairs and talked about Jesus 'healing power...he left feeling better and got up the next morning telling his mother how good he felt and wanted to go to school.

Thank You Jesus for choosing to give me a porch of Your presence... Amen.

Good Morning

May God be gracious to us and bless us; look on us with favor
Selah... Psalm 67:1

Good morning Holy Spirit, thank You for waking me with the songs of the wind from the storehouse. Good morning, this sunny day with your sun rays making ballerina pirouette on the windmill. Good morning light turning gracefully on the blades of the windwheel pointing to the northern sky. Good morning tree leaves dancing in harmonized step with the songs of the wind. Greeting Corinthian bells singing duet as the finger of heaven directs the eastern breeze to a sing along. Good morning loving breath of heavenly bliss, breathe on me. Good morning storehouse of heavenly life and the voice of God's love serenading me with peace as I arise to this new day. "Our God, will bless us"(Psalm 67:6). And He does. Have you realized where your help come from this new day?

Hello, this day which woke me with heaven's delights and the voice of God through the wind saying, "sing."
Every part of my yard from the trees, leave, wheels of the mills going around and around, birds, grass, flowers, Corinthian bells, and the sunlight are singing and dancing in the presence of God's love heaven graced this day with. I'm out of bed singing because I sought God first as I awoke, and He greeted me with a love song. Hello, heartbeat that which carries my blood miles and miles through this body God allowed to rise again to do His will.

The joy of God's love caressed me with glory hallelujah praise, because God wants to visit with me. He wants me to be in His presence, He never gets enough of me, He never gets enough of you, seeking Him is His desire. He calls us as He did Adam and Eve, "Where are you!" I'm learning to answer, "Here I am Lord!"

As a child, I didn't know I was seeking God, but He knew my child's heart because I sought the beauty of the morning and throughout the day the loveliness of my surrounding. A bee on the red coves fascinated me. The fish jumping in the pond as the fleas hovered over the water amazed me. The cows leaving the barnyard following the new dew washed grass disturbed me because I had to follow with the milk bucket to milk them (this what happens when you sleep too late). Smelling the turning of the spring soil excited me, yet a few months later I would be chopping rows of cotton in the fields. Braiding the grass like hair taught me for motherhood many, many years later. Making clothes from the leaves of the trees, I never got a hand of, but it was beautiful to watch my sister make clothes through the years.

God knew my child's heart, the innocence, yet boldness to always speak the truth. So innocent, my heart that visions were shown to me as a child. Beautiful White Lambs leaped before me and disappearing as they leaped. Heaven conversations opened to me. A child with wandering and owning a switch tree because of wandering and boldness to not be afraid to stand when something had wrong got me in trouble. God chooses who we will be and the anointing we will carry from the foundation of the world. Our personality God created. No one is a mistake, no one is a perhaps, we are each chosen to be a vessel God can use to be His light in this world created by God's heavenly plan. God proves Who He is moment by moment. It is left up to you and me to truly realize where our blessings come from and who supplies each one. Seeking God more and more have led me to seeing Him in every flower that blossom, only He can bring forth a rose without bruising it. Every bird song of the morning I hear God and smile. I see God in the clouds because He is the living water. But most of all, God sees me and laugh at my enemy because trusting Him like the birds on stormy days I am safe in God's care.

Walking with God through the songs of the birds, the touch of the wind, the sight of the sun rays, the smell of the fresh morning dew, I have learned to see God rather than the world. I hear His promises over the world's doubts and fear. I know my Redeemer lives and I know this because the sun still rises and the birds still sing, the death limbs still fall, the new ones still grow seeking the sun rather than looking downward seeking the roots to see if they are still there. We don't need to seek to see if God is still here, we know He is because we live, and the clouds haven't overtaken the sun.

I see God in His wonders too.

A Different World

Woe to me if I do not preach the gospel! 1 Corinthians 9:16b

We go through trials and tribulations in this life because we live in an imperfect world. World of faults and failures.
World of ups and downs. World ice cold or barely warm...
World of life and deaths...
World of joy and sorrow...
World that tells you to wait util tomorrow to forgive or not to forgive at all...
World of tears and sorrows...
World of joy and gladness...
World of forgotten promises...
World of lost hope and depending on dope...
World of blindness to God...
World where God fades from the man's memories before the fallen rain and dew on the morning grass...

But the truth be told, we see only with earthly eyes rather than the eyes spiritual eyes we were born to see the Creator. Before a child is told fairies protects him rather than his appointed angel. Bunny rabbits are the reason for Easter than Jesus' raising from the grave. Santa Clause is the reason for the season than Jesus' birth. Or the Lamb belongs to Mary rather than the Lamb dying for Mary. Drowns the hope of many in doubt and fears. Jesus took the pain of sorrow and shame upon His back so His yoke would be easy for mankind and burdens would be light. There is hope for each of us as we seek a closer and faithful walk with God on the narrow path prepared for me and you to walk on to see Jesus' face to face. Daily Word. Each holds its own wonders that will not come again. Be thankful for each heartbeat.

Gifts Are to Be Used

A gift opens doors for a man and bring him before the great... Proverbs 18:16

There was a time I felt as if I had nothing else to write in the daily post, I write each day. I write only what I hear the Holy Spirit say, but then the voices of the world can get in your ear, and you feel as if you have nothing to say that would make a difference in a person's life. But the loving thing about God is, He will not let us wallow in our sorrows and whoa-it-me because we are trying to please man's opinion of us. It is too easy to take our eyes off of God because He is not a dedicator, He never impose on our will. He reminds us because of His love for us that He wants us to move from the valley of despair and reject the lie that someone told us we are not good enough. He reminds us in His Word how special we are to Him, and He is the One who matter. So, I sat and did what He directed me to do:

I haven't written a post lately, but I feel the need to write one tonight because it may make a difference in someone's life. I'm writing with tears in my eyes. As I laid in prayer this lovely night, but it's a dreary night for a grieving family. As I laid in prayer about to close my eyes to sleep the phone rang. The voice on the other end said, "Hectic! What are you doing?" I replied, "Praying." "Good, pray for (she called the person's name) her granddaughter hung herself!" With my head on my pillow, I wept.

And I began to pray again. I asked the Lord to show me what to do to help the ones feeling hopeless. I asked Him to strengthen the hurting family. I wept again and said, "Lord cover the children. Put someone in their path to guide them to You."

The children are falling victim to the enemy. Cities are being burned down while the children are begging silently for help. Computers and cell phones are becoming their parents rather than mother and father having dinner around the table with their children. Hatred is taught rather than love. Jesus is only a Christmas tree ornament rather than the living Savior to many. Hope is waxing cold for the young.

Coronavirus is the name of the news as fear has become a god.

Jesus is made to look helpless because the doctor tells you what tomorrow holds, and many believe it rather than Jesus 'word that we know not what tomorrow holds. Hold your children close in prayer because the enemy is waiting for an opportunity to steal them. Put your children in God's hand because He promised nothing can snatch them out.

Daily Word...God's promises hold. His miracles stand. And His voice all creations listen to His command except man.

Listening

However, God has listened; He has paid attention to the sound of my prayer.
Psalm 66:19

Good morning, Holy Spirit! Joy is in the air because You are the breath I breathe. You are the victory song I sing in battle! You are the strength to my legs. You are the sight in my eyes! You are the heartbeat of pleasure I feel as I see the sun rays dancing on the grass as the squirrels run through each maze the sun rays make. You are joy I receive hearing the birds sing as the wind is still and the tree leaves rest from yesterday's dancing with the orchestra of the wind. Oh, the silent of the Corinthian bells are rehearsing in quietness until the next show of the wind. Thank You Holy Spirit for the grass growing in beauty under Your command, even though, it's time for the mowing once more before the week is done. You live because everything around me speaks of Your life-giving gifts. The crickets are moving their legs like the strings of a violin, keeping beat with the sounds of the rhythm of the blade of grass, the mosquitoes are seeking whom they can bite, the wasps are building their cone, but You are the creator of them all. Beauty surrounds me as I sit on the porch seemly nearer to God. The sound of the wind brings me in His presence to be bathed with His life-giving peaceful gift of love. My porch is my prayer closet and refuge of Jesus 'gift of love. I escape to the garden of love when my day becomes too full of the ways of the world. The hustle and bustle of preparing meals, answering the phone, washing clothes, writing letters, giving medicine, preparing messages for two services, just to name just a few. But God calls me to come and rest in His garden He prepared to meet me and wash me in His fragrance of love. Heaven declares glory of God and His handiwork Psalm19:1.

Have you really taken a close look at God's handiwork? The bumblebee is God's amazing work that man says shouldn't be able to fly. The ant is so small that man says it shouldn't be able to carry the weight it carries. The hummingbird is so unique that it stands still in midair. Looking at the hummingbird is a lesson for each of us from Psalm 46:10 "be still and know that I am God." God even made the dirt dauber special in an unusual way...it's the Predator for the spider that traps the good, bad, beautiful, and ugly in its web. God's handiwork of the invisible forces of evil that comes against us can be seen in the spiderweb. We fight the invisible when we walk into a web. God's handiwork also shows us how to trust Him as we look at the birds. How unique we are when we look at the bumblebee. How strong faith can be when we look at the ant. How He goes before us when hornet nest disturbed. We are fearfully and wonderfully made. We are one of a kind like the geese make designed ripples on the water uniquely one of a kind. How loving He is when we see a goose protecting her young. Yes, in the garden with Jesus is my refuge from the busyness of the day. Even in sickness God gives a resting place in Him as Job speaks about. "That path no bird knows, nor has the falcon's eye seen it. The proud lions have not trodden it, nor has the fierce loin passed over it" (Job 28:7-8).

Crying

Praise is rightfully Yours, God, in Zion; vows to You will be fulfilled. Psalm 65:1

Good morning Holy Spirit. Thank You for a peaceful and restful night sleep. Good morning, this windy just warm enough day I'm enjoying the breath of the Lord. Good morning, honking geese you woke me before sunrise to remind me that yesterday is gone, and this is a new day. Good morning clouds the dust under God's feet I feel God's presence. Each of the morning wonders is a word of encouragement for those of you still being tormented from the mistakes of yesterday.... Satan roams the earth seeking the ones he can keep reminding of their troubled past so he can keep them in a 'spiritual jail'. The geese are encouraging you that yesterday is gone, and God is welcoming you to a new day mistake free. God have given you 'spiritual keys' to unlock each cell door, His Word, The Holy Bible! The sunrise that brings promises and the sunset that cast the mistakes as far as the East is from the west.

God's Word is a weapon that blasts the missile of the enemy. God gave us mothers the world gave us drugs. Children are crying in the womb. Children are crying in the alleys. Where are the mothers? Where are the fathers? Do they know their children are crying? You hear the dog bark and feed it. You close your ears to the cry of a starving baby. A baby whose organs are being cut out as they cry in pain. Where is the compassion? Oh, I forgot, sin has no compassion. Sin doesn't share with sin partner, killing wants more killing! Hatred wants more hatred. Lying wants more lying. So where is the end to this? In the abyss when Satan is locked away forever. Father, mend the broken heart. Mold the broken pieces left has shattered...

Today's decision affects your tomorrow...
A word of hope brings a tree of hope...
A word of doubt brings a tree of doubt...
You are fearfully and wonderfully made...

So, when the enemy comes tomorrow to tell you that you are not. Let him see your roots of hope because of the positive seed planted yesterday...breaks the locked cell door of tomorrow.

Herticine Goree

God Is Not Blind

Listen, my people, I will speak; I will testify against you, Israel. I am God, your God. Psalm 50:7

Early Sunday morning with the cool breeze dressing my skin with a gentle touch of kindness as I watch the bird soar to the trees as if going to work, helps me to see God in His beauty. Woodpecker noisily flying to the top of the light poles as if flying in from a late-night Saturday dance sat in a hole as if in bed, makes me thankful. Tree tops dressed in early morning glow of the sun as wearing an evening gown carry me into praise that one day, I will wear a heavenly gown fitted only for me. Birds singing the morning song beneath the leaves on the trees, I hear God. Joy in the garden of Jesus 'love makes me celebrate saying yes to Him. Jesus opened my heart to love the unlovable, to give to the selfish, pray for the hateful, to forgive the unforgivable, but who am I to hold hatred when Jesus accepted me as I am? Loved me with a washable love which washed my sins away. The birds gathered in the tree to praise God with an early morning song, who I am to do any less? The wind sings the morning praise as it dances upon my skin this Sunday morning... As I take in God's morning hello as the light of the sun wraps the windmill with a glow only God can give, He is speaking to me, and I am saying more! As the wheels of the mills turn with God's touch, I know only heaven can speak to the hearts willing to be spoken to. Speak Lord, your servant is listening this early Sunday morning graced with heavenly love.
So Why Do You Think God Isn't Looking...

It's a sad thing when we think God is blind. Yes, too many of us treat Him as if He's blind, deaf and a secondhand citizen. Too many put fun and work of the week as top priority yet complain about tiredness and not feeling good on Sunday! Do you not think God sees your true desires? You teach Sunday, sing in the choir, attend Bible study, pray for others, yet you steal, lie, gossip, drink, and talk about the preacher as if God doesn't see and hear you. You see a wayward child, and you are thankful he isn't you. Don't you know God sees that you not caring?

Also, no one should have to run you down to do the will of God. No one should have to beg you to pray, you are not doing it for me, you are doing it for yourself but more so for God's kingdom! God doesn't need man's help, man can't feed Him, man can't clothe Him, man can't give Him what He already have...cattle on a thousand hills and everything else Psalm 50.

Pretending to be a Christian because you park your body on the pew each Sunday, it's the same as parking your Volkswagen in the garage and calling it a Jaguar. Others know it's a Volkswagen and not a Jaguar because it speaks for itself, just as God knows who Real is.

God sees our hearts and He's looking at our actions because nothing is hidden from Him. One day the trumpet will blow, and your name will be called for your final journey home...the fate won't make it in no matter how real man sees you, God knows everything. As He knows the songs of the birds 'praise, and the wind blowing in a love song from Jesus 'heart...

Then, I'm reminded that calling myself a Christian is one thing...being one is another. Saying I have faith is one thing...exhibiting faith is another. Saying I trust God in the storm is one thing...trusting Him is another. Being who you say you are and exhibiting who you are speak louder than words.

If I'm a bird, I need to fly... if I'm a chicken I need to lay an egg every once and awhile. If I'm an ant I need to be busy doing ant's things. If I'm a grasshopper I need to sit on a weed and do what I was born to do. But if I'm a butterfly let me exhibit God's beauty as I feed the flowers to make more flowers. Over the last weeks, I have seen and heard more fear about tomorrow than faith of Who holds tomorrow. Running around in a circle of fear brings more runners...but standing in faith brings the power of God to make us stronger and stronger. I'm not radical, I'm a believer in the unseen God of heaven and earth and doer of His Word. Coming against a person's faith is coming against God, our Redeemer. As the angel of death came to Egypt and killed the oldest of man and animal, but as long as the Israelites stayed behind the door of the blood nothing touched them. This is still true of the blood of Jesus...under the blood I'm off limits to the enemy. So, Lord, I ask You, why are the church doors close and the mall open? I ask you to help my unbelief when I take my eyes off of You and see the raging storms more.

The birds don't stop singing when man run in fear. The rain doesn't stop falling because man stops worshiping when troubles come. So, Lord, I'm sorry when I let the rocks and trees trust You more than me and out praise me. I'm sorry!

Daily Word...Fear is a bully until faith reveals its secret... Fear has no legs; it must have yours to carry it.

My Redeemer

For I know that my Redeemer lives, and He shall stand at last on the earth. Job 19:25

Physically, we go to the doctor yearly for a checkup. The blood pressure is checked, the temp, the oxygen level, the heart rate, the lungs, and or any other test needed to make sure we are in good health. We have house insurance in case of fire or floods, and a yearly termite inspection is done for any termite activity. Our cars are taken in for the needed oil changes and diagnostic check for any evidence of unforeseen problems. The lawnmowers and weed eaters are check for the seasonal use, the wood is cut for the winter heat, all the many things needed for a safe home, health, and protection of what we have need of and have paid for are done. If anything breaks down, I have the insurance to cover it.

Matter of fact, a rail on my porch was eating away and I called my termite company to come to check it. I am thankful it wasn't termites; it was just rot from the weather. The termite is the only creature of God who can eat wood, it doesn't want to live in the wood, it wants to eat the wood and then move on to the next meal at someone else's house. But have you had your spiritual checkup? Do you have everything right with God? Check out this checkup list and see if you are ready to meet Jesus if He comes today:

1. Are you holding unforgiveness?
2. Have you repented and confessed your sins. Confessing your sin is the open door to God's blessings.
3. Have you asked for forgiveness from the ones you know you have wronged?
4. Are you holding any form of bitterness?
5. Have you put any other god before Jesus?
6. Have you bowed down to an image?
7. Have you said yes to Jesus..." I will follow You!"
8. Ask God to search your heart and reveal your hidden and secret sins.

Sadly, but true many are running in fear of a virus that has to bow at the name of Jesus yet holding on to things which leads to separation of an eternal life with Jesus. The virus became a god to many because they trusted what man said it would do rather than knowing what Jesus did over 2000 years ago.

Have your spiritual checkups gotten a seal of approval from God? If not ask Him to search your heart and reveal anything holding you from walking with Him. There may be something needing repair and removal of things you are holding onto in your heart. If it is fear, seek God's presence and peace. If it's worrying, remember what Jesus said about the birds, and worry takes up room the Holy Spirit want to occupy. If it is jealousy, Jesus is the only One allowed to be jealous. All the insurance we need to walk a life pleasing to God is listed in the Bible free of charge.

Remember, do not fear, it's listed in the Bible 365 times...one for each day as a reminder... Jesus loves us so dearly that He reminds us of each day of our lives to not fear because there is fear in love; instead, perfect love drives out fear, because fear involves punishment 1 John 4:18. The Word of God is the Insurance policy for life.

Always Amazed

If anyone says, "I love God," yet hates his brother, he is a liar. For the person who does not love his brother he has seen cannot love the God he has not seen. 1 John 4:20

As a child when I kept asking my parent for something, they used this phrase, "You sound like a broken record." As I sit out each morning just to see the beauty in the garden of Jesus' love, I am amazed at the sounds of the birds in the coolness of the morning. And to see them fly together to the many trees in my surrounding is a revelation in itself. Now, I'm sounding like a broken record telling you about the birds again. But to see the birds fly to the feeders and eat together in harmony, amazes me, because I see the family God created man to be. I see joy, God desire man to carry. I see fellowship Hebrews 10:25 tells us to assembly together as believers. I see the friendship God desire each of us to have. Not friendship with the world, but friendship with each other as the Body of Christ.

I sit each morning and watch the birds drawn to the sun as it peeks through the trees and make wonderful, beautiful pictures on the wet dew grass. The birds fly to the trees the sun rest on early in the morning, and they sing as they fly to the feeder. Not one of the many different birds fight to keep the other one away. They even share their food with the birds which feeds from the ground rather than flying up to the feeders. The sparrow rakes out the best seeds for the mourning doves as they walk slowly to eat seeds saved for them.

In the early morning garden with Jesus is where He shows me the beauty of fellowship through the view of the birds of the air and the squirrels on the ground. The trees house and shelter many birds, and the grass feeds many as they seek the wombs hiding within the dew cover greenery of the grass.

I'm amazed how God desires man to be in fellowship with Him, and He is so loving and patient with us until we choose Him. He shows us what He desires for us when we seek Him like the birds and flowers seek the rising and going down of the sun. The sweetness of God's desire for a hurting world warms my heart with tears of sadness that I have disappointed Him too often, and tears of joy because He still wants to show me His amazing wonders and love.

In the Garden with Jesus is my separation from the world to be one-on-one with Him. He speaks through the sun rays dancing on the leaves of the trees as the birds sing. He holds me as the wind caresses my skin with the sweet touch of heavenly love. In the Garden with Jesus, I am safe in His care, I am saved from the grips of the world, I am pulled deeper into love I have never tasted or felt before. As I seek to be in the Garden with Jesus each day, I am reminded of the celebration of love in the garden: Song of Songs 5:1 I have come to my garden. my sister, my bride. I gather my myrrh with my spices. I eat my honeycomb with my honey. I drink my wine with my milk. Eat, friends! Drink, be intoxicated with love!

In the garden is where I fell in love with Jesus. In the Garden of Gethsemane Jesus saw my brokenness and my dangerous walk to the path of hell, and He went to the garden alone to save me... "Then Jesus came with them to a place called Gethsemane, and He told the disciples, "Sit here while I go over there and pray." Matthew 26:36

Choosing to walk in the garden alone with Jesus, I chose Him, and He chose me. From Calvary hill Jesus called and ordained me to see Him through the sunrise, hear Him through the birds singing with Him through the wind, feel Him as I sit with His as the wind caresses me with love as I rest in the garden of His love where Jesus taught me to love.

I'm Sorry Lord

He came into the very world he created, but the world didn't recognize him. He came to his own people, and even they rejected him. John 1:10-11

Good morning sunrise dancing as you arise for this new day God called you to shine in. Good morning birds singing a song of jubilee, I hear and rejoice in your praise to the Risen Savior. Good morning dew on the grass, thank you for showing me how I must obey God, because His promises never return to Him void, and your moisture will fade before noonday. Good morning wind blowing through the Corinthian bells, your praise takes my mind of thankfulness to Calvary cross where all sin were wiped away. Good morning flower in blossoms, thank you for showing me new life, because once I was lost but now, I'm found. Good morning, Father in heaven, I'm not making you last on my morning praise list. How can I when You are forever on my mind. Thank You for knowing me by name and looking over the times I didn't know You other than by a name in a book.

Jesus, you made this world, yet the world doesn't know; the One who created the diamond people like to wear; the gold people like to use to buy their wants more so than their needs; the oil You have given, yet many think man did it; the harvest You bring, yet all credit is given to man and fertilizer. Not knowing You is not knowing the breath we breathe, the water we drink, the love we have to give to others. Jesus, I'm sorry!

Years ago, I walked a path of loneliness because I didn't know You...a path of many windings turns, because I did not serve You. A road of many signs of bitterness and sorrow, because I did not want to give up the familiar for the road of faith. My daily conversation with Jesus is one of friend to friend because He knows me by name and have called me by name. John 1:10 tells us that Jesus created the very world He came into, but He was not recognized. Everyone who passed Jesus on the road, heard His voice, saw His love didn't even know He was the Creator of everything they had, even to their lives. The very tree Jesus died on knew Jesus created it. The very whip that beat Him, He created. The very spit spitted on Him, He created yet they didn't know Him.

I am reminded of a story a young man told me about the car he designed before he was layoff from GM. This young man became homeless and had no food to eat. He had no car to drive before of nor money to fix it. He walked everyplace he went. As he walked, every time the fancy car he had designed passed by him he would at first become angry. But then, he knew anger would not solve his problem. So later on, when the fancy car passed by, he smiled knowing God allowed him to design something so lovely. However, the one driving the car didn't know he was passing by the one who designed the car which bring him pleasure.

This is what the world did to Jesus. The world didn't know Jesus, its Creator when people passed by Him, He wasn't desirable to them. They didn't know He came to forgive and set us free of the grip of the enemy. They didn't know He was the Designer of everything we have. The world didn't recognize Jesus, but the Word tells us that we may have entertained angels without realizing it. Hebrews 13:2

Even with the world not recognizing Jesus He never fail to give directions for staying on the narrow path that leads to heaven. And to keeping down an infestation of mosquitoes are similar: Keep old stale water away from your surroundings and keep down thick weed where mosquitoes reproduce and hide. Same with sins that pull you from the path of righteousness...pour out stale things from yesterday that may keep bitterness reproducing...and weeds that seeds more weeds that blocks the path that keeps you from seeing where you are going! Jesus is real because He woke you today! Man can't do it...for you. He created this world and the pleasures of it. He gives the birds songs of the morning, and if you listen closely, you can hear the robin song praising Jesus as freedom is at His feet. Oh, how beautiful of the feet that carry the Word of the Lord.

My Rock

The LORD is my rock, my fortress, and my deliverer, my God, my mountain where I seek refuge, my shield and the horn of my salvation, my stronghold. Psalm 18:2

There is someone today needing to know that God is Bigger, than the liar; Higher, than any attacks of the enemy; Mightier, than hurts of the heart or any pain of sadness; Stronger than any needs in your life; Restorer of any hopelessness. And God keeps His word of any promises He promised in His Word. As He said to Jeremiah, "For I will hasten My word to perform it" (Jeremiah 1:12).

Hope is never lost when you truly trust God at His word...He is not a man that He should lie. If God said, He meant it! Even in the wilderness there are blessings; even though, we can't see them when our eyes are only on "whoa it me" rather than the promised land. When God leads us through the wilderness, our clothes and shoes will never wear out, because He is with us. We will never hunger because He is the manna from heaven. We will never thirst because Jesus is the Rock of living water! At the end of each road is a turn leading to another road, it's left up to each of us if we allow God to show us the way or trust our own navigation system to lead to the road we want. God's appointed road may seem rocky, but He is with us to strengthen us through the path. When our chosen road seems smooth and clear of any roadblocks, remember human's eyes can't see what lies ahead. In every wilderness path there is a promised path ahead when you trust God to be your guide. In your life you will have wilderness, time of hardships, losses, challenges, tears, as well as times of waiting, or of simply not being in the place you want to be. Remember then this truth: In God, even the wilderness can be part of the Promised Land. No matter where you find yourself, no matter what your circumstance, no matter what your surroundings, rejoice, press forward...choose to live in victory even when hope seems beyond your reach, which it is, but God's arm is not too short to reach you. What the wilderness path meant for harm...God used it for good to get you to the Promised Land He planned for you.

Hidden Gifts

Finishing is better than starting. Patience is better than pride. Ecclesiastes 7:10

Do you have a goodies basket? I do. I keep one filled of the things the children like who comes to visit during the week. However, extra special things are added to the basket when my grandchildren come. As the basket is replenished...after it becomes low in items, some of the best treats are hidden away under the new things...and they are missed or overlooked until one of the children take time to dig beneath the surface to fine them. The one who digs deep finds some of the amazing treats my grandchildren left behind...and he or she is allowed to take it as a special gift.

This is the same with the promises God have for us...we sometimes only see what's on the surface overlooking what God has hidden away...until someone takes the time to dig deep enough to discover the gifts needed for such a time as this! Look within yourself today...and discover the wonderful promises awaiting you!

God is real and so are His promises...I see the bird trusting Him for its daily bread! Listening to the birds singing and watching them playing in the water after the rain I had an amazing revelation about faithfulness... Many use the statement, "I'm grounded and rooted right where I am, but I'm going to go on over to the other side for a while!"

Well, if they are grounded and rooted where they are...want they pull their roots up and they will need to be re-rooted again? Seems to be...I would stay where my roots are planted and being fed, because the next soil may not be the same...and also poor in nutrition where nothing grows! Faith in Jesus is the root system to overcoming the enemy's attacks. Like the sequoia tree linking its roots to roots with the sequoia tree next to it. Linking our faith to the promises of God strengthen each step we take in faith. We are not uprooting faith in Jesus. Our promises are hidden in the faith we have in Jesus.

Rejoicing

Let the fields and their crops burst out with joy! Let the trees of the forest rustle with praise. Psalm 96:12

Jesus 'love and forgiveness are above what I can think or imagine. Beyond what I can reach. His love is wider than space and time. Bigger than the world can hold or record. His love lives when I no longer breathe in this earthly life or enter through the pearly gates. His love is deeper than the sea has ever been explored or the planets that haven't been discovered. Only Jesus 'love and forgiveness can keep me whole.

The leaves are clapping with the breeze...I see God...

The trees are rustling with the wind...I hear God...

The sunrays are dancing with the movement of the trees obeying the wind...I feel God...

The aromas of the flowers are swaying with the cool breezy summer wind...I smell God.

The bowl of early picked blueberries covered with the morning dew are bursting with watery sweetness...I taste God!

God wants to show Himself to you today too!

Moses saw the glory of the Lord. The children of Israel saw Him in the fire by night and the clouds by day and heard Him in the fire on Mount Sinai.

How do you hear God?

I hear God in everything around me...

The birds singing...

The grass straying...

A newborn baby crying...

God has no limits of His presence...rejoice in the goodness of Jesus' love.

His love which moves mountains of troubles. His love that changes the stony heart... His love time cannot stop. War cannot kill. Hatred cannot defer. Bitterness cannot sour. Pain cannot wear out... Tears cannot wash away. The sun cannot burn away because Jesus is the Sun of Righteousness and healing is in His wing.

The sky cannot contain this love. The depth of the earth cannot hide its wonders. The seas cannot drown it aromatic flowing. The seas of trouble cannot keep back the love of Jesus. Death cannot bury it; the cross threw it and defeated the attacks against love. The grass rejoices in this love as it receives the fresh morning dew. The flower bloom in this love as only Jesus can unfold a rose without bruising it. The birds fly high as the cloud hides the sun. But the clouds cannot hide love since the clouds are the dust under Jesus' feet and He was taken to heaven in a cloud and will return to get the ones who loved Him in a cloud. World, can't you see Jesus? Can't you hear Him. He is speaking to the ones willing to listen. Listen, the birds they sing the song of heaven. The flowers can't water themselves. The bees can't feed themselves. God gives the flower, and the flowers invite the bee to come and for-take of their sweetness. The bees are God's promise that He will never leave me, and He is forever and forever because the bees make honey which last forever and ever. The crops in the field rejoice...this is the day to rejoice because God is not limited, He is everything everywhere.

Forgiven

"I do believe; help me overcome my unbelief!" Mark 9:24

As I sit here at 3:32a.m. in my prayer room asking God to forgive me for my lack of faith... I looked up and noticed the writing on the door of my closet "Blessed"! So, you know I bowed before God and asked for His forgiveness again. Why was I asking for forgiveness this time of morning? We too often forget how blessed we are with whining over a broken toenail, when there are people just getting news that they have bone cancer, and a nineteen-year-old sleeping in her car because the mother is a drug addict, the father may be whoever, and the grandmother doesn't care.

This is a question for you to ponder over this morning: Do you know how many teenagers have no place to sleep because the ones who once kept them now have put them out because the welfare checks ran out? You may be surprised by the numbers right around you. There are many! I found this poster "Blessed" yesterday after I gave this teenager many things to go into her new apartment another lady helped her to get. Her needs came down to needing soap to take a bath to a pan to cook in. After loading her car, she had slept in many nights unknowingly to us, I walked back to my Prayer Room and found this gift folded away with many gifts I received for Christmas, and it said, "Blessed." After giving this child a carload of gifts, my closets are still running over. She left my house with "Thank you." But what she didn't realize, I needed to be thanking her for allowing me to give of my blessings I too often overlook. So, God reminded me as I awoke to pray...with a mere beautifully written poster on my closet door, "You are blessed."

Thank You Father for the needed reminder, I'm blessed because You are my Father and I shall not want. And You have given me my needs and so many of my wants so I can share with others who need. Amen.

Set Apart

"Know that the LORD set apart the faithful for Himself; the LORD hears when I call to Him"(Psalm 4:3).

Things seem awful now, when they are in man's sight but not in God's. As I was walking around my bed making it up this morning I began hearing, "Listen, I am here. Listen, I am here." Quite naturally, I began to weep because I know the voice of Jesus and He was speaking. He knows when I'm feeling a little weary because He lives in me, and once again this morning I gave the Holy Spirit permission to occupy my temple without me trying to do it my way. "Listen, I am here. I am here." Are the only words I could hear as I walked around my bed again.

I walked back to my reading chair and began writing what I had heard. This message is for each one reading this as well as it is for me. Jesus knows the weariness too many are carrying needlessly; He knows the blindness to His blood the enemy has blinded too many with. Jesus knows this narrow path isn't easy because He said so Himself, but He knows the ones who trust in Him and is calling on Him now. Many are still going to the church buildings, but their faith is left outside the doors because they have no hope that God is in control. Where there should be prayer gathering, watching TV has taken up that time. "The effectual fervent prayer of a righteous man availeth much"(James 5:16). A young lady in prison sent this Scripture to me attached to a beautiful picture of a flower. This was her hope knowing prayer works.

Where are the prayers? The enemy shouldn't be having as much fun as he is now...but where there is a lack of faithful righteous prayers the enemy increases. Yes, there is troubles in the land, but Jesus 'blood is the shield of protection. Praise is the sounds of victory without guns and bullets... Praise confuses the enemy and Jesus 'blood blind the enemy to our path. Listen, Jesus is here! He is able! He is willing! He is available! He is the victory in the clouds. So, know this truth today, the enemy of the virus, and troubles in the street are dust under Jesus 'feet. Who are you trusting today...man or manna? Your prayers matter to the kingdom, and they defeat the enemy... Amen.

Not Abandoned

I keep the LORD in mind always. Because He is at my right hand, I will not be shaken... Psalm 16:8

I once was lost in sin, but Jesus took me in... Oh, what a Savior! Jesus loves me just as I am. Oh what endless love! Without Jesus I would be a leaf flowing uncontrollably in the invisible wind. My, my, my what deep love! These thoughts came to mind this morning when Jesus brought to my mind the conversation I had yesterday with a man sitting at my table. I met him with love, and I welcomed him to sit at my table with no judgmental thoughts or action. He came to my house two days back-to-back...so to speak. Yesterday, as he sat at my table, he looked at me and asked, "Were you told about my background and what I did?" I smiled and said, "yes, I was told." But I'm not allowed by God to go into the sea of forgiveness and pull up what you have confessed and repented of to God. God has forgiven you and now your mistakes of yesterday are sealed under Jesus 'blood. We are in today so let go forward. Big teardrops were welled up in his eyes. Then he told me about his freedom from twelve years of another life of destruction...now ten years of freedom as a new man. Yet a bad day had him bound because he did not know how I would react by knowing about his yesterdays.

Fifteen years ago, I asked Jesus to let me feel with His heart...not knowing feeling with His heart meant seeing a person's faults yet praying rather than accusing! Forgiving what I once would have cursed and held to in hatred. Seeing and hating the spirit rather than the person. Yes, feeling with the Father's heart causes you to be quiet rather than gossip. Pray rather than talk. Give rather than keep. Be uncomfortable rather than comfortable when others are suffering. I'm Sleeping hugging Jesus 'love rather than fearing. Awakening early and kissing Jesus with a good morning salutation rather picking up the remote to the TV. Oh, I'm thankful God shared His heart of love with me...and knowing my mistakes are in the sea of forgiveness and anyone who thinks it's ok to dive in to get them...God sees. I'm free but whoa to them who seek after someone's forgiven sin because Jesus 'blood sealed each mistake with forgiveness, and no one has the rights to retrieve not one. If God forgives and forgets our sins when confession and repentance are made who am I to do it my way!

The man left with a smile and wanted to hug me because he was shown God's Word in action. "Forgive other's trespasses so we can be forgiven." this is not a request from Jesus. It's a step to the stairway of heaven. I rather do it God's way.

Heart of Tears

You Yourself have recorded my wonderings. Put my tears in Your bottle. Are they not in Your records? Psalm 56:8

Good morning cloudy day the birds are singing a slow song in harmony with the gentle wind... Good morning clouds, the transportation of Jesus going into heaven and His arrival carriage when He come back. Good morning tree standing still in the cool summer breeze, your leaves are caressing you with thankfulness because you are the source of each of their lives. Good morning semi-silent and still day draped in loveliness under the clouds and your sun shining in beauty above each one. Good morning Holy Spirit, this day is still and cool. It's the day you have made, I am rejoicing and glad in it.

The birds are quiet today. Holy Spirit do the birds get sad and cry? The weeping willow cries. The dog whines, the cat's meow, but why should I ask You if the birds cry. I know they are compassionate to their chosen mate; many are devoted to one mate until death. Is this the love mankind should pattern after and the devotion we should have for the ones we choose as a mate? The birds obey and trust You, so thank You once again Lord for showing me myself and if we seek You, we can see and hear You all around us. Birds cry when they are sad... they have tears, and they cry because they have a heart which hurts also.

I cry when I am happy...I cry when I'm sadden over the path many are traveling to destruction...I cry when a child is lost, stolen, abandoned by his parents, misled into sin...I cry when the lonely feels there is no hope, and just merely breathing a breath not knowing God has given another day of His grace and mercy...I cry when the hungry feel they have no hope...I cry when the handicap is mistreated...I cry when the helpless in the nursing homes are forgotten by family and the ones paid to care for them...I cry when people speak a Christian life but walk a hellish path...I cry when strong men play with the 'strange woman 'and lose themselves. Proverbs 5:3-4 "For the lips of a strange woman drop as a honeycomb, and her mouth is smoother than oil: But her end is bitter as wormwood, sharp as a two-edged sword." I cry when a father and husband have sought a path of tears in days to come and have forgotten their loved ones, they have taken a vow to love, obey, and protect through sickness and health. The birds cry over their mate sickness and death. Father, did the birds take a vow before You? If so, they obey and honor their vows. Some birds choose their mate by beauty, some by song, some by running their mate down with flattery. Then some birds like man cheat on their mate after the family come.

Male birds are unfaithful to ensure they father as many chicks as they can, but females will cheat with males of better 'genetic quality '...ones that are fitter and can produce stronger offspring. researchers say that cheating comes with a cost...the cheating female's partner will provide less food for their nest of young. Cheating mates turn into deadbeat dads... Birds father mating monogamy. If a male house sparrow detects that his mate is cheating, he provides less food for their brood, a new. But an alternative explanation is that cheating families and lazy males tend to pair up naturally.[1]

I cry now because some the birds act like some human's waywardness. I cry when people believe a liar over the one who walks in truth...I cry when people use Jesus 'death on the cross like a Christmas gift you step on and throw away when it's old...I cry when the lost dies without repentance...I cry when people think they can do any sinful act and still go to heaven...but today I cry because many have sisters and brothers, nieces and nephew but are left alone during their time of sickness.

But I also recall what Jesus said," Who is My mother? Who is My brother? But those who do the will of the Lord." So right now, my tears are slowing down because I have to make a decision...cry or do God's will. I choose to do His will, to be a willing vessel to be used as God desires. Like the birds that walk in faithful obedience as God designed them. They sing in the morning light and follow the light until it's time for them to rest to sing again another day. Even during the darkness of the night, the birds sings as they were

---

[1] *The American Naturalist. Volume 188 Number 2*

designed to do. Thank You Holy Spirit for showing me this day the beauty of Your creation and how we each designed by You in similar ways, we each have tears and cry when our hearts are broken.

Visiting

Don't neglect to show hospitality, for by doing this some have welcome angels august without knowing it. Hebrews 13:2

When I go out of town to visit my son, grandson, and two nieces, I have four different houses I have to go to while I'm in the city. One house is in a gated neighborhood with a security guard at the gate to let in the ones on the resident's list of visitors; another one is gated, and you have to call their phone so they can unlock the gate from their phones; one is in a new neighborhood, and you just drive to their house without having to use a code, and the other one you park in front of their house if their driveway has other cars parked there. One of the neighborhoods feel like home because most of the neighbors know each other...and at the gate early in the morning is always one of the neighbors checking the area...and watch over the children as they get on the bus.

This morning, I thought about each of the neighborhoods I visit when I'm away from home...They are beautiful, and look safe, but at one of the gated neighborhood people come in from the back through the woods on their four wheelers. Then this thought entered my spirit..." Man can't keep you from harm, when one key was made a duplicate was made also; when one gun was made, a hundred were made just like it; when an alarm was made, a manual how to disarm it was made too; with a surveillance camera people wear masks...

So once again, God in His amazing way let me know and you are too I hope that: The enemy wears disguises to make you think the uncreated God can't take care of what He created.

1. He is our only protection the enemy can't cross over or get through.
2. He is the only Gate which needs no code to enter... Just each of choosing Jesus as our One and only Savior.
3. He is with us wherever we go...
4. If I live in the ghetto or mansion on a hill, He is with me...and no thief or security gate can keep Jesus away from me."

This is the question today. How do you see Jesus as your Helper and Guide in times of troubles around you?

When the disciples saw Jesus' walking on the water fear gripped them until they recognized it was Him. Then they said, "Lord don't pass us by!" I relayed this message to a lady I met in Newark a few weeks ago when she said blessings don't pass us by. Blessings can pass us by...by too often rejecting the one God puts in people's path to bless them. For example, last week the Holy Spirit directed me to give someone a much-needed monetary gift, but each time I called, the person would be too busy to talk to me. I would call back, and the person would be on the phone with someone else. This week I tried to give it again, but the person still never had time for me to tell of the blessing God directed me to give. Zephaniah 3:17 says God is "Mighty to save" but we must want to be saved. So today, I realized even more that we allow blessings to pass us by when we enjoy the conversations of the world more rather than taking time to hear God through His servants. Be watchful because we never know when we are entertaining angels (Hebrews 13:2).

So, have you ever taken time out of your busy or lazy day to thank someone for what he or she has done for you? Remember, even weeds need soil and moisture to grow and produce other weed seeds! You didn't change your own diaper or fixed your own bottle when you were born...someone helped you! Think about it before you think you became who you are all by yourself. Even the birds need each other.

Word of Encouragement

Search me, God and know my heart; test me and know my concerns." Psalm 139:23

I have never seen a night that didn't turn into day; rain that doesn't water the soil; a lie that will not be revealed; or wrong trying to force its way on right. But I have seen clouds that don't give rain; a chicken that doesn't lay eggs; salt without taste; and people who never say they are sorry no matter what they say! But this is the good news... God knows how to handle each one, because He is the Battle Fighter! Just believe He can and will do the impossible on each of our behalf.

During your childhood someone may have spoken negative words over you, and you still hear and believe what was spoken! Take a small journey with me to the lowly donkey that carries burdens. Jesus chose it over the horse to carry Him. A little insignificant seed that sprouted into a tree was chosen by man for something bad. However, it held our sins as Jesus hung on it. So today, seek to see yourself as God sees you, chosen to do something someone else can't do for the kingdom. You may be the one who leads a blind soul to the light!

1. When life throws you an apple core...make jelly! Remember, jelly is desirable to the eaters, and they never ask how it got to the table...they just know it's well! Trust God with your problems, He knows how to make beauty from ashes!

2. What do you think will carry you to hell? The rich man in Luke 16 didn't go to hell because he was rich, killed, hurt, or stole, he went because of selfishness and not feeding the hungry. The poor man didn't go to heaven because he was poor, he went because he didn't blame, cursed, or talked against the rich man. And God even sent a dog to comfort him before he passed!

3. No matter where you are or where you work...show kindness even if bitterness wants to drown it out...your eternity depends on it!

4. A few years ago, I sent out a message on "Forgiveness." We must forgive to be forgiven. Hell is as real as heaven, but hell has tormenting benefits. Forgiven and God forgives and forgets (Hebrews 8:12). Reply, "We are not God, and you must have amnesia if you forget! This is my stand today. since I can't go to heaven if I don't forgive and stop reminding the person what he or she have done to me. I rather have amnesia than a home in hell!

5. There is nothing as beautiful as righteousness... Righteousness is being like God in character. So today, let your makeup be inside more than outside, and if you are cut in two let the seers see pure gold right through you. Makeup washes away...pure gold gets purer with each level and intensity of heat.

6. A cup half full is like almost being a Christian... It can become full and keep running over, or empty and dry out... Same with serving God...either you do which brings joy...or you don't that bring misery before the lasting fire! Choose wisely today, because tomorrow may not come!

Read the Book of Jude.

Rescue Me

Rescue me, LORD, from evil men. Keep me safe from violent men who plan evil in their hearts. They stir up wars all day long. Psalm 140:1-2

Today, Jesus wants each of you to know that He's in the exchange business, and no receipts are required to come and exchange the things of the evil one for the things of God. Matter of fact, He wants you to destroy each receipt of the things you were wearing and eating from yesterday! His exchange desk is opened twenty-four hours a day...so bring your weariness and receive peace...your pity and receive assurance...your doubts and receive faith...your fears and receive love and a sound mind. There is also more good news...Jesus' exchange desk never closes, and transportation is free; He paid for it all already!

I don't need to tell you what you need to confess and repent of your sins because you know better than I do what you are holding inside. God wants to rescue you from yourself. Many may say, "God knows my heart." You better believe God knows your heart better than you do, and He knows what you need to repent of from your heart. Jesus is a recuse worker and first responders to your needs. The sins of the world you are carrying are deleting your oxygen level each day. The forgiveness of sin was created at the Cross when Jesus breathed His breath for our rescue. This is the 'season of repentance, deeply searching your soul and asking God to reveal your secret sins because tomorrow Jesus may come. Today Jesus may come. He is not coming to rescue the unrepentant this time, He is coming to rescue the ones who have chosen His as Lord and Savior. I'm just the messenger it's left up to you if you seek God and do what He ask. Jesus is asking for your life to shine so brightly that and your children, the church, and this country will see and be pulled to the Light in you.... God is not asking you to walk this this path alone, He is with you and carries you when you are too weak to go. God needs willing vessels to say yes to His calling to be disciples in order to make more disciple.

Thought for today: God has no part in my failures just my blessings. My desires are God's delight when I delight in Him. My wishes are my laziness when my faith in God is my mountain mover. Being a servant of God is my action rather than my talk.

You Are Good

Humble yourselves before God. Resist the devil, and he will flee from you. Come close to God, and God will come close to you. James 4:7-8

Wow, is too mild...
    My goodness is too worldly...
    Holy cow is too idol...
    Woo wee is too common...
    I can't believe, it is doubt disguised...
    So, all I can say with my excitement is...
    God is amazing...
    God is faithful...
    God is sho'nuf good...
    God speaks to the ones willing to listen...

How? Through our ears when we hear the thunder. Through our eyes when we see the lightning followed by the rainbow. Through His Word when we read it. But more so, when we enter His presence...miracles happen, spiritual ears are opened, spiritual eyes see, the heart understands God is realer than the heat in summertime, and promises met. Saying all this to say...this is the epiphany of the morning. People are struggling with loneliness, rejection, being alone even with family members all around, yet never see or hear from anyone.

So, yesterday, as cards were written to different people, one was written to a man without a leg who felt as if life was merely to wake each day to sit and wait for night to come...then sleep and wake again to face another day lonely. He felt abandoned by family because no one called him or came to see him. A statement was made by one of the writers, "He has Jesus. He's not alone."

This morning God showed me. Jesus was surrounded by His disciples during the day...and He was in His Father's presence at night. However, when the Father turned away from Jesus on the cross, Jesus cried out to His Father and said, "My God why have You forsaken Me?" This man (without a leg) feels this way...he just needs to know someone cares.

Also, Jesus sent the disciples out two by two... David had his fighting men with him...Paul walked with Silas, and even Jesus carried Peter, James and John with Him to His transfiguration. He was never alone, and even on the cross one of thieves received Jesus as his Savior. Even God gave Balaam a donkey who served him, and God allowed it to talk to him...to remind him how he had served him, and actually saved his life. He wasn't alone on his path of destruction...

So, the revelation for today is...yes, we have Jesus, and we are never alone, but we, each is here to make a difference in someone's life. And we need a word of encouragement when the journey gets hard. I'm sitting here in the doctor's office now for my follow up exam... The nurse turned and looked at me as she was leaving the room and said, "I'm praying for your trip to South Africa, and your ministry here. You will do good wherever you are." The doctor said, "When I was doing my roster yesterday for today...I saw your name and was glad you were coming today. My nurse said, "Mrs. Goree is coming today. I enjoy it when she comes...hearing her adventures (my adventures with God).'" I smiled with thankfulness knowing God uses me wherever I go. Then God showed me one more thing...I received a letter from a seventeen-year-old young man saying, "You help and do so much for everyone else...you need encouragement too." I smiled even bigger knowing God sends a word of encouragement to us when we need it...through the least likely person to keep us from feeling alone. God knew I needed a word of encouragement, as He knows the lonely abandoned one leg man needed a friendly word of hope through a paper card coming through the mail. Five minutes, a card or paper, a stamp, and a walk to the mailbox made a difference in someone's life. Before you say again that a lonely, homeless, rejected person has God...yes, he/she does, but God wants to use you for His plans for that person to never feel forsaken. Are you willing to be used even as the trees clap their hands doing God's will? A kind word from a kind heart can break the stranglehold of lost hope from a wearily heart.

Your 'Wow Message' for today:

Many people today are in the midst of a great river of life but are dying of thirst because they do not dip down and take it. Doubts and fears are cankerworms that eat up faith.

Pages of Life
Be strong and courageous all you who put your hope in the LORD... Psalm 31:24

It amazes me how people read the obituary of the deceased person line by line during his or her services. Even though, some are fabricated from the loved one's perspective rather than God's. God wrote the stories for our life, but we began deleting each page to do it our way. Yes, God wrote the story for our lives, but He also gave us a 'free will', and He also gave a blueprint to follow so we would not get lost. He didn't write in our story to be a liar, a thief, a blasphemer, or an unbeliever etc. God wrote our stories, but it's left up to each of us to read His plans for our lives and follow. So, when you see your neighbors blessed, happy, peaceful, walking the path of favor, maybe they followed God's written stories for their lives page by page... But you erased yours by choosing the ways of the world. Today, let people see your life story written by God because the plans He have written for you are not fabricated, but changes lives because they see Jesus through you... We are to be a ship on the seas for the lost drowning in despair, the lifejacket to cast out to the ones in the raging waves of troubles. A word of encouragement is hope in a storm. An extended hand is the oar when there is no sail in the ship. Each page of our lives is a page of prayer when a child is lost. A hammer hammering the word when a child is stolen, a safe haven to lead the weary to the Rock and Shelter of the Almighty.

Take this word of encouragement, the ones who think you can't take another step because you are too weak, and it's too painful to move! The answer is, you can't, but God can. The Holy Spirit is our strength in our weaknesses, He is our Comforter in sorrow and weariness of not being able to do what we once did. The Holy Spirit is the same yesterday, today, and tomorrow. You may not be able to do what you use to do, but God can do far more than what our minds can imagine when we trust Him.

This morning as I got out of bed, my feet were still swollen from a long day's work yesterday. Also, I had tossed in pain from my shoulder that was over worked from writing and typing all day. But through prayer and praise around 3:00 a.m. the Holy Spirit touched my shoulder, and I went back to sleep, then woke up without pain or discomfort, matter of fact, I lifted it up to the blue sky and thanked God from healing me!

Back to my walking. Walking in the morning now is harder than usual, but to sit and wait for tomorrow would be a lack of faith. I put my walking clothes on, walked outside still in discomfort. The flowers were pointing their blossoms toward heaven and the birds were eating from the feeders. As I looked at each, I thanked God for His beautiful morning. Then I took my first my steps toward the direction I was taking. "Lord be my strength. Carry me this day. Amen"

I walked faster and farther than I have since I began to walk again seven weeks ago. I couldn't do it on my own, I needed Jesus' strength, and He faithfully did what He promised He would do. "Ask and it will be given." Be of good courage as you trust God to strengthen you. Each page of life turns as the days turn, and each brings a new wave of hope, because doubts are not allowed. Yes, we can do all thing through God who strengthens us, but we can do nothing by ourselves.

Only God's Voice
LORD, listen and be gracious to me; LORD, be my helper. Psalm 30:10

Good morning Holy Spirit. Thank You for a peaceful and restful night sleep. Good morning, this windy just-warm enough day I'm enjoying the breath of the Lord. Good morning, honking geese you woke me before sunrise to remind me that yesterday is gone, and this is a new day. Good morning clouds the dust under God's feet trampling out the enemy. Each morning the Holy Spirit gives a word of encouragement of His grace to strengthen the heart of the mistakes of yesterday, because Satan roams the earth 1 Peter 5:8 seeking the ones he can keep reminding of their troubled past so he can keep them in a **'spiritual jail'**. God in His amazing way shows us His hand of comfort through the geese honking to encourage the geese up front to keep up their speed. Hearing the honking of the geese is a sound of encouragement to encourage the ones seeking peace from mistakes made yesterday that yesterday is gone, and God is welcoming us to a new day mistake free. God have given His 'chosen one' Luke 18:7 **'spiritual keys'** to unlock each cell door of despair; by His Word, The Holy Bible! The sunrise brings promises and the sunset cast the mistakes of each day as far as the East is from the West.

God's Word is a weapon which blasts the missile of the enemy in two when we are attacked with the spirit of abandonment. God gives His children the best He can give naturally, a loving mother because Jesus called Himself a 'mother hen'. God gave us mothers the world gave us drugs. Children are crying in the womb not to die before their time. Children are crying in the alleys for mommy and daddy to tell them who they are. Where are the mothers? Where is the father? Do they know their children are crying? You hear the dog barking in the alley and feed it. You close your ears to the cry of a starving baby. A baby whose organs are being cut out as they cry in pain. Where is the compassion? Oh, I forgot, sin has no compassion.

Sin doesn't share with sin partner, killing wants more killing! Hatred wants more hatred. Lying wants more lying. So where is the end to this? In the abyss when Satan is locked away forever. Father, mend the broken heart. Mold the broken pieces life has shattered...

Lives are shattered in many pieces man cannot repair. Your tomorrows begin today where the mending hand of hope reaches out with mercy and grace to restore, mends a heart hearing false echoes from the alley where innocent was stolen... But Jesus heard the cries of the children left wanting, but what, they don't know what, because the world painted their minds with rainbow color lies and false dreams.

A word of hope brings a tree of hope...

A word of doubt brings a tree of doubt...

You are fearfully and wonderfully made My child...

So, when the enemy comes tomorrow to tell you that you are not. Let him see your roots of hope of the positive seed planted yesterday to harvest hope for tomorrow.

Lazy Day Breeze

"Give us a king to judge us." 1 Samuel 8:6

The wind is blowing half between a warm and hot breeze this morning. I'm a little lazy this morning, no, I'm a little tired this morning because I had a long... long day at the poll yesterday. Very few came in to exercise their rights to vote, but I have found out over the years, it's not about how many come in to vote, but the ones who come because there is someone there to talk to. Many of the ones who come in feel rejected because of their finances, some feel down because of divorces, some feel isolated because of caring for a sick loved one, some feel lonely because of the death of a loved one, some comes just to hear a kind word of concern about his or her well-being. Yesterday, one man came in not to vote (because if you voted one political party the first of the month you couldn't change to another party yesterday), but just to talk. His wife of 60 years is now too sick to do for herself, and he has to take care of her completely. He just needed a break to talk and know he was in our prayers and his wife too. He came in with deep wrinkles of weariness, he left out with a smile. God uses His servants to do His will no matter where we are. One man comes in rain or shine during the election to be blessed with a word of God over his illness. However, yesterday I was blessed with freshly picked blueberries, onions, tomatoes, apricots, grapes, and more grapes because I was thought about before I got there. The thoughtful kindness made me cry. Some came with heavy hearts but left with a word of hope; some with weary hearts, but a word of, "How are your children" melted weariness to a gentle smile of "Thank you for asking."

I came with cheese and crackers and left with fruits for a week, and a glad heart in a tired body to be chosen by God to do His will at a country-side election poll...

This morning's epiphany... If you say Jesus is your Savior, why is Satan allowed to take up room in your belief, and you welcome him to stay with your doubts and fears? Either you truly trust Jesus with everything, and I mean everything, or stop fooling yourself and others that Jesus is your all and all. Oh, yea, don't use the old excuse, this is just my human side... Paul only wavered in his complaints when he asked God to take the thorn from his side. but God said to Paul as He is saying to each of us. "My grace is sufficient."

So, start today to trust God with all your needs, wants, and desires. It's not easy trusting what you can't see a head. But it's not for you to see beyond the mountain, because you may turn away from God's promises if you see the peaks and jagged rocks to go through to reach them. Just trust the One who moves mountains and the One who walks with you through the valleys.

The Holy Spirit gave me a message the first of the week to write and post. I wrote it, but I didn't post it because I felt I was writing out of my own thoughts. God took me into Unquenchable praise and prayer even to the point I found specks of gold on my sheet Wednesday morning. I still didn't post this until yesterday, but in my sleep during the night the Holy Spirit spoke these words, "Must Be Born Again." I jumped up from my sleep at 2:30am this morning knowing I must post what the Lord had given me Monday. I failed to do what He had given me to do and I'm sorry.

96 and 1

Sing a new song to the LORD; sing to the LORD, all the earth. Psalm 96:1

After reading Psalm 96 there began a stirring in my spirit...and a shifting in the atmosphere. Whenever I feel a stirring, something is taking place in the spiritual realm that is going to touch the earth... The Sunday before the government asked the churches to shut down, schools to close, and businesses to close during service there was shifting of the atmosphere, and I told each one in service that the atmosphere was too thick. Sure, enough people began crying in fear. Fear of tomorrow. Fear of the day. Fear of family even coming around. The news media was pouring fear into people who loved to get out but was now too afraid to leave their homes. Then some people had no regards of other people safety. The Monday afterward fears began covering people the calls began coming from people too fearful to get out of bed. Even to the point of people believing they were going to die.

This morning the atmosphere is shifting with a falling away. The true believers are being revealed and the religious are being exposed. I almost cried as God revealed this stirring, but I can't cry or become disheartened because God had already told us these things would happen. The trees, birds, rain, wind, clouds, and sweet aromas of the morning are still doing what they were created to do...praising God in His holiness.

My friend either you believe and trust God or you don't. You can't be trusting God and fearing at the same time. God is not a partner with fear. You can't worship and hide in doubts that someone near you is sick with a virus...we are required to pray and use authority given to us in... Mark 16:17-18 which tells each born again Christian, "And these signs will accompany those who believe: In My name they will drive out demons; they will speak in new tongues; they will pick up snakes with their hands, and if they drink any deadly poison, it will not harm them; they will lay their hands on the sick, and they will be made well."

Are we believers in Christ Jesus, or like fake news? Sounding good isn't working, we must do the will of the Lord to stand in the fire knowing it can't touch us because the angels are encamping about us.

Micah Stampley sang a song about ten years ago called *"The War Cry."* There is a war going on now, and it's not a war of flesh and blood, it a war in the spiritual realm. Put on your battle gear of prayer and fasting because the enemy isn't hiding nor playing! He is bold and looking for casualties of souls. Move from your slumber and prepare for this war for souls through steadfastness of repentant and humbling yourself before God and He will fight our battle. If you are not born again. Do it NOW!

So, Good morning beautiful day the birds sing together as if having an early morning coffee time. The sunrise greets their songs as the Robin sings a welcoming praise and the sparrow reply in echo praise of thankfulness "Jesus our Creator holds us in His protection."

Standing in Truth

The house of the wicked will be destroyed, but the tent of the upright will stand. Proverbs 14:11

We often look at the time of slavery and the hardship of the ones of color being abused with hatred. But God was with each one serving Him then as He is with the ones serving Him now. God's grace of forgiveness is for each of us to use when the attacks come, and they will come when we walk with God. However, in times of troubles I think we forget where our help comes from, and who our Helper is, because we too often whine as if we have no Helper.

Now, I love the story of Sojourner Truth (whose birth name was Isabella Baumfree), because it gives a different outlook on faith. All of her children were sold as slaves, but she and one of her daughters escaped to freedom. Even though, it was the time when slaves had no rights in court, Sojourner took legal action to regain her small son Peter back when he was sold. Now, knowing she couldn't raise her children without God's help, she became a believer in Christ, and she changed her name to Sojourner Truth to show that her life was built on the foundation of God's truth.

With God's faithfulness we are walled in and shielded from the stones and arrows of the enemy. Sojourner's faith in God was amazing and is an example for each of us. One day a friend asked Sojourner if she was afraid for her safety because she'd received death threats, recommended she carry a gun. Sojourner replied, "I carry no weapon; the Lord will [preserve] me without weapons. I feel safe in the midst of my enemies; for the truth is powerful and will prevail." Sojourner built her house on the Truth, the Word of God the enemy can't teardown. Proverbs 14:1 says, "The wise woman builds her house, but with her own hands the foolish one tears hers down." Guns make war, the Word and trust in God tears down the enemy's camp. After reading about Sojourner Truth, I'm inspired to walk even more in truth and stand when the enemy wants me to run. Sojourner knew who she was, and she didn't let man dictate her path. She never was slave minded because her freedom was in serving God, and He honored the path she chose because she was a sojourner of truth what I desire to be.

Who God Says I am

The reflections of the heart belong to man, but the answer of the tongue is from the LORD. Proverbs 16:1

Zion Williamson signed a forty-five million dollars NBA contract, is he more important than you? Simone Biles broke the Women Gymnastic's record...is she more gifted than you? Mahalia Jackson is known as the greatest gospel singer of all time...is she more favored than you? You may not be tall and play ball, short and flip well, or hold a tune in a bucket, but you hold an extremely rare gift...Your Life!

Your days on earth come around only once in an eternity only once. Every moment you have, comes around only once in an eternity and never again.

How must you live? Appreciating every moment and the calling and gifts only God put in your life to do.

You may not be on the news for your gifts, but you will be in the most important Book of all...the Book of Remembrance in heaven. You may not have millions of dollars, but your heavenly rewards are priceless...

Therefore, make the most of every moment. For it will never come again. Whatever good you would do, do it now. Treat every moment as if it was infinitely rare and of infinite value...because it is. With each day, ask God to give you wisdom to live life His way to make a difference in this world of uncertainties. Treat this day as if it comes around only once in an eternity...because it does.

"So teach us to number our days, that we may gain a heart of wisdom"(Psalm 90:12). God brought you forth at this time for you to make a difference. He knows what it is, it now time for you to search it out.

My Own Faith

Do you really speak righteously, you mighty ones? Do you judge people fairly?
Psalm 57:1

How often do you hear statements like, "Pastor Joe Joe is sho'nuff anointed, I'm following him!" The truth to be told, Pastor Joe Joe is a mere man, the One living in him is the One you follow. If any leader seeks fame and fortune rather than seeking God over riches, then you better refocus your thoughts. It's sometimes not the leader who has more faith... Matter of fact, the leader is not responsible for your faith, he or she is responsible to walk a path which leads you to the narrow path where faith lives.

The wilderness is an example of the narrow path of faith. Israel spent forty years being tested in the wilderness. Of the generation that left Egypt, only two out of the original 600,000, Joshua and Caleb, entered the Promise Land. Joshua and Caleb entered the Promised Land because they had immovable faith in God. Moses is an example of a leader leading complaining people, and the people's complaining wearing away a walk of faith with God. Listening daily to complaining made Moses and Aaron stumble. Joshua and Caleb each kept their faith trust in God.

God talked to Moses' face to face, gave him the Law, showed him His glory, lifted His hands from destroying the people when Moses asked, but the sins and complaining of the people made Moses angry for God that he stumbled into disobeying God. Moses struck the rock rather than speaking to the rock. Remember, this one thing, God doesn't need yours or my help, just our faith like Joshua. Numbers 20:11-12 "Then Moses raised his hand and struck the rock twice with his staff, so that a great amount of water gushed out, and the congregation and their livestock were able to drink. But the LORD said to Moses and Aaron, "Because you did not trust Me to show My holiness in the sight of the Israelites, you will not bring this assembly into the land that I have given them." Prime example, of reacting in anger because it blinds our thinking.

The children of Israel entered the wilderness they crossed the Red Sea and journeyed on to Elim the place of twelve wells and seventy palm trees. There they camped, received physical refreshment and fresh hope before entering the next phase of their journey to the Promised Land. Elim was a picture of God's grace and the rest that we find in Him and in His kingdom.

The actual distance between Elim and the Promised Land was not great. The children of Israel could have arrived in probably less than a month. But they needed to pass through the wilderness on the way because God had many things to teach them. If they had entered the Land immediately, they might have been destroyed by their enemies. When the nation of Israel crossed the Red Sea, they were 'baptized 'into Moses (1Corinthians 10:1,2).

In the wilderness they would learn through Moses, and through their trials and temptations, that their hearts were sinful, unbelieving and rebellious against God. Similarly, we need to be convicted by the truth of God's Law and His mercy and grace. Israel spent forty years being tested in the wilderness...this is an example for each of us to follow. We see what happened to the ones wanting their own way. They never saw the Promised Law, but sadly, their sins and complaining wore at Moses 'patient causing him to do it his way rather than following God's instructions. As of today, a message is giving warning to each of you of the ways not pleasing to God. But do you listen? No, because Monday you are doing it your way... God asked Moses this troubling question." Moses, "How long will this evil assembly be murmuring against Me? I have heard the murmurings of the children of Israel which they murmur against Me. Say to them, "As I live," says the LORD, "just as you have spoken in My ears, so I will do to you. In the wilderness your corpse will fall, and all who were numbered of you, according to your whole number, from twenty years old and upward, who have murmured against Me, you will not go into the land which I swore by My hand to cause you to dwell in it, except Caleb the son of Jephunneh and Joshua the son of Nun"(Numbers 14:26-30). Complaining against God stops the plans for a fulfilled life in His hands... Is your mouth causing you trouble?

Walk With Me Lord
Jesus, Son of David, have mercy on me! Luke 18:38

Right now, allow God to take a walk through your heart to remove any debris that would cause you to be a day or moment late that you will miss His coming! When the rain came and Noah's Ark began to float...the people were a day late in repentance, and they all drowned. Will you be a day late when your time comes to face God at death, or when Jesus comes on the cloud? If you are reading this book...you still have time to get it right! Do it Right Now!

I have never seen night that didn't turn into day; rain that doesn't water the soil; a lie that will not be revealed; or wrong trying to force its way on right. But I have seen clouds that don't give rain; a chicken that doesn't lay eggs; salt without taste is useless. People who never say they are sorry no matter what they say are stumbling blocks to the ones seeking the narrow path!

But this is the good news... God knows how to handle each situation; He is the Battle Fighter! He is the Redeemer and He live. I know He lives, not that I think Jesus lives, I know He live because I live the promised fulfilled victory of His knocking the stone from the tomb with the key to life in His hands. I am redeemed because my redeemer lives. Now is the time to just believe He can and will do the impossible on each of our behalf. He is the Gift Giver of the undeserving and the unfaithful because He give another breathe to breath is His gift of live. I know my Redeemer live!

Listen, the hour is coming, yes, it has now come that you will be scattered, each to his own home, and will leave Me alone. Yet I am not alone, for the Father is with Me" (John 16:32).

We are not alone because the Father is with us. Even in the times of passing through the fires of trouble which seen unquenched, He is the water which calm the fire and He is the Fire which calms my fears. Jesus wants each beat of the heart to beat for Him. Even if your world says Jesus doesn't live, it has forgotten one important thing...Jesus is the world's heartbeat. The computer cannot breathe for you, the idol gods held in the hands can't see for you. The computer is man-made...the idols are craved by hands, and an idol god has to be carried by human hands made and created by God. As Jesus walks through your heart allow Him to wash it clean with His cleansing DNA which have never been touched by human blood John 1:13. Father, remove the scales off the world's eyes so they can see You. So, they can think beyond the opinions of blind foolish men. Father, have mercy on me. Amen.

Thought...Iron lungs cannot keep itself from rusting.

Heavenly Confession

The LORD is gracious and righteous; our God is compassionate. Psalm 116:5

I'm seeing more and more how The Word of God is being fulfilled. The wicked will come to their knees and God hears the cries of the righteous. I'm seeing the ones who have abused the ones who loved them all alone now and under the hand of the one once rejected. I'm seeing the ones who used a loved one like a maid now wanting to die because the maid is not able any longer and gone from home. I'm seeing the ones who looked at pornography and rejected prayer now wanting a touch from God just to breath. I'm seeing the abuser now lacking the abused. I'm seeing the one who used racial slurs now hope the one called names will bring a meal. I'm seeing the one without compassion needing compassion. I'm seeing the ones who cherished and worshiped material things finding each as a burden to use.

God opens the pages of life to show us His Word in action, but more so, His Word as true. His heart pours out for each soul because Jesus died for each of us. God knows how to soften each heart, how to save the ones who think life is in their hands and that Jesus is forgotten and rejected as the Giver of each breath. In lowness, looking up is the only answer to our needs and God will put someone in our path to lead us to Him. Life is precious and short and there is no time to waste on wickedness, and thinking you need no one. Even if you have riches, riches can't buy a loving hand to wipe away the tears of pain. Riches only buys a hand that only last until the money runs out. God smiles when we follow Him, because when this life ends on this side, I want my step into eternity to be sweet in God's sight "Precious in the sight of the LORD is the death of His godly ones." Psalm 116:1

Yes, I have everything I need because I chose Jesus as my Savior...I have everything I want because He is my Shepherd...There is no lack in serving the Lord and allowing Him to be Lord of my life. I'm in the shelter of the Most High when I chose to follow Him. Choosing Jesus and obeying His will in my life, my cup runs over. Giving to the needy, God sends me more:

My cupboard runs over. My closets are bursting opened. My prayer room has no other space for books. My porch overflow with visitors.

Last week, a visitor filled her car with her needs from my cupboard, refrigerator, laundry room, and bathroom. Yesterday, as I was walking (a half mile from home) a car stopped, the window rolls down, and a friend said, "I have something for you!" She gets out of her car, lifts up her back door, and gives me five to six pounds of sweet white grapes and sweet carrots (I had just given grapes in my refrigerator to a young lady four days before). I had to walk the half mile home with bags of sweet grapes and carrots in one hand, and my dog stick in the other. My refrigerator is full again with grapes sweeter than the ones I had given days before... Not only grapes, but also, I was given a full box of my favorite food, organic zucchinis. Delighting in the Lord...He will give you the desires of your heart! So good morning, birds that sing a song of trust. Good morning noonday, rose climbing on the trellis reaching for the sun. Good night daylight, frogs singing croaking song to the watches of the night. Good night Holy Spirit my Guiding Light. The Lord is my Shepherd I have all I need... Psalm 23:1

Zephaniah 3:17 The LORD your God is among you; He is mighty to save. He will rejoice over you with gladness; He will quiet you with His love; He will rejoice over you with singing."

New Morning

For his mercies never end. They are new every morning; great is Your faithfulness! Lamentation 3:22b-23

Good morning, beautiful sunrise with the trees as portrait of your light breaking the storm clouds of the night. Hello one-of-a-kind morning I have never seen before because each morning is new. Thank You Father for each fading day one more promise is fulfilled or sadly deferred. Good morning, Holy Spirit! What is on your heart today? Lingering in expectation of a Rhema word, I'm waiting needing to hear the Father's voice. Smell His fragrance. Feel His breathe. Lingering to meet with my Father who never lets me go unaware.

So, as I emerged in prayer this morning, I heard in my spirit, "Many roads." I stopped in prayer because I knew a lie was trying to creep in." Many roads lead to Jesus." I rebuked this lie, and then I heard deep within me," No, only one road leads to Jesus and that's the 'narrow path'. I realized then how there's a war of truth raging inside of each of us. Remember Paul said, "So this is the principle I have discovered: When I want to do good, evil is right there with me" (Romans 7:21). Praise God that He guarded my mind and spirit because I seek the truth and He granted me wisdom to know and recognize the enemy's lie. So yes, there are many roads painted with despair, guilts, worrying, temptation, doubting, disbelief, whining, complaining, half-truths, and the bright...bright signs blinking, "Follow me to the exciting places!" Which each lead to destruction.

After I finished praying and began with the next part of my day, I began to think, "How did that liar put a lie and temptation in my prayer time? Did I not go to that secret place where the falcon's eye can't see in, or the lion's feet have never trodden?" But then I rejoiced because I knew the voice of temptation of the enemy, but I knew the voice of Truth and obeyed the voice of the Father in heaven. I felt bad, then I rejoiced because I passed the test. This reminds me of the boy who copied from the boy's paper next to him on the mid-term test. He copied so that he even copied the final statement the other boy made... "you should have studied for this test because all my answers are wrong." So, yes, the enemy's answers were wrong this morning, because seeking God and studying His Word prepared me for the test. The enemy's path leads to destruction. Then, I realized I have been listening to too many voices and opinions about John's rehab stay, when the only, yes ONLY voice I should follow is the Holy Spirit my guide and teacher.

Isn't it amazing how God gets our attention? It took a lie in my prayer time for me to see the truth and close out the voices of others who see only the old John rather than the John God is molding in His hands. When we are broken God is the Potter who mends us to the creation of His choosing. And He wants us on the road less traveled...the Narrow Path which leads to eternal life with Jesus.

One road led to Jesus and that's the 'narrow path'. I realized then how there's a war of truth raging inside of each of us. Remember Paul said, "So this is the principle I have discovered: When I want to do good, evil is right there with me" (Romans 7:21). Praise God that He guarded my mind and spirit because I seek the truth and He granted me wisdom to know and recognize the enemy's lie. So yes, there are many roads painted with despair, guilts, worrying, temptation, doubting, disbelief, whining, complaining, half-truths, and the bright...bright signs blinking, "Follow me to the exciting places!" Which each lead to destruction. After I finished praying and began with the next part of my day, I began to think, "How did that liar put a lie and temptation in my prayer time? Did I not go to that secret place where the falcon's eye can't see in, or the lion's feet have never trodden?" But then I rejoiced because I knew the voice of temptation of the enemy, but I knew the voice of Truth and obeyed the voice of the Father in heaven. I felt bad, then I rejoiced because I passed the test. This reminds me of the boy who copied from the boy's paper next to him on the mid-term test. He copied so that he even copied the final statement the other boy made... "you should have studied for this test because all my answers are wrong." So, yes, the enemy's answers were wrong this morning, because seeking God and studying His Word prepared me for the test. The enemy's path leads to destruction. Then, I realized I have been listening to too many voices and opinions about John's rehab stay, when the only, yes ONLY voice I should follow is the Holy Spirit my guide and teacher.

Isn't it amazing how God gets our attention? It took a lie in my prayer time for me to see the truth and close out the voices of others who see only the old John rather than the John God is molding in His hands. When we are broken God is the Potter who mends us to the creation of His choosing. And He wants us on the road less traveled...the Narrow Path which leads to eternal life with Jesus.

All Around Me I See Jesus

I am the rose of Sharon, and the lily of the valleys. Song Of Solomon 2:1

The morning light reflects the beauty of Jesus the rose of Sharon Song of Song 2:1. The aroma of the fresh morning breeze is the fragrance of my Savior. The dew which rests upon my skin is His kiss of love. "His cheeks are as a bed of spices, as sweet flowers"(Song Of Song 5:13). I feel Jesus.

How can I say no to such a love, such a friend, such a light, such a sweet bed of love overflowing with heavenly peace which gives me sleep?

Jesus is knocking with His gift of love. Gift of salvation. Gift man cannot give nor take away. Don't you hear Him? He is singing a serenade of comfort. Don't you feel it? Jesus is seeking your love. He is reaching through the moment of times desiring to hold you...His left hand is under my head...and his right hand embraces me. Song For Solomon 2:6

Want you receive Jesus' awaken love, His sweet aroma of love which beckon His beloveds. My beloved spoke, and said to me: "Rise up, my love, my fair one, and come away" Song of Solomon 2:10. Jesus is waiting to receive you this day. He's standing at the door of each heart wooing with His sweet voice and lovely face. Do you see His face? Look around you, look within you, look at the reflection in the clear blue water of love in Jesus' eyes, as He looks back at you with the reflection of love. Each blue sky above you, each white cloud beneath the sky, each sunrise of the glow of new life, each sunset calling for rest is Jesus' show of love. Oh, the fragrance of love is calling with each dawn, with each bird song, with each cove of the grass, with each chicken announcing the arrival of a new laid egg, Jesus is showing Himself.

Jesus' gentleness is softer than the clouds; His seeking lost sheep outshines lightning from the storehouse. The roses in May can't compare to His fragrance of love. He is the Rose of Sharon, the Bright Morning Star, the Lily of the Valley, the Sun from the east to the west Who forgives our sins and cast them from where the sun rises in the morning to where it sets at night.

Who is like Jesus? Who can shine like Him? Who can forgive like Him? Come sinner and receive your rest. Come burden to loosen your transgressions. Come weary to the fountain of peace. Come blind to see the Lover of mankind who let you see His smile heaven can only give and earth can't imagine. Come with faith. Come with assurance. Come receive this heavenly gift.

But what if the sun would only shine when we obey God's commands, and it stops shining when we don't? What if we could only breathe when we forgive? What if we could only hear when we seek to hear God's directions? What if we could only see when we walked the narrow path? And what if God would forget about us as we do Him...where would each of us be? In the valley of the shadow of death without hope...

Father, set me as a seal upon your heart, as a seal upon your arm; for love is as strong as death. Today, I seek to come away with You Father to the path which leads to Your unquenchable love. Amen.

Jesus' Love

The street of the city shall be full of boys and girls playing in its streets...
Zechariah 8:5

Good morning, lovely day after the storm of the night. The storm passed over because the birds were singing before six and the geese were sounding their victory song of praise. Praise because God kept them safe during the night. The mockingbirds were sounding like dogs barking and the Robin Redbreasts were running in the grass three by three as the hummingbird was still drinking from its feeder. As usual Sugar, my elected deaf dog was misbehaving by walking where she wanted to go. Oh, how beautiful the bird's song this morning, which made my heart rejoice. My heart rejoicing by the sight of the morning celebration of the birds dancing in the water, and the trees housing the birds during the storm still standing in victory because the storm had passed over!

I see God handiwork of love. His speaking in the thunder and showing Himself in the lightning. How wonderful is His faithfulness to shelter us during the storms of life. The storms which rages seems impossible to hold on to the tree of faith when the winds of troubles are hitting on every side. The wind so mighty and nosily, the flesh wants to cry out, "Lord where are You?" But the spirit knows where He is, holding me in safely in the stormy winds.

God daily shows the birds flying and singing, the trees swaying, the sun rising, this morning the birds singing after the storms but were silent while in the storm helped me to trust. I heard Psalm 46:10, the birds are examples of being still and knowing that God is their Protector. Then, as Sunday service began, we sang "Jesus Loves Me." My heart filled with admiration for Jesus' love for me and His children in the womb and out of the womb... Because of His love Jesus gave a warning to the world, "Whoever causes one of these little ones who believes in Me to sin, it would be better for him if a millstone were hung around his neck, and he were drowned in the depth of the sea" (Matthew 18:6).

Yes, we are loved by Jesus, and He showed His love beyond measure on Calvary hill. He cried over Jerusalem when they rejected Him as their protector and provider of all their needs... "How often have I desired to gather your children together as a hen gathers her brood under her wings, and you were nor willing" (Matthew 23:37-39). Hurting children are the sparkle of compassion which moves Jesus' heart. He came as a child, and He knows how easily a child can be misused and abused. Lost and stolen, hurt and rejected, forgotten and left hungry, sold and killed for their blood so others can stay young. Jesus' compassion goes through the years of time. Jesus loves the little children then as He does now.

Yet commercial after commercial comes on the TV about saving wounded and abandoned dogs, but I have never seen a commercial to save the unborn baby from abortion and the hurting children from abuse. Soft music is played during the commercial to draw people's attention to the sad look of a dog or cat. But Jesus sat a child on His knee and said, "What you have done to the least of these you have done unto me." He didn't put a dog on His lap or a cat. Jesus loves all His creations, but He didn't say kiss the dog and curse the child. "A child shall leave the way." Jesus said. Where is the heart of mankind? Is a dog more important than a child? To some yes. Too often, a child is cursed with name calling when the dog is kissed with lipstick lips.

However, there is good news when we serve God, His spirit will be poured out on the children, He is the Mother Hen who takes the lonely forgotten child under His wings to shelter and love. The one the world is abusing Jesus comfort the child the world says has no hope. Even if a child is conceived in ways not pleasing to God, He is the Giver of life. Tamar dressed as a prostitute to get pregnant by her father-in-law Genesis 38:6 "but God blessed the womb with twins Perez and Zerah Genesis 38:28. He used what the enemy meant for bad for His glory.

Lots daughters committed incest, but God is the One who gave life to their wombs, yet the sin led to Moab and Ammon fighting against the Israelites even to this day because God will not impose on our wills good or bad. Yes, this is a good day because even in the storms of life God gives shelter to His servants, the storm may rage but Jesus gives calm to the storm.

Each morning when I awake, I hear the birds singing and see the wonders of the new day. Yet too often we never look at the beauty of God around us as His way of speaking the daily message of His heart to us. We count it as the birds doing what they were born to do. This is true, and there is a wonderful revelation to draw from it. God use the many things He created to show us through the Scriptures how He speaks to us through His creations:

The rocks will cry out if man doesn't praise God.

The church was built upon a rock.

The heaven declares the glory of God.

Jesus as a mother hen.

Birds of the air carry what is spoken in secret to tell in the open. Birds are used 42 times in the Old Testament, 7 times in the New Testament. Fowl or Fowles are used 74 times in the Old Testament 11 times in the New Testament. Dove, doves is the most mentioned 47 times. Eagles 27 times. Owl 27 times. Sparrow 7 times. Quail 4 times. Swallow 2 times. Sheep is mentioned 212 times. Lamb 203 times. Ram 162 times. Goat 172 times. Bull 171 times. Donkey 154 times. Horse 166 times. Lion 145 times. Ox 98 times. Camel 71 times. Dog 42 times. Eagles 30 times. A cat is not mentioned in the Bible.

Waking to the songs of the birds lets me know that Jesus lives, and He shows everyone willing to hear and see Him in the beauty of His glory.

Somebody's Child

It is not good to take the children's bread and throw it to the little dogs. Matthew 15:26

How often do you look at your children and thank the Lord for keeping them from danger, and for carrying them through an accepted temptation? And then, how often do you look at your parents and thank or thanked them for giving of themselves and for keeping you on the path of righteousness? But more so, thanking them for opening their arms to hold you even with the mistakes you have made.

Even with your faults and failures they never have given up on you, they cover you with prayer knowing God loves you as they do. Stumbling is not failure is what their actions say. No need for words, the hugs and the words of encouragement speak louder than a thousand words. You hear, "stumbling isn't failure." Isn't this what Jesus speaks over us when He forgives faults and failures in the lives of the lost sheep? Jesus spoke loudly from the cross, not by words but by the drip, drip, drip of each drop of blood. Blood which gives life, He spoke "I love you." He spoke, "You stumbled but you didn't fall nor break because I caught you first."

Each drop of blood spoke loudly, each agony of breath hard to breathe He caught me. Each drip of each drop of blood spoke, "Mercy, mercy Father, they know not what they do. Mercy Father, I'm shedding each drop of blood because they have stumbled but I have caught them. These are the children I want. The world says they are somebody's child I know who they are. They are mines Father; I have prayed for them."

Matter of fact, God loves you even more because Jesus suffered and died for your mistakes. Drip by drip of each drop of blood He caught me, he caught you. Mistakes aren't failures, mistakes are stumbling blocks in your path that each drop of Jesus's blood moved away...Moved away by grace...moved away with love...moved away because I am His child.

Right now, is a good time to thank God for giving you a heart to love and care for the ones He blessed your womb to have, and even for giving you a heart to love the ones you chose as your own because God didn't allow you to have one by birth. Unfortunately, there are many broken children with heartless parents who only care about their pleasures. There are children behind prison bars because they were born in this world to fend for themselves. The promises of God are being deferred because their mental prison is keeping them prisoners in their own body. Too many children have gone to an early grave because no one told them they had a purpose in this world. No one told them they were fearfully and wonderfully made.

Jesus sees the pain of the ones who are rejected, He sees the sorrow of the one who never being hugged, He sees the spirit of pity of the ones left on the doorsteps, in the alleyway, in the garage cans, He sees the spirit of rejection coming closer and closer because the mother isn't there to comb the baby girl's hair. The father isn't there to take the son to the mall to get a pair of roller skates. The preacher isn't there to lead the child to Christ Jesus whose is dripping drip by drip to cover the hurting child with a shield of love, the shield of protection, the shield of worthiness, the shield of blood which speaks loudly of Jesus who loves...

Is this message breaking your heart? Good? Because we too often overlook what we have right before us. Hug your child, love your child, guide your child, speak the promises of God over your child, because if you don't the world will, and the world is not kind.

As you read this today, tonight or tomorrow of years to come, pray for the motherless and fatherless children; the ones walking the streets late at night is someone's child. The ones who have chosen drugs as their closest friend, is someone's child. The ones sleeping in the alleys, is someone's child. The ones behind prison doors, is someone's child. The one who is called ugly names is somebody child, the handicap is someone's child. You who have been rejected from birth you are someone's child, the ones who was given away, you are someone's child, the child sold in the street is someone's child. If you don't know their names that's alright, God does because you are His child He saw from Calvary as each drop of blood dripped for you.

Hugs of The Morning

Oh, taste and see that the LORD is good; Blessed is the man who trust in Him. Psalm 34:8

Good morning, sunshine and the birds singing in the trees. Hello sun hugging my skin with warmth of the morning. Sorry morning if you hear my sadness from yesterday; even though, the birds sang a good night lullaby to the day as night caressed each tune as it called for the moon. Good morning is my song of praise for God keeping me through the night. He didn't have too, but He chose to hold me in His unfailing hands.

I wake up with the joy of the morning surrounding me with praise. I find it amazing how God shows Himself with the touch of the wind, and the voices of creations celebrating a new day. How I have missed knowing the voice of the Lord for so many years of my life. It took a reawakening of my spirit to know God greets us before we greet Him. Now, it is not for me to get caught up in the creation but the Creator and how He gently holds me with His love as He calms my anxious spirit when I don't know that I am.

However, we must realize that the enemy brings attacks so we can take our eyes of faith off of Jesus. I promised Jesus the beginning of this year that I would keep my eyes eye to eye with His. I would seek Him over the many things around me. One thing we, each need to learn and be aware of, the enemy doesn't care about your promises to God, he only cares about his own self.

This morning, the feelings of emptiness over the passing of a loving friend have turned to a smiling heart because she gave herself to God years before she met Him in the sky. I miss our talks together, the sharing of canning tip, but most of all, her coming to God and loving Him more since we began worshipping together.

Why am I sad when I know she accepted Jesus as her Savior and was praying for her husband and children to be saved. Her husband had a nasty habit that she surrendered to God and put him on the altar to be saved from himself. I rejoice each time I think how faithful she was to Christ, and how she didn't fear death even though, she had cancer. She lived in victory knowing her Redeemer lived Job 19:25. Jesus hugged her will comfort each time she would have a pain. He became her comfort in the storm man said would be unbearable. God never left her side; He sang love songs of His presence to her. When the chemo got so bad (that was worse than the cancer) she turned from man's way and decided to follow Jesus to His healing stream.

So right now, I'm looking at the birds still about their daily routines of flying about from feeder to feeder eating and singing their different bird songs. The sun came up this morning as usual without delay as it smiled with warmth as it greeted the trees. The bugs of the morning attacking a peaceful remembrance of my friend caused me to move from my peaceful place heavenly rest. Well, I guess they have to eat too.

The dew watered the grass, and the spiders still made their webs as the mosquitoes are doing their best to sting me before noon. So once again God has spoken softly and clearly that He knows the beginning from the end, and He knows the time clock of each of our lives...the days fashioned for me. Psalm 139:16

Time goes on...it's left up to each of us how we use it. Once again today, I'm observing two different mourning for a passing of a loved one: One mourns with sadness and tirelessness because everything human's possible was done to care for a loved one. But there aren't any regrets.

One mourns with regrets of not being there for a loved one during illness. I received a thank you card from a man whose mother passed in April thanking me for the card and gift I mailed to him. He had stop going to see his mother. Regrets of yesterday are the only thing he sees now! This is what he wrote in the card, "I didn't know what it meant to lose a mother, but now I know. It's a weird feeling, which comes and goes." Condemnation is always weird because there is no condemnation for those in Christ, but for those walking in the flesh.

Don't waste time thinking only of yourself, because there will come a time when you will be by yourself and Satan reminding you what you didn't do when you had a chance.

Regrets will hug you tighter and tighter until bitterness takes the place of regrets and then blames come. Following the will of God always hugs us with comfort and then joy comes to push aside regrets of a loved one passing away. Jesus cried out form the cross "My God, My God why have You forsaken Me" Psalm 22:1

Matthew 27:46 Alone in blackness beyond man's imagination hugged Jesus, but the hugs of the Father raised from the tomb. The Father will do the same for each of us calling unto Him.

Try to live this life doing God's will so there will be no regrets.

One Road Leads to Jesus

Most assuredly, I say to you, I am the door of the sheep. John 10:7b

Good morning, beautiful sunrise with the trees as portrait of your beautiful light, breaking the storm clouds of the night. Hello one-of-a-kind morning I have never seen before because each morning is new. Thank You Father for each fading day, and one more promise fulfilled or sadly deferred because of you wanting to have your way.

Good morning, Holy Spirit! What is on your heart today? Lingering in expectation of a Rhema word, I am waiting needing to hear the Father's voice. Smell His fragrance. Feel His breathe. Lingering to meet with my Father who never let me go unaware. So, as I emerged in prayer this morning, I heard in my spirit, "Many roads." I stopped in prayer because I knew a lie was trying to creep in." Many roads lead to Jesus." I rebuked this lie, and then I heard deep within me," No, only one road leads to Jesus and that's the 'narrow path'.

I realized then how there's a war of truth raging inside of each of us. Remembering Paul said, "So this is the principle I have discovered: When I want to do good, evil is right there with me" (Romans 7:21). Praise God that He guarded my mind and spirit because I seek the truth and He granted me wisdom to know and recognize the enemy's lie.

So yes, there are many roads painted with despair, guilts, worrying, temptation, doubting, disbelief, whining, complaining, half-truths, and the bright...bright signs blinking, "Follow me to the exciting places!" Which each lead to destruction.

After I finished praying and began with the next part of my day, I began to think, "How did that liar put a lie and temptation in my prayer time? Did I not go to that secret place where the falcon's eye can't see in, or the lion's feet have never trodden?" But then I rejoiced because I knew the voice of temptation of the enemy, but more so, I knew the voice of Truth and obeyed the voice of the Father in heaven. I felt bad, then I rejoiced because I passed the test. This reminds me of the boy who copied from the boy's paper next to him on the mid-term test. He copied so badly he even copied the final statement the other boy made... "you should have studied for this test because all my answers are wrong."

So, yes, the enemy's answers were wrong this morning, because seeking God and studying His Word prepared me for the test. The enemy's path of many roads leads to destruction, listening to his lies would have caused me to doubt. The road of doubt leads to the road of faith deferred. Then, I realized I have been listening to too many voices and opinions about John's rehab stay, when the only, yes, ONLY voice I should follow is the Holy Spirit my guide and teacher.

Isn't it amazing how God gets our attention? It took a lie in my prayer time for me to see the truth and close out the voices of others who see only the old John rather than the John God is molding in His hands. When we are broken God is the Potter who mends us to the creation of His choosing. And He wants us on the road less traveled...the Narrow Path which leads to eternal life with the Father is the road less traveled each fading of another day. One more promise is fulfilled when we follow the narrow path or sadly deferred when we follow the wide one.

Good morning, Holy Spirit! What is on your heart today? For me to seek You over the opinions of man. I have learned a valuable lesson over the last nine months. Life doesn't stay the same. God is the God of today, yesterday and the days to come. He never put more on any of us than we can bear. It's easy to sit and feel sorry for yourself when you see others doing their daily routines and you are starting over so it seems. It seems as if life have changed because of illness, which it has, but not Jesus!

You sit and think, "If they only knew how hard this is they would come and help. If they only knew how I feel they would call to check on me. If they only knew how it feel to see a loved one seemly fading before your eyes, they would help." Yet, I'm a not allowed to have a pity party because Jesus banded the guest list of whoa-it-me from my hands and reminded me that He is my every source.

By not complaining many around me have grown in faith and casted off the spirit of fear which led to infirmity. Many watched my walk rather than my talk during these last nine month and have grown closer to Jesus' breast. We don't understand why Jesus allows the attacks of the enemy to come through our doors, He knows as with Job the enemy only can touch us when He allows him to do so.

This walk with Christ Jesus these last nine month have pulled me closer to Him. I no longer look at TV, I no longer sit and feel sorry for myself, I no longer look at my husband as being ill. During this time religion has broken from him. He never accepted me as being called to preach the gospel of Jesus Christ. He never supported me or heard a message I preached twice a week. But during this time, he has felt the true touch of Jesus on his heart. He has tasted the goodness of the power of the Holy Spirit and the touch of His presence. He now tells people about the services of Sunday and Thursday. He now goes with me to do the broadcast at the radio station. He has been born again into the family and kingdom of God, and he divorced denomination. We see the natural God sees the spirit realm where Michael the archangel is winning the war over our lives.

Promises Without Holes

May the LORD fulfill all your petitions. Now I know that the LORD saves His anointed. He will answer him from His holy heaven with the saving strength of His right hand. Psalm 20:6

Right now, allow God to take a walk through your heart with a bucket of His cleansing blood to remove any debris that would cause you to be a day or moment late missing His coming! When the rain came and Noah's Ark began to float...the people were a day late in repentance, a moment short of confession, yet on time to drown as each one floated away with the thrills of the world that could not give them a boat, and all drowned in the depths of sin.

Will you be a day late when your time comes to face God at death, or when Jesus comes on the cloud? If you are reading this book...you still have time to get it right! Do it Right Now! The Word of God is true. Not one of God's promises have fallen to the ground. His promises stand because He is not a man, that He should lie, nor a son of man, that He should repent. Number 23:19

If Jesus said He is coming back for a Church without spots or blemishes, He is coming. Jesus' faithful word is shown to each of us through our surroundings. I have never seen night that didn't turn into day; sun that doesn't rise and set; wind that doesn't blow; water that isn't wet; rain that doesn't water the soil; a lie that will not be revealed; or wrong trying to force its way on right. But I have seen clouds that don't give rain; a chicken that doesn't lay eggs; salt without taste; and people who never say they are sorry no matter what they say! But this is the good news... God knows how to handle each one, because He is the Battle Fighter!

Just believe He can and will do the impossible on each of our behalf. "Listen, the hour is coming, Yes, it has now come that you will be scattered, each to his own home, and will leave Me alone. Yet I am not alone, for the Father is with Me" (John 16:32). Birds are singing a late afternoon lullaby as I sit in wonderment as the day is resting and night covering it with starry wonders. Each late afternoon I hear the beautiful voice of the same bird or couple of birds singing a tone like a whistle. This same song is sung just before sunrise.

As I stand watching Sugar, my dog disobeying my command, this beautiful song began by the lovely bird serenading sunset. It is the Robin Redbreast whistling its nighttime song. Oh, how beautiful the act of love for a day gone by. Oh, the questioning of the love song from the robin to heaven...how I see the years as a blessing of Jesus' love to allow the birds to sing goodbye to the day gone by and welcoming a new one of Jesus' love, as another year of thanksgiving I give to my wonderful Savior praise...
Want love gives love...
Want blessings give blessings...
Want kindness show kindness...
Give what you desire for yourself...

Once again, I'm thanking God for His kindness. I'm still excited about turning 70th and the things God is doing in this season of my life. I'm seeing the Holy Spirit pulling more to Jesus. Seeing a lost soul born again is more excitingly than receiving silver and gold which fades, but the gift of salvation is a gift that never fades nor drowns...

More so, God is faithful to His promises too! Serving God and obeying His commandments bring blessings and fulfillment the mind can't imagine. Blessings you can't contain...As of today, I'm still looking for places to put my many birthday gifts. Clothes the closet has no room. Minister Bible the selves have no space. A and C note Corinthian (chimes) Bells gracing my porch with beauty and harmonious sounds. Pictures covering the walls in beauty. Crystals giving shades of beauty to my glass tables. Flowers, books on Israel, writing tables, jewelry, lotions, even to ones wanting to give me washing powers to protect my hands from making any. Cards filled with money, gift cards...hug and kisses and love speeches of gratefulness from friends driving long distance in cars and vans just to say thank you...for the things God allowed me to do over the years. No matter, what you do for others in times of needs, or just to give because of ones 'desire to have a piece of cake they can't bake or breads they can't make, God is the One who gives me the strength and ability to do so. We can do nothing without God not even love. So right now, I thank God for Him using me in this life...Thank You, Father for the things You have done for me. Thank You Father because Your promise is hole free. Amen!

The Aroma of Love

The dew which rests upon my skin is His kiss of love. "*His cheeks are as a bed of spices, as sweet flowers*"(Song Of Song 5:13).

How can I say no to such a love, such a friend, such a light, such a sweet bed of love overflowing which gives me sleep. Jesus is knocking with His give of love. Don't you hear Him. He is singing a serenade of comfort. Don't you feel it? Jesus is seeking your love. Want you receive it. His gentleness is softer than the clouds; His seeking outshine lightning from the storehouse. The rose in May can't compare to His fragrance of love. He is the Rose of Sharon, the Bright Morning Star, the Lily of the Valley, the sun from the east to the west Who forgives our sins and cast them from where the sun rises in the morning to where the sun set at night. Who is like Him? Who can shine like Him? Who can forgive like Him? Come sinner and receive your rest. Come burden to loosen your transgressions. Come weary to the fountain of peace. Come blind to see the Lover of mankind who let you see His smile heaven can only give and earth can't imagine. Come with faith. Come with assurance. Come receive this heavenly gift. But what if the sun would only shine when we obey God's commands, and it stops shining when we don't? What if we could only breathe when we forgive? What if we could only hear when we seek to hear God's directions? What if we could only see when we walk the narrow path? And what if God would forget about us as we do Him...where would each of us be?

Today, thank God for His grace and mercy...through these are the only reason we are forgiven and not forgotten.

Unquenchable

Jesus answered her, "If you knew the gift of God and who it is that asks you for a drink, you would have asked him, and he would have given you living water."
John 4:10

From June 20, 2020...The Holy Spirit gave me a message the first of the week to write and post. I wrote it, but I didn't post it because I felt I was writing out of my own thoughts. God took me into Unquenchable praise and prayer even to the point I found specks of gold on my sheet Wednesday morning. I still didn't post this yesterday, but in my sleep during the night the Holy Spirit spoke these words, "Must Be Born Again." I jumped up from my sleep at 2:30am this morning knowing I must post what the Lord had given me Monday. I failed to do what He had given me to do and I'm sorry...

This is the post written Monday After reading Psalm 96 there began a stirring in my spirit...and a shifting in the atmosphere. Whenever I feel a stirring, something is taking place in the spiritual realm that going to touch the earth... The Sunday before the government asked the churches to shut down, schools to close, and businesses to close during service there was shifting of the atmosphere, and I told each one in service that the atmosphere was too thick. Sure, enough people began crying in fear. Fear of tomorrow. Fear of the day. Fear of family even coming around. The news media was pouring fear into people who loved to get out, but now were too afraid to leave their homes. Then some people had no regards of other people safety or feelings. The Monday afterward, fear began covering people and the calls began coming from people too fearful to get out of bed. Even to the point of people believing they were going to die. This morning the atmosphere is shifting with a falling away. The true believers are being revealed and the religious are being exposed. I almost cried as God revealed this stirring, but I can't cry or become disheartened because God had already told us these things would happen. The trees, birds, rain, wind, clouds, and sweet aromas of the morning are still doing what they were created to do...praising God in His holiness. My friend either you believe and trust God or you don't.

You can't be trusting God and fearing at the same time. God is not a partner nor friend with fear. You can't worship and hide in doubts that someone near you is sick with a virus...we are required to pray and use authority given to us in... Mark 16:17-18 tells each born again Christian, "And these signs will accompany those who believe: In My name they will drive out demons; they will speak in new tongues; they will pick up snakes with their hands, and if they drink any deadly poison, it will not harm them; they will lay their hands on the sick, and they will be made well."

Are we believers in Christ Jesus, or like fake news...? Sounding good isn't working, we must do the will of the Lord to stand in the fire knowing it can't touch us because the angels are encamping about us. Micah Stampley (sp)sang a song about ten years ago "The War Cry". It's a war going on now, and it's not a war of flesh and blood, it a war in the spiritual realm. Put on your battle gear of prayer and fasting because the enemy isn't hiding nor playing! He is bold and looking for casualties of souls. Move from your slumber and prepare for this war for souls through steadfastness of repentant and humbling yourself before God and He will fight our battle. If you are not born again..., do it NOW!

Through The Eyes of a Child

"Take heed that ye despise not one of these little ones; for I say unto you that in Heaven their angels do always behold the face of My Father who is in Heaven. Matthew 18:10

As a child I loved to greet the morning with joy with its beautiful meadows under the fresh sunlight. But joy faded for a while because I had to milk the cows! I still remember as a child going to my father's watermelon patch on the far northern hill of the land to gather watermelons. As I walked through the patch, I would gather the largest melons and put them in my croaker sack. Now, this wasn't wise at all because I was a little girl carrying an overly filled sack of watermelons hill by hill all the way home. And was a fox in the path but it was afraid of me...

The bag was heavy across my little shoulders.... but I was determined to get them home. As I walked, I would put the bag down to rest awhile, then pick it back up to go another hill. I would put the bag down again to rest, then pick it back up and go another hill. When I would see the barn, I would breathe a sigh of relief...but the barn was still between another hill and the house. But when I got to the barnyard...I could see my house, and oh how happy I would be! "I can make it now" were my thoughts. When I finally got to the back porch of the house, I would be so tired that I promised myself I would never pick up that many watermelons again to bring home at once. But I did each time I would go to the watermelon patch...it seemed better to bring a lots home than one...but the unneeded suffering of getting there was awful!

Isn't this the same way we carry our burdens? You put them down and then pick them up. When Jesus set us free on the cross from the curses of life...He forgave us and released us too. When Jesus saw a woman suffering from a condition that caused her to be crippled for eighteen years. He said to her, 'Woman, you are loosed from your affliction.' She was forgiven and released. If you don't forgive, you won't be released...like the heavy watermelon sack. You'll stay bound and imprisoned. Forgiveness is linked to healing and the lack of forgiveness to the lack of healing. Those who cannot forgive cripple themselves. If you don't forgive, you won't be able to move on or to let go of the old. Nor will you be able to be sent forth and fulfill God's calling for your life. Forgive and you shall be forgiven. Forgive and you shall be released. Forgive and you shall be healed. Let it go, and you shall be set free.

I taught my children when they were upset because someone did something to them to try to pull them down...These were my words of encouragement to them..." In order for someone to hold you down, they must stay down to hold you there." Anytime we hate the ones who hurt us...you are holding God's love and forgiveness away from yourself...

Just as the croaker sack of watermelons kept me from climbing the hills with ease...the weight of unforgiveness hold you back from a joyous and peaceful life.

Words of Harm

For there is nothing reliable in what they say, destruction is within them; their throat is an open grave they flatter with their tongues. Psalm 5:9

The eye doctors tell you to wear sunglasses to block the rays of the sun that's harmful to the eyes. Troubles tell you to wear blinders of worries to block you from the promises of God. Weariness tells you to hide from the truth so lies can live. Doubt tells you to lie so wrongs will be right, and rights will be wrong. How often have you noticed people turning away from God when an unexpected tragedy comes, or when they are hurt from someone in church?

This is the epiphany of the morning, when you turn from God, Baal is waiting to welcome you to come to a promise that fails and fades...and lies which kills! The Israelites turned to Baal when they wanted to have their way. When other countries had a king, they wanted one even though the King of Kings was their Protector...not insane Saul!

Crying to have the ways of the world brings trouble and darkened painted tomorrows. Tomorrows of "woe is me", and why did I do this? I should have listened, I should have waited, I should have over and over played a game on the mind of what should have not been! To block grace from taking care of yesterday's mistakes.

Mistakes of yesterday are shadows that have no life only misery of something that cannot be undone. Hope dies in the yesterdays, steals from today, and kills tomorrow promises and peace which lies ahead when we stay in yesterday. Shadows cannot harm because there is no life, but it deceives you that it breathes and lives. Yesterday's sunrise died when yesterday's sunset went over the western sky, same with yesterday stumbling, is it a shadow that cannot be change, it can only be learned from where not to walk that path again.

What is Baal...Baal Zevuv means the Lord of the Flies. Translated into Greek is Beelzebub...the name of the devil. Baal is the devil. Jonathan Chain

The devil wears many masks...Baal is one of them. Baal is the substitute god for the ones looking for visible gods. So, if one turns from God, the devil is always there to fill in the gap with lies of hope. He's the god of one's turning away from God. This is the good news to the devil, but bad news for your soul...whatever you choose in place of God, the devil will take the form to make you feel justified in your decision not to follow Jesus.

He will have a preacher on the news who has committed a hideous crime so you will think all preachers are the same. Yet the devil fails to tell you that he has his preachers disguised in sheep clothing to mislead and blind you to the truth of the true God.

When a nation turns from God, it becomes satanic. When a person turns from God, he become entangled with bondage of false hopes. Then the enemy destroys those who worship him. God blesses the ones who worship Him with more than enough peace beyond measure; joy overflowing; hope that frightened the enemy; faith which moves mountains.

So, beware of serving other gods, even the god of your desires. Guard your heart, because Beelzebub has flies waiting to hatch confusion where the Living Water should be with fulfilled promises of today and so many more for tomorrow.

Is there anything you are living for today other than God's desires within you. Desire God's presence as you desire your dream car and flee from the fly trap of destruction. Elijah came to all the people and said, "How long will you stay between two opinions? If the LORD is God, follow Him, but if Baal, then follow him. And the people did not say a word" (1 Kings 18:21).

What about you? Yesterday and today don't mix well together, one is a shadow, the other one is live. Live in your today, not yesterday or tomorrow because today have enough troubles of its own. "Therefore, don't worry about tomorrow, because tomorrow will worry about itself. Each day has enough trouble of its own." Matthew 6:34.

Playing Church

But you were confident in your beauty and acted like a prostitute because of your fame. Ezekiel 16:15

Each day is a new realization of the Holy Spirit revealing power. Playing church is like wearing a mascot suit, sooner or later the suit must come off for cleansing or the filth will take it over. As I seek a closer heartbeat with Jesus, He reveals the real walk with Him. There is no pretense, either it's a straight walk with God or your leg getting hung crossing the fence...I love talking in parables because this is how I hear the words from the Holy Spirit.

My grandchildren are no longer surprised when I call with directions for safety because they know the Holy Spirit has shown me. Yesterday, I texted my oldest grandson with this message, "When you said, "I Do" Alex became my granddaughter. Never make her cry that will ricochet a bad report into eternity. Also, always give a fair day's labor for a fair day's wage. Never side with wrong because staying on the narrow path leads to blessings and favor. Wrong decisions stall the blessings."

I want my children and grandchildren to want and receive my Godly advice more than my money. To be kind to the unlovable and give a helping hand to the downtrodden and the ones in need. I want each of them to know that kindness ricochet to the Heavenly Kingdom where blessings are created and poured out. Matter of fact, God sees the small minute things we do in secret for others. While in the nail shop today, a lady walked in and our backs were to each other, but everyone in the shop was in one conversation about traveling. When I washed my hands and came back to my seat, I noticed her face and she noticed mines. We knew each other from teaching at the same school years ago. She began to tell me how she was just talking about me earlier. How I worked so hard and cared about my students. Also, how I started special programs for the student and made them feel as if they were somebody. How I fought for their rights and future. The nail shop owner said that I knew so many people, and the shop was a meeting place. I smiled.

I go to get the flowers for the sick and the florist was troubled over his father being on life support after a four-wheeler accident. We talked and a word of encouragement was given to this kind man... He felt as if he was wasting time working there the few hours he does, but I let him know the difference he is making in many lives by the flowers I pick up each week. He hugged me and he said, "I started not to come to work today, but I'm glad I did, because to see you today." I finished getting all the things I needed, and the things I thought my mother-in-law would enjoy eating. I walked out of the store, got into the car, turn the key, and it went click-click without the motor turning to start the car. I picked up my phone and called a friend, but no answer. I called another number, and a tow company was called. Before the tow company got there, my phone rang, and it was my friend, she called another friend and help was on the way. I called the tow company back, and they waited before coming to see if my car would start. My friend pulls up with everything needed to get my car started. A lady was parked in front of me, when she saw my friend lifting my car hood, she started her car up and moved so my friend could pull his car hood to hood to mines. I got out of the car and thanked the lady for being so kind to move her car. She said, "You were having problems, hopefully if I had car trouble someone would do the same for me." This lady looked like the lady who votes at precinct I work. I always ask about her son who has a form of Asperger. When my friend was sick with the flu last year he asked if I had made winter tea for colds...I gave him what I had.

So, today I'm a living witness that kindness and good deeds are never in vain. Kindness is like a boomerang when released from your hand it always returns. In my time of need today, God had someone in place, and when I called, each one said yes without hesitation. Never do anything to get some back, God sees the hand and heart of His servant's faithfulness to His will, and He has a ram in the bush before the ax falls. So, today is another realization that playing church keeps you in direr need, being the church moves mountains.

Why I Do What I do
I will not die, but I will live and proclaim what the LORD has done. Psalm 118:17

Why do I smile? Because God is my Rock in the wind!

Why do I laugh? God is my Shield in the stormy rain.

Why do I sing? Because God is my Keeper when the enemy wants his way.

Why do I write? Because God is the Hand which helps me tell of His goodness.

Why do I pray? Because prayer keeps the enemy outside looking in. Also, God is my Standard that a flood can't break through. Hail can't shatter. Fire can't burn through. Tornado can't blow down. Missiles can't blow up, and dogs can't bite.

Why do I praise God? Because He is good and better than coffee to the very last drop.

Now, don't stop reading because the reason for my joy follows:

My cell phone went off at 12:25am in the morning. Now, this is the amazing part, I never have my cell phone turn on at night. I keep it on silence whether it's day or night. But this morning it was on but silent. When a text came in at 12:25am, I turned over and picked it up to see who was texting me that time of morning. It was my newly wedded grandson with pictures of his wrecked car and these words, "God kept His hands around me tonight." I saw my life flash before my eyes as I was flying over the ditch and crashing through a fence. I missed every single tree in my way and was able to eventually stop. Neither me nor Bentley (dog) was hurt, but my car is ruined. Idk (I don't know) why God loves me so much, but He saved me tonight. I love you guys and I'm glad I get to tell you"

I called him, and he answered. He was home with his wife by his side. Both were nervous and shaken up. But he said, "Nothing touched me as I was flying through these people's yard holding on to the wheel.... missing the trees until the car stopped."

Yes, I sing because I'm thankful! I sing because Jesus loves me. But more so, I serve God because He's faithful, and I know He watches over me. But most of all, God watches over His Word to perform it (Jeremiah 1:12) ... just as He did this morning. "Do not be afraid or discouraged, for the LORD your God is with you wherever you go"(Joshua 1:9). Is one of God's promises to His servants...He kept His promise, God moved the trees back as the car passed through.

Do I need to say any more? Good morning this blessed day! I guess I did need to say a little bit more. Birds of the morning I'm singing along with the praises of joy beyond the clouds of understanding. Wind in the trees I hear your praise to the Savior, thank You Holy Spirit for using the wind as Your reminder You are with me and hear my prayers.

Oh, wait a minute...Sweet Hour of Prayer was playing on my phone when the text came in.... Now tell me if God isn't real!

Crooked Steps

A man's heart plans his way, but the LORD determines his steps. Proverbs 16:9

When you take your eyes off God...and put them on things that perish...you will have crooked steps in the sand. There was a king who had a beautiful daughter, and he sent out an invitation to any prince that could walk a straight line over a long journey of varying landscapes to his castle could have his daughter's hand in marriage. The first man came to accept the invitation, and he looked to the right and to the left as he walked to make sure his steps were straight, and he didn't get off the path. But when he got to the castle his lines on the path were crooked. The next man came, and he looked down, to keep his eyes on his feet as he walked to make sure each footstep followed in the same path was straight. But he too went badly off the path.

But the third man came, he looked neither to the right nor the left, nor down at his footsteps. And yet at the end, he had walked a straight line. No one could figure out how he did it. Then he told them his secret: "All I did was look into the far distance to the light on the crown of the castle tower. I didn't look at my path or the landscapes to my right and left. I just kept my eyes on that light and kept pressing forward to the light until I arrived there. The secret is to your walk in God." We are all called to walk a straight path in God which leads to the light.

Even if today brings news of cancer, or the pain of a wayward child keep your eyes on the victory of the Cross. Your footsteps may become weak, but your straight path will reach the promises of God, because in your weakness God is strong. God your Healer and Redeemer never fail. "Jesus did it all" is a humbling thought and reality. But when troubles come, we whine. When blessings come, we rejoice. When sickness comes, we fret. When healing comes, we give the doctor the credit. When sorrow comes, we blame someone too-too often. When disappointments and unanswered prayers come, questions go before God, "WHY!" The meek are picked on and given the lowly seat...while the prideful are respected to their face and talked about behind their back, but yet given the best seat.

Jesus did and gave His best...He did not do less than best...He took the stand which says... "Good, better, best...
Good isn't better...
Until better is best...

So why is it so easy for hurts, disappointments, mistakes, attacks and failures from yesterday causing too many to walk away from Christ Jesus to the crooked path of failures and pain? His suffering wasn't enough...His body drained of blood, His unrecognizable face, His uncovered spitted on body, His nails pierced hands and feet, His rejected sin covered body, His agony of pain for my sins were not enough for the world to love Him. What more does He have to do? He loves us beyond suffering...but it's not enough for this sin sick world...

It's so easy to talk about someone when he or she hurts us, but Jesus intercedes for us... It's so easy to stay at home from church because of tiredness, but Jesus still intercedes for us. It's so easy to blame others in hurts, but Jesus never blamed us in His pain on Calvary...He forgave and asked the Father to forgive us because we know not what we were doing.

Do you know what you are doing when you reject Jesus? Do you know what you are doing when you won't receive Him as your Savior? Do you know what you are doing when you walk away from His love?

Satan knows and smiles. And as my friend told me yesterday about her husband who insisted on owing **IRS** when they told him that he didn't His wife's reply to his foolishness "You're about to lose my mind!" When you look to the world for your answer...it's about to lose your salvation!

Booster Club for Christ

The God of heaven is the One who will grant me us success. Nehemiah 2:20

I am my children and grandchildren biggest booster club. I boo them when they are wrong and cheer them when they are right. I guide them through the obstacles in their path with learned and bought wisdom... I cry when they cried, and smile with thankfulness with their achievements. I cook their favorite meals, but they must do the dishes and sweep the floor they messed up...It's a house affair not mama/grandmama doing all the work.

When times are hard, I do my part through prayer and giving a helping hand if needed. I'm a Christian and I try my best to follow the leading of the Holy Spirit. If Jesus said it, I do my best to do it! Jesus said if you have two coats, give one to someone who doesn't have one't. You know, it's hard being a servant of God because it's so easier to be selfish! But then Jesus said the narrow path would not be easy, and it isn't.

With each thing God calls me to do, it's a test of obedience... As Samuel told Saul when he disobeyed God, "Obedience is better than sacrifice."

This morning I had to let go of my 1985 Silverado Chevrolet pickup truck. I almost cried when my grandson was driving it upon the trailer. This truck is older than my grandsons...but still useful. How could I say no to my grandchild in need of a truck... Over the years I have said no to every person who stopped by to ask to buy it. Not my Armada or F150 people wanted, but this old 1985 Silverado. Why was I holding on to this truck? Why would I almost cry seeing it about to be used daily? Because it is mines and I paid for it...I had the right to let it sit or let it go! Sound selfish? I told you it's easy to be selfish...and walk a crooked path.

But then Jesus quickly reminded me that I am His, and He paid the cost for me. But He doesn't complain. He uses me. He doesn't lose. Sitting causes dry rot. Now, I got my correction for the day, and it put me back on the right path! Also, Jesus reminded me that the way I wanted to hold on to the truck is the same way we hold on to old things that takes up room in our heart. Mistakes of yesterday. What someone did to us yesterday.... wow!

So, I smiled with joyfulness after my heavenly chastising. I rather be obedient than having clutter in my heart...and God is not pleased with me. I love Him and I know what He says leads to victory over my selfish desires.

We prayed on the porch and blessed our grandson as he pulled away with a gift older than he, but desired by many. Psalm 37 says the wicked watches the righteous...and God sees all of us. Amen

So, I am in the booster club of Jesus Christ because He paid the price for my redemption and paid for my salvation with His holy blood. Yea, Jesus, yea Jesus You are the Master of my soul, and the gift of life to me.

What Do I Want for Mother's Day

You, LORD, will guard us; You will protect us from this generation forever. Psalm 12:7

Over the last few weeks my mind has been pondering over the things I wanted for Mother's Day: Walking shoes, but I have many new pairs hidden behind other shoes I have never worn; Fitbit, but I do not wear clocks; clothes, my closets run over; chocolates, I eat very little, vacation, where do I want to go...perfume, my shelves are full.

So, my oldest grandson called me yesterday and asked, "Grandma, what do you want for Mother's Day?" A Fitbit was my reply. As I woke during the night and I was reminded that I don't wear watches, so I need no Fitbit, shoes, perfumes, or chocolate. What I desire for Mother's Day are as following:

My children and grandchildren give their hearts to Jesus completely.

They choose Jesus over the world.

They love Jesus more than me or anyone else.

They walk in obedience to His Word.

In everything they do allow Jesus to guide them.

With these gifts each of them will live full lives that the moths can't eat, and time cannot wear away. These Mother's Day gifts assure me that I will meet each of them in heaven.

So, my grandson, this is the gift I desire this Mother's Day...the gift that never fades! You are making Jesus your gift to yourself. I think about God's gift to Hannah that she returned to Him, her son, Samuel. Samuel, whose prayers never fell to the ground.

But What If ... But What

The people who live in darkness have seen a great light, and for those living in the shadowland of death, light has dawned. Matthew 4:16

I'm sitting here on my porch watching a bug caught in a spider's web. I see it moving as the spider pulls it closer to its legs. As I look at the spider wrapping the bug in its web...I want to sweep the web down to set the bug free, but it seems as if I'm too late because the bug isn't moving now. Then a thought entered my head... "Do I need to interfere with the spider's meal? God made every living thing in a special way...the bug is the spider's meal, like a chicken leg is mine." After I looked at the bug in the web, I began to think, if the bug was flying around, I would kill it with the flyswatter.... uhh...ugh!

For me to sweep down the web isn't for me to do, this is the reason so many things are out of order now, because the mind is webbed with the world's way, rejecting what God says in His Word. For example, animal rights group wants to bring dogs and cats inside when it's too hot or too cold outside. God equipped dog and cats with survival skill. The Circus is fading out because man says it's abusive to train the animals now. People walk alligators on a leash like a dog...when the alligator will eat its owner as well as a stranger. Rats are trained to preform and are kissed on the mouth like a man kisses a woman on the fifteenth date. A person will go to jail quicker for hitting a dog than abusing a child. People will clean their cars and trucks to shine like a mirror but throw the paper on the ground. Jesus didn't ride a horse from place to place, He walked, but it's too hot for us to walk (go figure). Jesus cooked a wonderful breakfast of fish for His disciples before He went to heaven.... but we eat out even though the cabins are running over with food.

So, the epiphany for today is...If Jesus did it, I will too! He made everything His way, it's not for me to tamper with it...even the webbed bug I felt sorry for but was going to kill it myself with the flyswatter. But I will tell you that Jesus died so the webs of the world are swept away for the spiritual eyes to see.

Elm Tree

The righteous thrive like a palm tree and grow like a cedar tree in Lebanon. Psalm 92:12

We never know what God have surrounded us with until He reveals it. Good morning is my daily song, and anthem of praise. Good morning today the wind is blowing warm with heat like a dryer. Good morning to the birds finding shade in the trees. Good morning sunrise resting on the treetops with serenade of love. Good morning people passing by with an early morning salutation. Yes, good morning this new day, and thank You Holy Spirit for welcoming me to this day. Oh, the beautiful wonders of God's creations are rejoicing in the light of a new day as they do what they were created to do. I walk on my south side porch each morning to greet the day with excitement. I look at the trees surrounding the houses with amazing wonders and thankfulness. I look at the leaves on the trees hiding the clouds behind them. I look at the birds finding protection under the leaves. And I smile with a smile of joy because God has something to teach me as I look at the Elm tree many want to be cut down.

This morning as the tree company was pruning the Elm tree one of the workers walked over to me and said, "This is a lovely place y'all have here. It is so nice. You have something rare here. Years ago, in Mississippi the Elm trees got a blight and the majority of them died. People always wanted Elm trees around their house for the good shade and how the tree flourishes. You have the biggest Elm I have ever seen. What you have done by cutting the limbs back, you have taking some of the pressure off the tree. The tree is health and the way it is pruned the top will grow into a mushroom top. The foliage will grow on the top limbs to fill in the space. I have a degree in trees." I thanked him and he said, "God bless you. And thank you for letting me share a conversation with you." I said, "No, thank you! And God bless you."

It still amazes me how God keeps things concealed until we search them out. I was debating with myself, should I cut the Elm tree down, should I just pruned...let it stay, let it go, let it stay, let it go? God never told me to cut this unusual tree because I never asked Him. But God overruled my thoughts of cutting down this tree by sending a stranger to tell me what God wanted me to know about an Elm tree. This Elm tree have sheltered the family from storms since before I was born... It's not the tree, it's the message God sent through the tree. No matter, the winds, the blights, the age, the weakness, He is the Healer, Keeper, Protector, and Deliver. What man call useless and old God use for Him glory. The Elm tree the storms have attacked, but God kept it when every other Elm was dying. I see even more why we should welcome a stranger because you may be entertaining an angel (Hebrews 13:2).

This man wore no shirt and was carrying the spirit of rejection, but when I welcomed him to look at my fig tree and welcomed him to share the fruits, rejection died. Elm tree or man usefulness is revealed when God appoints a receiver. As God appointed a plant to grow over night to give Jonah shade, He also appointed a worm to attack the plant, and it withered. God appointed a scorching east wind to wake up Jonah from depression. (Jonah 4:6-8)

God send a man to cut down an Elm tree to encourage him and to let him know hope is not deferred. He was not useless, and neither is the Elm tree. The Elm is swaying in the cool breeze of July and sheltering the birds from the storm as I write this daily word.

Thank You Father for speaking over my thoughts and having Your way. Amen.

Portrait of Heaven

When I observe Your heavens, the work of Your fingers, the moon, and the stars, which You set in place. Psalm 8:3

Good morning, beautiful sunrise with the trees as portrait of your light breaking the storm clouds of the night. Hello, one-of-a-kind morning I have never seen before because each morning is new. Thank You Father for each fading day which one more promise is fulfilled or sadly deferred. Good morning, Holy Spirit! What is on your heart today?

Lingering in expectation of a Rhema word, I am waiting needing to hear the Father's voice. Smell His fragrance. Feel His breathe. Lingering to meet with my Father who never let me go unaware. So, as I emerged in prayer this morning, I heard in my spirit, "Many roads." I stopped in prayer because I knew a lie was trying to creep in." Many roads lead to Jesus." I rebuked this lie, and then I heard deep within me," No, only one road leads to Jesus and that's the 'narrow path'. I realized then how there's a war of truth raging inside of each of us. Remember Paul said, "So this is the principle I have discovered: When I want to do good, evil is right there with me" (Romans 7:21). Praise God that He guarded my mind and spirit because I seek the truth and He granted me wisdom to know and recognize the enemy's lie. So yes, there are many roads painted with despair, guilts, worrying, temptation, doubting, disbelief, whining, complaining, half-truths, and the bright...bright signs blinking, "Follow me to the exciting places!" Which each lead to destruction. After I finished praying and began with the next part of my day, I began to think, "How did that liar put a lie and temptation in my prayer time? Did I not go to that secret place where the falcon's eye can't see in, or the lion's feet have never trodden?" But then I rejoiced because I knew the voice of temptation of the enemy, but I knew the voice of Truth and obeyed the voice of the Father in heaven. I felt bad, then I rejoiced because I passed the test. This reminds me of the boy who copied from the boy's paper next to him on the mid-term test. He copied so that he even copied the final statement the other boy made... "you should have studied for this test because all my answers are wrong." So, yes, the enemy's answers were wrong this morning, because seeking God and studying His Word prepared me for the test. The enemy's path leads to destruction. Then, I realized I have been listening to too many voices and opinions about John's rehab stay, when the only, yes ONLY voice I should follow is the Holy Spirit my guide and teacher.

Isn't it amazing how God gets our attention? It took a lie in my prayer time for me to see the truth and close out the voices of others who see only the old John rather than the John God is molding in His hands. When we are broken God is the Potter who mends us to the creation of His choosing. And He wants us on the road less traveled, the Narrow Path which leads to eternal life with Jesus. Blessings,

Ballroom Dance

Praise Him with tambourine and dance; praise Him with flute and strings. Psalm 150:4

I close my eyes as the birds sing early in the morning, as I sway in pleasant peace with the sounds of their many voices. As I sit motiveless the gentle wind rest upon my face as I think of God's wonders and amazing grace. Slowly, I open my eyes and bask in the beauty of God's smile upon the treetop as the sun caresses each with its morning glow. Only the tree top sway silently in the early morning breeze, as the birds sing the new morning song. I sit and in silent as my heart dance within me with joy. Words cannot tell of the wonders of beauty in the morning light. Pictures cannot be drawn of the untapped love of Jesus calling in the morning mist, and the sunlit tree top man cannot create. Sights unexplainable, sounds desirable, touch of the breeze calls to the heart seeking Jesus to come and dance with Him in the morning light. Just Jesus and me, Jesus and you, Jesus and the ones seeking more of His love to heal their fears, to comfort their weariness, to guide their thought from the shadow of yesterday. Jesus, is calling in the morning light, come to the garden with Me. Come as you are and take of my love for you. Take My hand and dance in the presence of Love unlimited. Jesus is calling, don't you hear Him? Come to the garden alone with Me... Take my hand...

NOW....

Close your eyes for just a moment. Now, imagine you on this grand ballroom dance floor, dressed in the more glorious ballgown. You are dancing with the love of your life, the fragrant of love fills the room. A fragrant beyond human imagination...an aroma of Love. Then you feel this gentle touch, you turn, you see Jesus extending His hand for a dance with you. You smile as you accept His invitation.

You lay your head softly on His breast... You hear His heartbeat as you allow Him to lead you in dance as your heartbeat meets His. You no longer feel the floor beneath you because Jesus is carrying you. A love song fills the atmosphere as Jesus wraps His pure white beyond beautiful robe around you as He leads you around the ballroom floor. Every worry fades there; pain drowns there; sickness dies there; and broken pieces of the heart are healed there on the dance floor with Jesus.

So today, let more than your imagination dance with Jesus...because He is willing to dance with you each moment of the day...so right now dance...as the love song plays.

Come to Me with your seeking heart
Come to Me with your desire
Come to Me be filled with the aroma
Of forgiveness as you dance
With Me as your heart beats
With Mine
And your desires become Mine...

Walking In Forgiveness

Therefore, no condemnation now exists for those in Christ Jesus, because the Spirit's law of life in Christ Jesus has set you free from the law of sin and of death... Romans 8:1

I love to walk among nature not the walking track because I see the same rock each time, I make a round. Walking the path of the road I see something new each round I make. I see God:

A flower blooming and some drying up and dying...God's hand giving and taking away; bumblebees giving and taking from the flower and weed nectar...God's provision, the reason He tells us not to worry; even new trash lies among the green grass to be picked up by my walking partner...God's strengthen His servant to be a good steward over His domain.

Now, God desires to walk with us each day, and if He sees a rock of unforgiveness in our hearts one day, but we repent of it before the day is done, He keeps walking with us. But when hardness takes control of the heart, He doesn't walk with us. As He didn't walk with the Israelites in their disobedient in Leviticus 26. Unforgiveness is an idol because we choose the ways of the world rather than what God says.

Walking the path of God's promises we must choose His path of righteousness rather than our own way... On my daily walk I must choose the path that leads me home. If not, I will be lost and have to find my way through crooks and turns unfamiliar to me. God paved a path for each of us to walk, and Jesus is the door we pass through to enter the path that keeps us mindful of home. We never get lost when we follow the lit pass. There will be detours we must choose to take or reject. There will be paths of many lovely things which fades, but the path laid out by Jesus' hand is paved with blooms of blessings awaiting us... Sweet nectar of God's unfading provisions lies ahead...even when the path has trash lying in our sight, God gives us strength to walk around it.

Jesus never promised the narrow path would be easy, matter of fact, He said it would be difficult, and few find it. (Matthew 7:14)

Jesus didn't say there would be no trash on the narrow path...God knew Satan would put anything in the path leaving to

Him to make us not trust the promises for our lives. Jesus knew the enemy would throw the pain of a wayward child in our path...but this is the reason God said in Isaiah 49:16, 25 that we are inscribed in the palms of His hands, and He would contend with him who contends against us, and He will save our children.

God knew the enemy would try to block the narrow path with doubts that a son or daughter will be free of drugs or come up again from the fiery pit of despair...but God says in Isaiah 59:1 "Surely the arm of the LORD is not too short to save, nor His ear too dull to hear." God hears your prayers...

God's walking with us is more than an honor, it's a promised from God in heaven. He will not leave or forsake us...He puts someone in your path to bring you a word when you least expect it.

For example, my computers needed cleaning, a new one set up, and a printer installed to print from all my wireless technology. The technician came at 11:00am and left at 2:15pm. He wouldn't take a penny for servicing all my computers, printer, iPad, and phone. He said, "Ms. Herticine, I can't charge you anything. I keep hearing or see it on something each day, "'Much given much required." Ms. Herticine, I was drinking out of a cup this morning which said, 'Be encouraged'. And each day I read my devotional I think of you. You are the one who gave them to me, and the DVD 'The Devil in Your Bedroom'. You just don't know how much you mean to me and how you have helped and encouraged me!'"

I covered my face with my neck brace with tears in my eyes, as I said, "Oh, my! You are making me cry. I had forgotten all about those! How many years have that been? "About six years, and I'm still using each one.'" The devotional and cup were given to him when his brother died suddenly, and the DVD for his birthday. Once again, I learned today that God helps to keep us on the narrow path by a testimony and a reminder of Him keeping us when we need a word of encouragement...and His eyes are on the smallest things we do to help His servants in times of sorrow and in need of a touch of care from God through His servants.

There's no broad meeting in heaven about our needs...God already knows each one. This morning's epiphany... If you say Jesus is your Savior, why is Satan allowed to take up room in your belief, and you welcome him to stay with your doubts and fears? Either you truly trust Jesus with everything, and I mean everything, or stop fooling yourself and others that Jesus is your all and all. Oh, yea, don't use the old excuse, this is just my human side... Paul only wavered in his complaints when he asked God to take the thorn from his side...but God said to Paul as He is saying to each of us." My grace is sufficient."

So, start today to trust God with all your needs, wants, and desires. It's not easy trusting what you can't see a head. But it's not for you to see beyond the mountain, because you may turn away from God's promises if you see the peaks and jagged rocks to go through to reach them (the promises). Just trust the One who moves mountains and the One who walks with you through the valleys holding your hand as you go.

Blessings...

Jesus Is Worthy of My Boasting

But as for me, I will never boast about anything except the cross. Galatians 6:14

Bragging on Jesus is one of the best discussions I have with people. My heart is always so touched with tears...that each tear holds me from saying a word. Matter of fact, the presence of God is so mighty that my strength is gone after a discussion. But I'm renewed each time and be ready for the next discussion. As I see it..,Jesus manifested His presence mightily because Heaven inhabits our praise.

However, today's praise won't take care of tomorrow's praise, and we must do God's will to receive heaven's ear. So, this is the question..." Have you repented of your sins...? If you hadn't...let me remind you that unconfessed sin is leprosy to your spirit...I have noticed many who have not confessed their sins carry hurts which causes suffering in ways, the mind never imagined. Their joy is gone, and they become withdrawal.

This is how it was with leprosy; the person was isolated from society and loneliness set in. they became withdrawal until their death. There are reasons after reasons I brag on Jesus. For one, the leper ran to Jesus to be healed with all his sores...the world wouldn't touch him, but Jesus willingly touched him with love and healing. As Jesus touches each of us with forgiveness when we run to Him for our spirit healing from the cesspool of hell rather than hiding in despair. Jesus reaches out and cleanse us.

When we look at the rejection of a leper, this is how heaven will reject each of us if we do not repent and be cleansed by forgiveness from Jesus' hands. "Now the leper on whom the sore is, his clothes shall be torn and his head bare; and he shall cover his moustache, and cry, "Unclean! Unclean!" Leviticus 13:45 Sin is unclean...

When a leper was diagnosed, he had to tear his clothes and bare his head because he was 'unclean' before God and man. He was expressing his grief and despair at his condition and ensuring that others did not touch him and so become infected and unclean. In contrast the priests were kept ritually clean. They were never permitted to tear their clothes or bare their heads in the service of the tabernacle (Exodus 39:23, Leviticus 10:5, 21:10). They were to deliver people from their ritual impurities. It was only when Jesus claimed before the High Priest, to be the Son of God, that a Priest tore his clothes (Matthew 26:65).

The High Priest had made himself unclean by accusing Jesus of blasphemy. At that moment the old order of the priesthood ended. It was no longer holy. It was stricken by God with spiritual leprosy.

The disease of leprosy is symbolic of sin. The Hebrew word for leprosy, 'tsars' means to be scourged and stricken. King Uzziah was stricken on his forehead for presuming to act like a priest...(pride)... 2 Chronicles 26. And Miriam was stricken with leprosy for speaking against Moses...(jealous)... Numbers 12:10.

Sin has no respecter of person.

The actual disease of leprosy leads to the eventual decay and rotting of the flesh, causing terrible deformity, pain and finally death. This is a picture of what sin does to us if we do not repent. When allowed free rein, it takes us down a path of spiritual decay, to death and hell. Highly infectious, it begins small, but grows to eventually consume the whole person. Only Jesus can make us clean again by forgiving our sin and healing our desires.

Consider the seriousness of sin and thank Jesus for being your High Priest to cleanse you. If you think you can go through this life without repenting of your sin...think again. Sin eats your promises of a sane life...the enemy knows you hadn't repented, and he smiles because he knows your peaceful life will be eaten away...and your eternal life will be agony. This is why I brag on Jesus because He sets us free from the danger of hell and renew us for the promises of a home with Him in heaven.

Hebrew 5:1-11

The Reason I Sing

Sing to Him; sing praise to Him; tell about all His wonderful works! Honor His holy name; let the hearts of those who seek Jesus rejoice. Sing to the LORD, all the earth. Proclaim His salvation from day to day. 1 Chronicles 16:9-10; 23

Why do I brag on Jesus? I watch the sunrise many mornings from my porch. Jesus did it, so I sing and brag! I hear the birds sing from my rocking chair. I feel the breeze on my face as I walk. I feel the pavement under my feet as I move along the path, I walk each day. I hear the voices of my child as they call me "Mama". Only Jesus can do this...so I brag on His goodness in a joyful song of praise.

Why do I brag on Jesus? He un-webbed my mind when hope had failed. He answered my prayers when I didn't know the roads to take. He wrapped me with the Rainbow of His promises when doubts were squeezing me tight. He bathes me with His love when hatred screamed louder than hope. He fights my battle, even when I don't know I need a Defender. He anointed me with His oil so Satan couldn't have his way. He laid me down in green pastures of rest when sleep was evading me. And my Wonderful Savior directs each step of weakened legs as I walked through valleys of uncertainties.

The hands which hold me in attacks is the reason I brag on Jesus. He is the calming waves in the storms of life...is the reason I brag on Him. He is the unmovable Rock of my salvation is the reason I brag on Him. But there are so many more reasons I brag on my Lord and Savior Jesus Christ. In every Book of the Bible, we can see Him. He reveals Himself so each of us will have hope and fear which fades.

Jesus promised we will be with Him even when this earthy life is over. This is the reason I brag on Him to everyone I meet. Through my walk and action rather than my talk...I brag on Him. I sing because I'm happy. Jesus promised I will be with Him in Paradise...I sing because I am happy. I sign because Jesus' promises never fail. All the prosperous of the earth shall eat and worship, all those who go down to the dust shall bow before Him. Psalm 22:29 This gives us the hope of Heaven. You can't help but brag on our

Savior...I'm never away from Him.

The prosperous are those who have received God's grace. There is no one richer on the earth than someone who has received the abundant grace of God and the love of the Father...I brag and sing. With Jesus, we are richer than the richest multi-millionaire in the world, because we have a heavenly hope in our hearts. The save will eat of the bread of the broken body of Jesus. His life given for us. His life is our life and sustained by Him we worship the Father. For the saved, their worship does not end when they die (go down to the dust), but continues in the world beyond, where they will bow before the Lord of Heaven and earth.

Even on the cross Jesus received the one giving Him his heart and accepting Him as Savior. Jesus was crucified between two thieves. They faced death, with the Messiah in between them. Luke, called them criminals. At first, they both mocked and reviled Jesus, but then their true hearts were revealed, and one of the criminals joined in the mockery of the soldiers, blaspheming and saying, "If You are the Christ, save Yourself and us." (Luke 23:39). His heart was hardened, and he had lost fear of the Lord. In his anger and bitterness, he failed to recognize his true need. He thought he needed to be saved from the cross. He didn't realize he needed to have his soul saved. The other criminal however acknowledged his guilt before God and he recognized that, unlike him, Jesus had done no wrong. So, he said to Jesus, "Lord, remember me when You come into Your kingdom." Jesus responded, full of grace, "Assuredly, I say to you, today you will be with Me in Paradise." (Luke 23:43).

I brag on Jesus because He is the:
Ram which substituted for my redemption...

Every aspect of the life of Jesus fulfilled God's holy Law, and He became the substitute for our failures and lacks in keeping God's law...

The peace offering speaks of Jesus' peace with the Father being conferred on us through His sacrifice. Through His blood we receive thanksgiving, God's life in us. As of today, remember our desires can only be our desires when God place them in our hearts. Exodus 35:21, lets us know God placed His will and desires into our hearts, so that even sacrificial giving becomes a joyful sacrifice and privilege. God loves a cheerful giver (2 Corinthians 9:7).

Why do I brag on Jesus?

He is a jealous God burning with godly jealousy for the love of His Bride (Deuteronomy 4:24). I bear His fragrance and I'm His bride...and every wife brags on her husband if he is a man of God.

Jesus's blood covers us from the fall of man in Genesis 3...so I have joy, peace, love, forgiveness because of my Wonderful Savior Who knows me by name...the God of Herticine... And I brag because Jesus said... "I, even I, am He who blots your transgressions for My own sake and will not remember your sins. Put Me in remembrance; let us plead together; state your cause, that you may be justified. Your first father has sinned, and your teachers have transgressed against Me. Therefore, I have profaned the princes of the sanctuary, and have given Jacob to the curse, and Israel to reproaches" (Isaiah 43:25-28).

This is only the beginning of why I brag on Jesus..." who is wonderful in counsel and excellent in wisdom" (Isaiah 28:29). If I don't brag on Jesus, the rocks will shoutout how great and wonderful He is...

Hearing God

So, the LORD God called out to the man and said to him, "Where are you?"
Genesis 3:9

Jesus said in John 4:34 that His food was to do the will of His Father who sent Him. and to finish His work. Wow, we can all lose weight doing it Jesus' way! The field is reaping with people in need of prayer, and a touch from God, but too many don't think it's real! They are going through the day feeling unworthy to be near the ones they work with. Their confidence level is low in many ways, and the attacks of the enemy for their peace and health are raging.

This morning, I didn't go out to the porch to pray. I didn't want any distractions, not even the beautiful sun rays or the sounds of the birds. So, I went to my 'prayer room' and the only sounds and sights I wanted hear was the voice of the Holy Spirit. I prayed Ephesians 1:18 for my spiritual eyes to be enlightened. As I prayed the Holy Spirit called three names...one He said felt unworthy, one losing confidence, and one He showed me from her head to her lower chest He was touching her with His healing touch.

Within fifteen minutes 6:53am the first person's name the Holy Spirit called...called. He felt unworthy and rejected because he wasn't included or offered food at an office party...I prayed for his self-worth. Then 7:25am the second call came...this person was dealing with his confidence...Hebrews 10:35 was prayed over him..." Do not throw away your confidence, which will be greatly rewarded."

Then at 7:52 am the third person called from her ICU bed. She was upset because she was hungry and thirsty, she could not have any food or water... I quoted John 4:34 "My food is to do the will of Him who sent Me, and to finish His Work." But she was too sick to understand the food God wanted her to crave was His food to do His will... So, the Holy Spirit led me to sing "Oh the glory of God's presence. Come from Your rest and be blessed by our praise... We worship You in Your embrace." So, she had to calm down to receive the prayer about to be prayed for her. Her anger lifted, and the prayer of God's peace went forward.

With the touch of God she felt, her nauseous lifted. Within five minutes after the prayer, she was allowed to eat. She would be moved to a regular room as soon as one opened. Satan wants each of us to doubt the power of faithful prayer. He wants us to doubt Jesus is real. He wants us to doubt that God listens and hears our prayers. But more so, the devil does not want you to know that he is fearful, this is the reason he wants you to be afraid. He wants you to stay in the past where things are not real and cannot be changed. He wants us bitter and bewildered. He wants the world and even the body of Christ to believe Jesus' healing touch of yesterday is dead, and His Spirit of Peace is a fairytale. But God has given us the authority to strangle Satan to death by our faith in Jesus' victory over Satan on the cross.

Yes, God still uses His saints, and yes, Jesus' stripes still heal. As of right now, this trembling frightful young lady in ICU is now sending out names of the ones in ICU from accidents and on life support to be prayed for, and she's praying also. She has asked the hospital chaplain to bring her a Bible to read. Who would have thought a song sang to fearful and angry people would turn a tormenting spirit into a praying one? The Holy Spirit knows what calms a fearful soul, His guidance to the peaceful River of Jesus Christ.

So, do you know how to strangle Satan to death in your life? By your faith in Christ Jesus put in action.

Old Saying

In the morning, 'O, LORD, you will hear my voice; In the morning I will order my prayer to You and eagerly watch. Psalm 5:3

There was an old saying when I was a child, "The early bird gets the worm." I don't eat worms, but I do love looking at the habits of the birds early in the morning before the busyness of the day begins. This morning after the early morning rain, I sat on my prayer bench praising God for another morning in His presence. Then He took my eyes to the birds feeding on the many feeders in my yard free of worries and rejoicing in song. Each bird was trusting God to take care of its needs. The ones not eating from the feeders were eating from the ground or tree, even some were eating from the flower blossoms. Then I understood better than the days before, I must trust God as the birds to take care of each of my needs...from my health to hearing and answering my prayers so I shall not want. The birds don't waver in faith, so I asked the Lord to help me to be a rock on unsinkable soil than a wave upon the sea moving from high too low.

Also, when the enemy comes to disturb my peace...I rejoice because each attack from him helps me to die to the flesh to live in the spirit where faith and peace increase! It's sad how we so often limit God by thinking with a human mind of the things He has done and is doing for us...Rather than knowing we can't make it through the minute without God's mercy...it's so vast, so beyond human understanding, and we limited the move of God by uncertainties in our thoughts.

Now, I have heard this statement made too often, "I hope he or she had an opportunity to hear about Jesus before he died!" Read the following of God's unlimited grace: Last night, I received a text from a young nanny who takes care of this very privilege, intelligent, rude little boy whose parents are too busy in their careers to have anytime with him. He has gone through many nannies over his six years of life, but this nanny is making a difference, even his teachers have noticed a difference in this child's behavior since this young lady began taking care of him. Tuesday night she(nanny) prayed over him (little boy) ...and this is the text I received confirming God is always on time: "I started praying over.........(boy's name) last night and he liked it. So tonight, he comes, and he was like, "can you do that thing again like you did last night?" And I was like, pray? And he said, "Yes, pray for me please. I want to pray like you. Can you teach me?'" By the nanny praying for this little boy, she introduced him to the sweet touch of Jesus' love. The touch he had never felt before, and the name of Jesus he had never heard before.

God will put someone in each of our path to introduce us to Him. What a Loving Savior! There's no limits to His arms of love.... they can reach to the highest mountain to save us, and to the lowest valley to deliver us. There are no hiding places He can't find...and no ocean He can't swim. Oh, how I love Jesus because He first loved me! The little boy didn't only hear about Jesus, he met and received Jesus. Hearing about Jesus without receiving Him is like King Agrippa (Acts 25-26) an almost received Jesus. Almost can go either way, up or down.

When you take your eyes off God...and put them on things that perish...you will have crooked steps in the sand, and a home with the worms that never die.

Song In the Wind

He rode on a cherub and flew, soaring on the wings of the wind... Psalm 18:10

Some people don't like the morning. They sleep to noon missing the fresh breeze which smooths the skin. The sweet sound of the bumblebee twirling in the blossoms of the Rose of Sharon. The eastern sky hugging the delight of the sun. The honeybees on the grass drinking in the morning nectar of heaven. The geese flying low to land on the lake like a 747 coming in from an overnight trip. The breath of God is breathing on me the comfort of love through the gentle wind. I look at the trees and they sway with the wind. They obey the movement of the wind, and with each breath of the wind they become stronger to stand against the forces of the storms to come. Oh, how God wants to meet with His lovely ones to caress us with His wind song of love. He directs the birds to sing with the wind in harmony of gentle love. The morning songs carry me deeper into the embrace of heavenly bliss. God wants to meet hug to hug with His beloveds to pour His sweet nectar of assurances of His tender care.

Song Of Song speaks of "My lover puts his hand through the latch..." This is how the Lover of my soul puts His hand on the latch of my heart to awaken me to His love call of the dawn. I'm beautiful in my Savior's sight. Sadly, man calls what God have created ugly when it doesn't meet the standard of worldly beautify.

Also, man's standard of love and beauty have caused many minds to be crippled with doubt of who they are. How lovely they are with short legs and crooked teeth. How needed they are, even if they were not number one in their class. The birds let us know God made us different because there are robins to cockatoo, and each has a purpose. Man says who should live, "Not the handicap, not the blind, not the deaf, but I am the reflection of God...Which is beautiful... So don't call me ugly or how God made us ugly, because when you do, you are talking about God, I am in His image, you are in His image.

What heaven began in you the devil can't stop. Some of you are lying in bed in a darkened room of pity because of troubles of the past. Guess what? God is there with you, just look up because He is the Light that lights darken places so you can see your way out!

Some of you think you are climbing an uphill battle that you will never get it over. Guess what? God didn't say to go over the valley, He said He would carry you through the valley. Reach out your hand from the locked cell you are in right now and God will unlock each one, because heaven's plans for your life must take place.

Remember, the devil is under God's authority.

Seeking

Know the God of your father and serve Him with a whole heart and a willing mind, for the LORD searches every heart and understands the intention of every thought. If you seek Him, He will be found by you, but if you forsake Him, He will reject you forever... 1 Chronicles 28:9

I like sitting out on the porch early in the morning. The sun rays form beautiful shapes through the tree limbs at the sunrise time of the day. The leaves dance in silent with the breeze as the windmill moves slowly in the direction of the winds. Sometimes it's as if I'm watching a silent movie with only the characters from God's habitat of obedience servants. Each obey God's command and forms a beautiful reflection of His beauty. The loveliness of the morning pulls the ones desiring God to want more and more of His presence. I love hearing God speak through the wind as the birds sings a duet with it. The dance of the eastern sunrise peeping through the trees carried me to wanting to praise God's goodness like David 2 Samuel 6:14. David whirled in excitement like the leaves whirl in the wind as each dance gently together on the tree which gives them life, God is the life Giver.

As I write this message, my thoughts went back to the times of my childhood and seeing my grandmother on the porch early in the morning. She would sweep the yard after she ate her breakfast and drank her cup of coffee. Then she would read the newspaper from front to back. She did all these things before my mother finished with our breakfast and set the table for the seven children, and she and my father to eat. There was never a time we didn't sit together as a family to eat a tasty meal my mother prepared from the harvests of the land. Thinking about it, it would take my mother longer to cook for nine people(uh). But each morning after the cows were milked and the milk strain for selling, the joy of a wonderful meal taught us to honor Jesus for His provisions. Honor and thanks to God was given by my father as each child bowed in thankfulness of the tasty meal to come!

Now, after sitting in humble thanks for God's provisions and guidance, I don't know if I will go to the rehab today because I'm waiting for Sears to come to repair the lawn mow (repaired the first of June and stopped in the yard 30mins later). Yes, I'm waiting, but as I wait, I'm listening to hear God. I'm reminded of 2 Kings 6; Elisha wasn't in the enemy's house physically but God opened his spiritual ears so he could hear the enemy's plans. Elisha even prayed and asked God to open his servant's eyes so he could see His protection. I love the Scripture from this chapter, "There is more on our side than theirs." Hallelujah! This morning while listening to nature singing, I'm hearing God say His angels are everywhere and there are more with me than against me. I'm where I need to be because John will not be in rehab much longer, and the home-front much be kept so he will have one to come back to.

When John looked at the picture of the lawn our neighbor mowed while I was gone, he smiled and said, "I need to be home." "Only when you have finished this time of restoration." Was my reply. He got his Bible, and we had devotion. He realized the day before that each time we have devotion in his room he gets stronger. And the last few days of devotion have been on trusting God from Psalm 34-38. He even talked about the conversations he and the therapists have. Also, there's a 20 min limit on riding the bike, he asked if he could ride longer. He's determined to come home. Through this journey, I'm learning to dive into deeper trust. I no longer want to be a paddle duck eating from the surface, I'm choosing to be a diving duck eating from God's deep hidden revelations. I seek to have the anointing of Elisha rather than be in dismays like his servant. I know John is fine with me there or with me waiting for the repairmen because there more with him than not. Also, this is a message for me, him, and each reading this, be determined to prepare for the eternal home because this earthly home will one day be left behind.

And I'm realizing that a hypocrite has God in his mouth and the world in his heart-Vernon Grounds. If I say I trust God with each of our needs, then I need to exhibit it more than talk about it. The Lord, says: "These people... honor me with their lips, but their hearts are far from me,"–Isaiah 29:13. Father, forgive me if I am not who I say I am. Help me to seek Your guidance...Amen.

Singing

While the morning stars sang together, and all the sons of God shouted for joy.
Job 38:7

Good morning, this windy day the birds are singing in harmony with the Corinthian bells, and the sun rays on the tree leaves are the backup dancers giving morning praise and welcoming this new day. Good morning, Holy Spirit, thank You for showing me true authentic worship because the sun and wind can't pretend, the birds and trees will not deny that You give them life this day and Your breath can take it away.

Good morning Holy Spirit this cool sunny day the crows are singing louder than all the birds in the trees. Squirrels are chasing each other as if they are in a wrestling match. The hummingbirds are gracing the feeders with stunning beauty. The new mornings welcome so many things too numerous to write about. The eyes can only hold one amazing wonder at a time as the ears hear each sound and the mind distinguish between the many. Who can do this other than You Lord? Who else can mix each wonder of Your wonderful creations so beautifully the eyes cannot take in and the mouth cannot explain how amazing the beauty of Your hands? Who other than You can tell the sun to rest on the top of the trees to give them hope of a sunny day? Who else can give a drink of water to roots of each tree and they have enough, and then there is plenty for the next day? Who else can tell the wind to lay the trees on their sides and their roots still feed from the ground? Who else can carry a hawk in the wind of Your hands and man cannot see it but the hawk trusts You? Who else can tell the sun not to burn too hot on the things below and the ocean water stay cool breath the heat? Who else can tell the wind to blow, and the wind blows against the Corinthian bells to sing the songs from the storehouse of heaven? Who else can tell the trees they are the protective shelter for the birds? Who else can give me ears to hear the birds sing but do not see them? Who else can give crickets legs like violins to play in a hiding place hard to find by man. No one but You, Lord can tell the sunlight to dress the treetops with silvery mist that my eyes can only see but my hands can't touch. This is why the stars sing at night and shine during the day but only the ones who seek more of You can see and hear them praise You.

The windmills obey the direction of the wind. I hear God. God says in...Ecclesiastes 11:5 "As you do not know the path of the wind, or how the bones are formed in a mother's womb, so you cannot understand the work of God, the Maker of all things."

And John 3:8 The wind blows where it wishes. You hear its sound, but you do not know where it comes from or where it is going. So, it is with everyone born of the Spirit."

I can't see the wind, but I hear it singing and obeying God's directions. The butterfly wings are graceful in the wind. The leaves of the trees shimmer in isolate beauty as the wind moves through each limb but God keeps each leaf from falling. I see God. God is everywhere and He knows every need. As I sit in amazement each day viewing the things that look like it did yesterday, but it is not, I thank God for His beauty. Even the windmills are pointed in different directions. New birds are eating from the feeder. The birds seem to be singing a new song. I know Jesus lives!

This morning, I received a phone call and the caller asked if I was at home. I said yes, I was here. The caller asked if he could come by to see me? I said yes. He came, and we sat and talked for a while. I looked at him and asked, "What is going on?" He reached in his pocket and said, "The last time I was here last week I heard something, and I came to fit it (taking batteries out of his pocket) your fire detector so you will be safe." I smiled with joy knowing God touched this man's heart with love and care to want to take care of me. This is a new day to celebrate the goodness of God for a new day...this is why I sing...because God's mercy is renewed every morning with a new bird song...

Two Cities

These are the worst of times yet the best of times- The Tales of Two Cities by Charles Dickens.

There are two cities and each of us has a choice of the one we choose. I can't even imagine what Moses went through dealing with millions of people wanting their own individual city (having their way). Each whining or complaining about something. Even in their threats and name calling against him, he humbly forgave them and went before God for them. Moses even risked his home in heaven and the wiping away of his name in the Book of Life for their wrongs. Yes, it was the worst of times for Moses, but he made it the best of times because he chose God, the place of peace and fulfillment. Moses standing in the midst of the people complaining about what God hadn't done...and Moses and Aaron's taking them out of Egypt... my, my who could bear it other than a called by God man of God?

Moses stood when pestilence, disease, and death came, he stood between the people and God's wrath. Moses saw the earth swallow the ones choosing the city of death over God. Numbers 16:28-32 "Then Moses said, "This is how you will know that the LORD has sent me to do all these things, for it was not my own doing: If these men die a natural death, or if they suffer the fate of all men, then the LORD has not sent me. But if the LORD brings about something unprecedented, and the earth opens its mouth and swallows them and all that belongs to them so that they go down alive into Sheol, then you will know that these men have treated the LORD with contempt." As soon as Moses had finished saying all this, the ground beneath them split open, and the earth opened its mouth and swallowed them and their households--all Korah's men and all their possessions."

It truly amazes me how Moses stood humbly still trusting God when disease and virus of troubles barked at him...he knew God always knows best. Another wonderful revelation in the wilderness of troubles it's testing our faith.

Also, God never let us face troubles alone even if we can't see who God has in place for us... "But My servant Caleb, because he has a different spirit in him and has followed Me fully, I will bring him into the land where he went, and his descendants shall inherit it" (Numbers 14:24). Out of twelve men, ten saw trouble, while only two saw God. Many today, right now see troubles and a few, only a few sees God bigger than any circumstances. Out of millions of people twenty years of age and older, only two out of all saw the Promised Land.

God used Caleb and Joshua to speak up in the midst of 'false reports. Sadly, the people chose the crowd's report over God's report, and they perished in the wilderness and opened graves became their city because of their unbelief. Hebrews 3:12 warns us: 'Brethren, beware, lest there be in any of you an evil heart of unbelief in departing from the living God.'

Two Cities Part 2

These are the worst of times yet the best of times- The Tales of Two Cities by Charles Dickens.

The Israelites hardened their hearts in unbelief, not trusting God. They did not really believe in God's goodness and sovereign power and ability to give them victory, or the truth and reliability of His Word. God was looking for hearts that were 'soft' toward Him, believing and trusting in His great love, kindness, faithfulness, compassion, and power. Instead, they thought the task impossible because of their enemies the Amalekites, Hittites, Jebusites, Amorites, Canaanites, and coronavirus were bigger and stronger.

Joshua and Caleb, the two believing and courageous spies, saw the good things of the Land and said, 'If the Lord delights in us, then He will bring us into this Land and give it to us, a land which flowing with milk and honey.' (Numbers 24:8)

They believed God's promise. God delighted in their faith and took them into the Land and enabled them to conquer it. Isaiah 30:15 tells that our victory comes with our quiet trust in God. Our wise planning has value which is prayer...prayer works...Listen carefully to this prayer from 2 Chronicles 32:7-8 "Be strong and courageous; do not be afraid nor dismayed before the king of Assyria, nor before all the multitude that is with him; for there are more with us than with him. With him is an arm of flesh; but with us is the LORD our God, to help us and to fight our battles." And the people were strengthened by the words of Hezekiah king of Judah." The same army of God is still fighting your, mine, and our battles. Let God fight Coronavirus for you...so which time and city are you choosing? City of fear, or city of faith knowing there are more with us than the enemy, God is the city without fading lights.

Lord Is My Light

The LORD is my light and my salvation...whom should I fear? The LORD is the stronghold of my life of whom should I be afraid? Psalm 27:1

Listen carefully, snake eggs will hatch in the slum as well as the king's palace. They will crawl on dirt as well as diamond carpet. They hiss at the president as well as the factory worker. They bit the queen as well as the prostitute. They live wherever there is food to eat; they have no friends among themselves; even the babies' mama doesn't care if they survive.

So, have you allowed or invited any snakes to have space in your house? They don't care if you are kind, loving, giving, old or young, they even bite the ones who feed them. Remember, snakes only stay where they can find food, this is one of the reasons the snake could stay in the Garden of Eve so long... Adam and Eve were feeding it with their unadvisable attention to his lie to them being like God. You don't have to be a gossiper in order for the enemy to stay in your house...all he needs is for you to listen attentively to his lies and not rebuke him. Garbage always needs a garbage can to empty into.

Inviting a snake to live with you will ruin your household and life...Adam and Eve found this out the hard way. A snake has no compassion...no love...no beauty...no family...only deception. With every kiss, is venom. With every squeeze is death. With every tongue thrust its counting your size to attack...

Why is a snake's conversation poisonous?

Because the snake in the Garden of Eve con Adam and Eve to receive the venom of death when its lie led them to eat the fruit of the tree of good and evil...Genesis 3:1-6

Lying is venom that leads to death. From the moment Adam ate the fruit death entered this world, and blood sacrifices from the lamb was needed to cover man's sins...Genesis 3:21.

From the snake's conning Adam, God had to make the first prophecy in Genesis 3:15 "I will put enmity between you and the woman, and between your offspring and her offspring; he will bruise your head, and you will bruise his heel."

From man's first stumble Satan has sought to destroy the Promised Seed that will destroy him...starting with the first murder in Genesis 4:6 "Sin is crouching at the door. It desires to dominate you, but you must rule over it." Cain allowed the snake to take room in his heart...he killed his brother, Abel. Abel, the first prophet sought to hear the voice of the Lord.

Lack of peace is like a slithering snake...that causes you not to be satisfied.

For example, Lamech who took two wives in Genesis 4:19... starting the absentee father...and welfare for the leased loved.

People accepting the poisonous venom of a snake brings more hatred and jealousy...Joseph's brother sold him. To stop the dream from being fulfilled.

Satan hated the first prophecy of God so badly that he used Pharaoh in Exodus 2 to kill all the Hebrews boys two years old and younger to keep the prophecy from being fulfilled. It didn't work...Moses was born and the promised fulfilled to let the children of Israel go...

Herod in Matthew 2:16-17 killed all the male children in Bethlehem two years old and under to stop the prophecy. It didn't work, Jesus was born, healed, delivered, taught, made disciples, crucified, died, rose, went to heaven and the enemy was defeated, not is defeated but was defeated!

Paul ran down the born-again Jews to keep down the population of heaven. It didn't work, he was saved, and more born-again believers added to heaven's roll.

Stephen was stoned to death to keep new believers away....it didn't work...more were saved, and Paul preached the Gospel.

Hitler killed millions of Jews so the apples of God's eye would be not more, and the seeds to His heart would die....it didn't work, more came to the faith, and lived to talk about it. Snake goes where there is food...the spiritual snake feeds on the food of hatred, anger, bitterness, unforgiveness, half trues, gossip, and all the things God's Word tells us not to do. Lock the snake out by sealing every negative hole in your life.

Today, know this mighty truth...there is a repellent for all snakes, and there is a place they can't enter. "A highway shall be there, a roadway, and it shall be called the Highway of Holiness. The unclean shall be for the wayfaring men, and fools shall not wander on it. No lion shall be there, nor any ravenous beast shall go up on it; these shall not be found there, but the redeemed shall walk there, and the ransomed of the LORD shall return and come to Zion with songs and everlasting joy upon their heads. They shall obtain joy and gladness, and sorrow and sighing shall flee away" (Isaiah 35:8-10).

So let not your heart be trouble...Jesus defeated the snake (Satan) at the cross. And even with the snake crawling in dark places...God even saved the snake from the flood...He let him slither on the Ark. Meaning, your sins are forgiven. God's covenant with its people.

Eyes On Man

Go to the ant, you slacker! Observe its ways and become wise. Proverbs 6:6

How many of us are guilty of putting our eyes and hope on man and in man? Many will say, "Not I!" like the barnyard animals and friends of Little Red Hen when she found the grains of corn. They kept their eyes on what they didn't want to do until the harvest came in and the meal prepared for the cold winter's meal. As the Little Red Hen ate in warmth her 'missing in action friends' in a time of planting and harvesting were standing in the cold. This is what too many of us have done, left Jesus out in the cold while we looked to man for the answers to our problems. How can man solve our problem when he is the problem? As the troubles rage around us, who are you seeking and keeping your eyes on man or God? Don't you think it's time to invite Jesus in from the cold where He should have never been in the first place? Man is only used by God to get His plan done, because man will fade away like dew on the grass, God never fades. Decide right now the ones who's weary and feeling hopeless whom you will keep your eyes of faith on in these troubling times. Remember, "You ain't got no problem, all you need is faith in God!" On December 26, 2020, God showed me this vision of His glory, hopefully it will strengthen you as it did me. Amen.

Song of the Morning

He put a new song in my mouth, a hymn of praise to our God. Many will see and fear and put their trust in the LORD. Psalm 40:3

Good morning, Holy Spirit! You allowed me to see another day. A day the trees are prettier than yesterday, and hummingbirds are at play. The mockingbirds have heard the morning dog bark and they are marking in song what they have heard.

The morning bird song with a dog bark between the musical rest, sounds like fellowship in morning worship of Your goodness. I heard the voices of the children on the bus as it passes by. Some are happy some haven't had much sleep during the night, some are struggling with who they are, some received hugs of love before their day's journey, some received curses rather than breakfast. Holy Spirit comfort the one who doesn't have a home to call their own, and the ones with a home left alone. Home alone isn't a child's joy; parents presence brings much joy. The pain of hurts and repairs of many of the children on the bus will lead to questioning, "Why am I here?"

During your childhood someone may have spoken negative words over you, and you still hear and believe what was spoken! Take a small journey with me to the lowly donkey that carries burdens...Jesus chose it over the horse to carry Him. A little insignificant seed that sprouted into a tree was chosen by man for something bad...however, it held our sins as Jesus hung on it with our names in His hands.

So today, seek to see yourself as God sees you, chosen to do something someone else can't do for the kingdom...You may be the one who leads a blind soul to the light! Too often, people will say, "I don't understand how people can be raised by the same parents but act so differently." Watching the trees move with the wind the Holy Spirit revealed the limbs not the leaves today so I can get a clearer understanding.

Each limb is a part of the same tree rooted in the same soil, but yet each limb is different from the other. They are side by side on the mother tree, but some are twisted, some straight, some pointing upward, some pointing downward, some covered with leaves, some stripped, some pretty and some ugly, but who am I to call it ugly when the Creator created it!

One tree limb is different in shape. Same limbs feeding from the same roots but grown in different ways. Some small some large, yet parents are the same roots. God shows life in everything He created, and we can learn from them the way of life. Children born to the same parents make their own decisions. Cain killed Abel; same teaching different choices made. God told Cain that sin was creeping at his door, Cain chose to open it to let it in, his choice made him the first murderer...and his brother's blood the first to cry out to God because innocent had been killed because of sin and hatred.

When the question comes, "Why is your sister or brother different from you?" We can get the answer from Jesus. Jesus said... "Who is my mother? Who are my brothers? But those who do the will of the Lord." Matthew 12:48-50

Following Jesus leads to a path the donkey traveled bringing eternal life to those willing to separate themselves from the tree bearing bad fruit to allowing the Creator to plant them in His soil which gives life forever.

Testimony

They conquered him by the blood of the Lamb and the word of their testimony, for they did not love their lives in the face of death. Revelation 12:11

A friend asked me yesterday if I would give this testimony. Three years ago, this month I went to my oldest grandson's graduation in Atlanta, GA, when I got back home my leg was hurting badly. But I was sure it would be better when I woke up the next day because I'm a true believer in God's healing powers. But it wasn't better when I woke up, matter of fact, I tossed and turned through the night with pain. I got up and I barely could walk. My leg hurt so badly that I literally had to drag it. I prayed, "Lord heal my leg. You sent forth Your Word to heal me. I trust you, Lord. I know I'm healed."

My leg got worse with swelling and pain, and the pain also moved to the other leg. But I kept going before God for His healing. I kept praying and claiming His promises that I was healed. However, I had to humble myself and ask for forgiveness because I had been taking my walking for granted. I'm a long-distance walker of 6 miles a day, but now I couldn't walk to my car without unbearable pain. I couldn't drive without my leg cramping. But I kept all this between me and God. No one knew when they would see me that I barely could stand.

People in my area were so used to seeing me walking every morning, (I was many of their alarm clocks because I walked the same time each day) that after not walking for a while some would stop by to see if I was ok because they weren't seeing me out. One man came to my house to see if I was alive because he hadn't seen me out walking, "I thought you were dead, because I haven't seen you out! So, I had to come to check on you!" he said as he stood in my door.

Two years had almost passed, and I was still asking God to heal my legs because I wanted to walk long distance again. Then He showed me Naaman in the Bible who had to dip in the Jordan River seven times before he was healed of leprosy, he had to do something first before he was healed. The invalid man of 38 years in the Book of John had to pick up his mat and walk before he was healed.

"Alright Lord, I see what I must do." I had to put on my walking shoes to walk. I started on my porch walking a few laps then rested, a few more laps and rested. Then to the mailbox and rested. A few more laps on my porch and rested... As of today, I'm walking two (2) miles, and just planted my garden. I received a phone call this morning telling me how nice it was seeing me out walking again.

Also last year, I had an awful pain in my side, after the doctor did an ultrasound it showed a gallstone. I was referred to a surgeon to have my gallbladder removed, but God would not give me any peace about having the surgery. Then once again I turned totally to God for my healing and had to do my part in my healing. The Holy Spirit led me to the Book of Daniel and how Daniel ate. I changed my eating to fresh vegetables and fruits only, and 96oz of water a day if not more. At the end of the week when I went to the surgeon, he did his examination and told me to come back in two weeks. I went back, another examination was done, and he said, "No surgery needed. Keep eating your 'clean vegetables and drink plenty of water.'" I make my vegetables pretty to sight and tasteful so the ones eating at my table will enjoy their meal.

God is our Healer, but He is not going to put our shoes on to walk for us or lock our mouth close. He will be with us with each step we take in faith. Jesus was willing and waiting to heal my legs and gallbladder, but He was waiting for me to take the first step of my healing by trusting Him to strengthen me with each step I take. Each of our healing lies within our faith walk with God's unfailing promises..."I will never leave you or forsake you." What a wonderful promise!

Sunrise of Promise

But for you who fear My name, the sun of righteousness will rise with healing in its wings, and you will go out and playfully jump like calves from the stall... Malachi 4:2

It has been a long day...but I'm thankful to have been awakened to another day. Up at 5:45 for a 6:30am walk with the beautiful sunrise peeping through the eastern trees. My days are long, and many say that I need to rest more! But I do rest two or three times a day when I walk on my porch to feel the breeze on my face (well, I guess they mean sit down)!

Most morning, before I can sit to enjoy the freshly brewed coffee and choose which breads, I will savor the phone calls come in with prayer requests for the sick, weary, and yes, often for someone on their death bed. This morning, before my morning walk a neighbor stopped by to talk (she was up as early as I was). Sometimes we must stop what we are doing to welcome a visiting soul to a seat in the rocking chair to listen to God commanding the wind to sing through the chimes to bring peace to a tired and weary soul.

Also, an expecting mom stopped us as we walked to thank us for the baby gift, but more so, for the book I gave her for expecting moms! She wanted me to know that she is using the book in her Wednesday Youth Bible study class. I rejoiced because God uses things many reject.

God is amazing as He shows us how to minister to the ones in need of salvation, and He does it in such unusual ways. I'm using the different colors of flowers to minister to the ones He wants in His kingdom. I laughed when the Holy Spirit showed me in service Sunday that He is using the Bouquet of flowers I give to the sick to reveal Himself to the ones receiving them, and to the ones carrying them. Each color has a meaning as God directs me to buy the flowers each week for the ones lying in the hospital or nursing home beds feeling hopeless. Souls are important to God, and He uses the ones willing to be used to get His plans fulfilled.

My morning walks are not easy, but the rewards from doing so are beyond words...only God knows how He is going to use each morning walk. So, I just trust He will strengthen me to go each day. God sees the needs of each person crying out to Him. Many are so lonely that the spirit of rejection comes knocking on the doors of many. A simple card or colored flower speaks to the lonely heart hope in the isolation of weariness.

Yes, God speaks through the many things He created. The color of a flower woke a man from darkness to light. His life was changed because of a yellow flower. I don't know what God said through the flower, and I don't need to know, I just need to keep doing what He directs me to do.

A man was spared hell because God had me to sing a song of heaven...and a prayer was prayed. The man gave his life to Christ Jesus on His bed of affliction. God took what I was told by man wasn't worthwhile and used it for a dying soul on the way to hellfire. How often, we listen to man's opinions over the gift God have given to be used for His kingdom. A plate of food bought with an offering of love gave a cancer victim the desire to eat. There are no small things with Christ Jesus, He directs, and we should seek and listen.

Morning walks have given me the opportunity to know each of my neighbors, and a loaf of bread from my oven have formed a friendship ordained by God. The simple things from a kind heart moves mountain and plants a harvest of fellowship with the ones needing to see Jesus as real, not a Sunday day god.

If I Would Have

Do not hide Your face from me in my day of trouble. Listen closely to me; answer me quickly when I call. Psalm 102:2

Don't wish you would have after I'm gone. "Would haves" are shadows without life. Would have hold you in fear of facing a new day because of the stumbling mistakes of yesterday. Fear holds you in yesterday where dead hopes never take life. In a place and time where mistakes can never be undone. Even the birds move from yesterday's memories as they follow the sun from the eastern sunrise to the western sunset, they trust God.

Holding to yesterday brings fades dreams. The only life in yesterday is wisdom gained and learning increased from the stumbling of yesterday so you will never walk the same path or fall in the same pits of faded colored dreams again.

I wish I could hear her teaching again. I wish my heart would have been opened to hear God speaking to me in my darken place of despair. Hearts closed to the teaching of the Word are left in darken, regrets as the promise passes by as a closed heart welcomes the world's failing promises which bring commendation to a seeking heart later. The heart is filled up with regrets of what if! Sinking more in weariness as the floods of hope washes aways as the boat of hope floats away to the mountains of promises.

Oh, how I wish I could feel the hugs from a heart of love. Keeping the 'eyes of hope' on yesterday's rejections steal today's promises of "never to leave you" as Jesus promised. Closing the heart and ears to the invitation of love knocking and failing to open the door, too often voids the invitation as it expires into dreams of yesterday. Hope for another invitation fades when the receiver decided not to come to the door to receive the Knocker. The Knocker is gone... "I opened to my love, but my love had turned and gone away. I was crushed that he had left. I sought him but did not find him. I called him, but he did not answer" (Song of Song 5:6).

You were invited to listen, but you were too busy with wanting to find your own pleasure. I wish I'd learned to cook my favorite cake; you could have but you wanted to show off to the neighbors and family. I wish I could taste that home cooked meal, you could have, but you were too busy wanting to be a guest rather than a child coming home. I wish I could have.... but complained when needed in helping needy hands.

Didn't you see me limping as I prepared your requested dish? Didn't you see me leaning as I washed the dishes? Didn't you see me silent when a joke was told? Didn't you see me needing help when the yard was covered with limbs? The little foxes of worldly desires ate your desires to be a helping hand... "Catch for us the foxes, the little foxes that ruin the vineyards that are in bloom" (Song of Song 2:15). Wishing will not replace what happened yesterday, move the foxes from your garden so you will not have to wish no more on eaten dreams...

Did you thank me for the special meal? Did you thank me when as I give you, my best? Did you think it wasn't good enough? Did you think you grew from the cabbage patch? Did you think I would always be here? Did you think you would not miss me when I'm gone? Think again because home is where you were taught to trust. Home is where you were introduced to Jesus. Home is where you were prepared for life's journey. Home is where prayers are prayed for your favor. Home is where fasting and prayer are prayed for your protection. Home is where Jesus seeks to meet with you. Are you too busy to sit for an awhile? Are you too important to know home is where you will return when time is said and done?

Jesus wept over Jerusalem when they rejected Him as the Mother Hen, He wanted to be to them. To pull the brood under His wings for protection and provisions. Matthew 23:37 Jesus stands at the door and knocking, but busyness will reject it. Wishing what would have been useless wishes, are shadow dreams which can't be repeated only learned from. As Jesus informed Jerusalem when they rejected His invitation, He is warning the stony hearts today.

"For I tell you, you will never see Me again until you say, 'He who comes in the name of the Lord is the blessed One'!" Matthew 23:39 Jesus' blood on the cross dropped drop by drop for the ones who gives honor to the world as their keeper rather than Jesus who carried each of us in His hands to the cross. Every mistake died there. Every stumble was caught there. Every need was met there. Every attack of the enemy was nailed there. Every blind eye was opened there. Every deaf ear was healed there. Every life was claimed there. Heaven received and destroyed the grip of uncertainties there. Every promise was fulfilled there, because Jesus ripped the dividing wall apart so each person with an invitation for everlasting life can come. Ifs fade as we answer the knock on the door from the Gift which never fades.

Wisdom

Give thanks to the LORD, for He is good; His faithful love endures forever...
Psalm 106:1b

I stood in my bathroom and watched a wasp move backward and forward trying to get free from an outside screen on a window. It couldn't see its freedom even though, nothing was blocking it from flying away, but it became weaker and weaker, and blindness killed it. This is the trouble with lies, they are deceptions which are sinful. Honestly is always the best policy. Furthermore, deceit often turns on its source, who pays an even higher price in the long run than if he told the truth in the first place. To be truthful, lying is an enemy to wisdom and truth.

Lies trap the ones who wants blindness to be blind to the desires of the heart. Lies trap its prey in blindness to the truth as the wasp was trapped in the open window. The only thing the wasp could see was failure to be free again. A lie is a trap which causes one to fail to keep what he has achieved. Because lying is false hope hoping to never to be found out.

We can see through the Scriptures how lies caused many to stumble and some even death. Hananiah, the prophet misled Judah by denouncing Jeremiah's unpleasant message and speaking his own prophecy, announced with the words, "Thus says the LORD." But the Lord had not spoken to him (Jeremiah. 28:10,11). False prophecy was a serious sin punishable by death (Deut.13:1-5), and it was no surprise when the Lord made Hananiah pay for his deception with his life (Jeremiah.23:15-17).

God hates dishonesty (Prov.6:16-17) and that "he who speaks lies shall perish"(19:9). Lying has consequences:

• A lie brought sin and death into the world (Gen. 3:1-7; 1Tim. 2:14).

• Cain tried to lie his way out of answering for the murder of his brother Abel, then spent a lifetime in fear of meeting a similar fate (Gen. 4:1-16).

• Rebekah and Jacob told Isaac a lie in order to steal the family blessing from Esau. The result was family estrangement and hostility, which endured for generations (Gen. 27:5-17,41-46).

- Joseph's brothers lied to their father Jacob about selling Joseph to slave traders, causing Jacob profound heartache (Gen. 37:28-35).
- Potiphar's wife lied in order to frame Joseph for attempted rape, resulting in an unjust prison sentence (Gen. 39:7-20).
- David caused Uriah's murder in order to cover up his affair with Bathsheba. His deceit caused his child to die and his family to suffer profound conflict (2Sam. 11-12).
- Peter denied knowing the Lord, bringing shame and sorrow on himself (Matthew 26:69-74).
- Ananias and Sapphira lied to the church and the Holy Spirit about a financial gift, inviting their untimely death (Acts 5:1-11).

Jesus spoke clearly about the nature of lying when he declared that lies are of the devil (John 8:44). By contrast, Jesus is the source of all truth, and those who speak and practice the truth demonstrate that they belong to Him (14:6; 1 John 3:19).

Life and death are in your tongue...

Father, speak Your servant is listening. Help me to be wise and reject the lies of the enemy no matter how good they sound. Amen...

Confidence

Therefore, do not throw away your confidence, which will be greatly rewarded...
Hebrews 10:35

The WORD of God break strongholds... Someone is in need of this Word today: "Therefore do not throw away your confidence, which will be greatly rewarded" (Hebrews 10:35). The enemy wants you defeated in your confidence, when God wants you victorious because only, He knows the plans for your life...and the traps of the enemy that lies ahead.

Don't throw away your husband or wife...work through the hills that you think are mountains. Ladies, there is someone waiting to collect your husbands...Isaiah 4:1 "On that day seven women will take hold of one man and say, "We will eat our own bread and provide our own clothes. Just let us be called by your name. Take away our disgrace!"

Don't throw away your children by letting them have their own way...someone is stealing, killing, and misleading them everyday. Proverbs 22:6 "Train up a child in the way he should go, and when he is old, he will not depart from it."

Don't throw away your job...there are hundreds of applicants waiting on it. Don't throw away your faith in God...Satan is waiting to handcuff you in doubts and fears which leads to a miserable life. So today, choose to live life God's way, in the end it's sweeter that way. And one day each of us will return to the dust. Genesis 3:19 "By the sweat of your brow you will eat your bread, until you return to the ground--because out of it were you taken. For dust you are, and to dust you shall return."

Passover

Clean out the old yeast so that you may be a new batch. You are indeed unleavened, for Christ our Passover has been sacrificed. 1 Corinthians 5:7

Good morning, this Passover day the birds are rejoicing with song, the clouds are forming with the voice of thunder and vision of lightening, the leaves on the trees are motionless, the windmills aren't moving, the grass grew taller overnight, these things are respecting the presence of the Lord. It is Passover, the Lamb of God took away my sins. Hallelujah to my Savior!

Being a recipient of Jesus' love this Passover day I rejoice in excitement because of Calvary and the love of the Passover Lamb, Jesus. His love speaks through the ages. His love which defeated doubts and fears. His love which took the key to death from Satan. His love which gives the sinner new life. I rejoice with love for my fellowman because of the Passover Lamb slang for man's sins.

C. S. Lewis wrote, "Do not waste your time bothering whether you 'love' your neighbor; act as if you did. As soon as we do this, we find one of the great secrets. When you are behaving as if you loved someone, you would presently come to love him."

Jesus didn't talk of love, He lived it, died for it, rose for it, ascended to heaven for it, and interceding in heaven for His love for us...The Love which became flesh. Jesus my Creator's love which moves mountains of stress, seas of weariness, valley of despair, and His blood which cleanse the world of sin and shame, is offered for each of us to claim.

Praise The Lord

Shout triumphantly to the LORD, all the earth. Psalm 100:1

Good morning, daylight the birds are singing an early morning prelude to your arrival. Good morning blue sky the clouds passed over for the sunlight to come forth. Good morning, green grass not growing back by man's hands. Good morning shadows on the barn door made by sunlight on the trees. Hello, breath from God and thank You for Your guiding light. Good morning Heavenly Father and thank You for Your reminder of Revelation 16:15 "Blessed is he that watcheth". But do I watch? Help me to be watchful and mindful of...

Jesus is coming and the bird of the air knows it because they listen. Jesus speaks and the clouds obey, and the thunder of His voice speaks to the storehouse of the lightning, and it moves across the horizon and make beauty man's hand cannot be captured on canvas. Microscopes cannot understand the sound waves. The drumbeat fade in comparison to its sound. You, Heavenly Father can only make things incapable of man's copying and selling it in a bottle or drawing a book. You remind each of us of Your coming through the wind and the singing of the birds at Your command. The trees bow in the raging wind as a reminder of Your hands of grace and mercy. The thunder roar and we hear you, but we call it thunder rather than Your voice. The moon comes if fullness at Your hand and we are reminded of Your loving hands, but faithful and true hand of Your Word never fail. You are coming again.

Jesus knew many faithful servants would forget to do the things He left for us to do...1 Corinthians 11:24 Jesus said to take communion as often in remembrance of Him. The reminders from heaven and who gives life are constantly before us, but we fail to see, hear, feel, smell, and taste the goodness of God. Yet with His loving kindness Jesus reminds us to remember Him. Creation is God's gifts to each one who believes or don't believe because rain rains on the just as well as the unjust. The birds wake me each morning with singing, unless there is danger from a storm, and they remain silent...they hear God. Birds are a choir make-up of the fowls of the air. The human choir is made up of four-part harmony, so is the bird choir. However, I believe there are more parts in a bird choir because there are so many different sounds of the birds. When I was in Israel during the month of the bird migration, which comes through Jerusalem. I have never seen so many different colors and kind of birds in my whole life. Songbirds and birds, I did know existed were there in the trees, bushes, flowers, sidewalk, parking lots innumerable in numbers. Only God directs the birds to migrate through a place He has chosen as the New Heaven. One day we, who follow Jesus will migrate from this place called earth to the New Jerusalem our final home.

I see God as the sun rest on the top of the trees in mid-day, but more so, I see the smile of God as some of the tree sway with the breeze as the other near stand motionless...they hear God too. Who can do such a wonder other than God who loves me! I know I'm loved as the gentle breeze sweeps my skin like a sweet perfume as I seek God's presence in the coolness of the day. I look around and see the grass cut a few days before growing back for the bumblebee to feed from the nectar of the coves. I look and see one side of my flower leaning toward the sunlight while the other side fail to keep up with its growing. God is calling even the flower to seek the sun.

Will we answer when God calls?

God is speaking! Will we listen?

God is watching! Do we see Him? God is singing with the wind! Do we hear Him? Are we receiving His gift of love? God is knocks but He doesn't enter where He isn't welcome. Just like the sun makes shadows on the doors and roofs of my garage but it can't make a shadow on the cars if I don't open the doors to allow the sunlight to come in.

Years ago, darkness was my company from hurts and disappointments of the past, but I decided to open the door to my heart when Jesus was knocking to come in. The light didn't receive the darkness, the light made darkness fade. The shadows of false hope were dispelled when the light was welcomed in.

Yes, I see Jesus in everything around me because He opened my eyes as I prayed Ephesians 1:18 and my life haven't been the same. I see my spirit walking through the birds that sing. The birds follow where the sun goes each day. The birds listen when God calls for their migration of the year. They follow the voice of the Lord to

Jerusalem each year when Jesus calls. Learn from the ways of the birds, when you do, they will teach you to trust Jesus as your guide.

Love Never Fails

A joyful heart is good medicine, but a broken spirit dries up the bones... Proverbs 17:22

Question, what does it mean to be truly blessed? I'm sitting looking at the shadows of the trees and hearing the neighborhood on a newly painted porch. I'm tired, but the men are more tired. The painting of the house went well in the cloudy coolness of Saturday and the "ox in the mire Sunday". The meal was good and feet and legs tired and sore from cooking...meatloaf, cabbage, mustard greens, macaroni and cheese, candied yams, baked beans, grilled chicken, sausages, brisket, banana pudding, slaw, cauliflower salad, cake, and another cake that wasn't so good. Laughter, babies playing, and the sight of the men carrying the ladders and pulled the floor coverings from place to place fills my memories.

Paint on hands and knees of the beginners...and me saying, "Be careful of my floor, watch my door, check the food in the oven." More cars and more cars filled my driveway as the passengers watched the men and my granddaughter paint with love and care. The smoke from the grill carried the aromatic aroma of the well-seasoned meats to the nostril of each person in the yard. Then, the call for the meal to be served...as my daughter filled each man's plate and the visitors filled their own. Every seat was filled with a warm body on the porch and the dinner table as well...and any other seat to be found. Nothing left of many of the things cooked because the men ate as hearty as they worked...but the amazing thing, the ones who haven't worked ate just as much!

As I sit writing this post my heart rejoices because all I had to do was to tell my daughter...and she coordinated the project of getting the house painted and my son planning the menu for me to cook.... How do I say thank for the kindness shown to me this weekend? How do I show gratitude to the ones who never say no when I call? How do I say how I cherish each moment of the gathering of love of the ones who love what I love? Simply by saying, "Thank You Lord for touching the hearts of the ones I call on with love. And thank You for letting each one remember the examples laid before them. Thank You, Lord for their hearts. Only You give such blessings. Amen

God Sees

"Beware of false prophets. They come to you in sheep's clothing, but inwardly they are ravenous wolves." Matthew 7:15

It seems as if each day I'm reading about pastors of Megan-churches abusing the ones under their authority, having someone drying the sweat from their face rather than him using his own hands, to human trafficking, to wives giving liquor and having sexual relationship with the teenage boys. Then we wonder why so many people stay at home rather than fellowshipping together as the Word says... and why so many children are missing. I cry when I see how too many leaders are misleading trusting souls into destruction. The Word tells us if eating meat causes your brother to stumble...don't eat it. I was so disappointed this week after reading about all the different church leaders being arrested for abused and human trafficking...I cried because it's causing too many not to believe Jesus is real...and there are righteous pastors still doing the Father's will. But then the Holy Spirit reminded me of His Word...Matthew 7:15 "Beware of false prophets. They come to you in sheep's clothing, but inwardly they are ravenous wolves."

Years ago, if someone had told me I would cry over wrongs against God's children...I would have talked about it rather than praying about it and confronting the sin. How do you confront sin...by rebuking the person to his or her face rather than behind the back. Paul confronted Peter's hypocrisy to his face when he shunned the Gentiles believers when his fellow Jewish brothers came (Galatians 2:11-22). Wrongs are wrongs and rights are right! "All Scripture is God-breathed and is useful for instruction, for conviction, for correction, and for training in righteousness, so that the man of God may be complete, fully equipped for every good work" (2 Timothy 3:16-17).

We must use the Word and live by it. I don't have to tell any of you this, but I'm broken-hearted over the misleading of children and the ones seeking God. The wide path is getting wider because people are trusting man's word rather than God's. I heard a statement the other day." My pastor hasn't told us that (talking about the Scripture)." But we must study to show ourselves approved. A month ago, I heard the Holy Spirit say this to me when I was concerned over hurting someone's feeling after correcting an out and out disrespect for the House of God... the Holy Spirit rebuked me doing my worrying over it with this statement... "You are worrying about man's feelings, what about Mines!" I repented right then...because God's feeling about me is my shield.

Attention Please

Take heed that ye despise not one of these little ones; for I say unto you, that in heaven their angels do always behold the face of my Father which is in heaven. Matthew 18:10

May I Have Your Attention Please! There are too many angels standing in the Unemployment Line because you are not commissioning them out in prayer for you and your children... (Matthew 18:10).

Also, God wants to promote you. He wants you to get away from your own thoughts and your own foolishness, and get to a definite place, believing that He exists and that "He is a rewarder of those who diligently seek Him" (Heb. 11:6).

Employ your appointed Angel with your belief and faith in God's Word

Keep on believing, Jesus is near,
Keep on believing, there's nothing to fear;
Keep on believing, this is the way,
Faith in the night, the same as the day.

God does not honor unbelief; He honors faith.

At times you may hear negative thoughts...or Satan has your imagination kicking at your faith in God's promises! At your lowest times Satan will come with questions of your role in life like he did John the Baptist while he was in prison. Starting today, don't allow the suggestions of Satan to dethrone your better knowledge of the power of God.

Some of Satan's suggestions:

You can't forgive. He did too much to you so your marriage is over Your household can't be blessed because of what you did years ago Your children can't be delivered because they are like their mama and daddy. You will never be well. These are just a few of the things he put in your thoughts. Remember, when these imaginary thoughts come from Satan...God is not a fairy. He is real and He only gives good things that never fade. Never fade is Jesus' promise.

Same Tree

A devious heart will be far from me; I will not be involved with evil. Psalm 101:4

❧ Good morning, Holy Spirit! You allowed me to see another day. A day the trees are prettier than yesterday, and hummingbirds are at play. The mockingbirds have heard the morning dog bark and they are marking in song what they have heard. The morning bird song with a bark between the musical rest sounds like fellowship in morning worship praising Your goodness. I heard the voices of the children on the bus as it passes by. Some are happy some haven't had much sleep during the night, some are struggling with who they are, some received hugs of love before their day's journey, some received curses rather than breakfast. Holy Spirit comfort the one who doesn't have a home to call their own, and the ones with a home left alone. Home alone isn't a child's joy, parents presence brings much joy. The pain of hurts and repairs of many of the children on the bus will lead to questioning, "Why am I here?"

During your childhood someone may have spoken negative words over you, and you still hear and believe what was spoken! Take a small journey with me to the lowly donkey that carries burdens...Jesus chose it over the horse to carry Him. A little insignificant seed that sprouted into a tree was chosen by man for something bad...however, it held our sins as Jesus hung on it with our names in His hands. So today, seek to see yourself as God sees you, chosen to do something someone else can't do for the kingdom...you may be the one who leads a blind soul to the light! Too often, people will say, "I don't understand how people can be raised by the same parents but act so differently." Watching the trees move with the wind the Holy Spirit revealed the limbs not the leaves today so I can get a clearer understanding. Each limb is a part of the same tree rooted in the same soil, yet each limb is different from the other. They are side by side on the mother tree, but some are twisted, some straight, some pointing upward, some pointing downward, some covered with leaves, some stripped, some pretty and some ugly, but who am I to call it ugly when the Creator created it!

One tree limb is different in shapes. Same roots feeding from the same roots but grown in different ways. Some small some large, yet parents are the same roots. God shows life in everything He created, and we can learn from them the way of life. Children born to the same parents make their own decisions. Cain killed Abel; same teaching different choices made. God told Cain that sin was creeping at his door, Cain chose to open it to let it in, his choice made him the first murderer...and his brother's blood the first to cry out to God because innocent had been killed because of sin and hatred. When the question comes, "Why is your sister or brother different from you?" We can get the answer from Jesus. Jesus said, Matthew 12:48-50 "Who is My mother and who is My brothers? For whoever does the will of My Father in heaven, that person is My brother and sister and mother." Following Jesus leads to a path the donkey traveled bringing eternal life to those willing to separate themselves from the tree bearing bad fruit to allowing the Creator to plant them in His soil which gives life forever.

Early Morning Sunrise

Very early in the morning, on the first day of the week, they went to the tomb at sunrise. Mark 16:2

Good morning sunrise as the crows sang calling forth the dawn. Good morning springtime as the winter sleeps and the spring awakes with aromas of praise. Good afternoon thunder bringing forth springtime showers. Goodbye winter as you take a long a spring nap. Hello new leaves on the tree. Welcome spring seeds bringing forth the joy of new birth. Fragrant flowers rejoice with beauty to a new season of God's love as God calls each bulb from its rest. "Rise up, my love, my fair one, and come away." Song Of Solomon 2:10

God's love calls me from slumber to awaken me to the sweet fragrance of Jesus' calling me to blossom in His favor from the desires of my yesterdays. I bathe in Jesus' wondrous sights of the morning; I'm carried back to the harvest fields of my upbringing. Crows were the predator of the planted seeds of the spring, summer, and fall crops of my father's fields, as scarecrows graced the fields dressed in clothes worn out through the years. The seeds called to the crows as my father called for the gun to scare them away. Planted seeds with poison covering were used to kill off the crows invading the fields planted with seeds of the spring...and scarecrows were planted in the fields that grew the fruits and vegetables. However, strange but true, the scarecrows scared me more than the crows, and they gave a hiding place to the ones sneaking in the vegetables fields to steal before my father arose to walk to the barn and check on the fields. Times store memories of good and bad, the memories of good outweighs the bad.

How is this? When the hand God reaches down to lead us through the day is a good day. Thinking back over the years about crows and scarecrow God is speaking. Man sought to control the crows by planting seeds coated with poison. Not only did it rear the field of crows but many other birds. Morning after morning the songbirds and all types of birds would sing in the tree, barn, grass, on the fence during the day. The bats which flew at dust began to fade. The flying squirrels stop coming during the dust of the early lite night. The owls stopped peeking through the trees they hoot was gone. No more did I hear the nightingales or whippoorwills; the frogs fail to croak because someone told man to kill the crows... The scarecrows left the fields that scared me rather than the crows. Then the Holy Spirit said, "Man's plans killed the crows, but I will restore their voices again." As I think of the scarecrow, I'm reminded that God did not give us the spirit of fear. Fear is false hope appearing real. The scarecrow couldn't talk, couldn't walk, couldn't move its hand so the crowd sat on its head. Fearing what appears to be real can't harm or run us down. We can sit on fear's head because it's false hope created by man that the enemy have more power than Jesus had in His hands.

Morning Praise

Praising God with resounding cymbals; praise Him with clapping cymbals. Let everything that breathes praise the LORD. Hallelujah! Psalm 150:5-6

Another, Good morning, this windy cloud laden sky as the birds sings as if waving for the clouds to pass by. The flowers stems are pointing to the sky as each one is asking the clouds to stay and pour on them the gentle rain. The Corinthian bells sang as I sang in choir duet praises to the Lord beyond the clouds. Yes, this is a morning of God's many mysteries to come forth in praise of His grace.

Each day amazes me with different sights I have not seen before. As I sit watching my disobedient dog, Sugar rejecting my call to come back from the road, a beautiful yellow and black bumblebee flew by seeking the holly tree nectar. Then I recalled the joy of serving God. But there was a time I rejected His call like my wayward dog does each morning. I once was in a foreign land of sin and a lost heart filled with bitterness like the lemon tree bears immature bitter fruits. The bumblebee was my reminder of God taking what man treats as if there is no hope and proves him wrong. As God take bitter lemons and make lemonade showing the world that it can taste and see that He is good in the bitter times and well as the sweet.

After service today, I sat on my south side bench watching the clouds when this man walking on the road talking to himself decided he wanted a person he could see walked in my yard. He had a bag in his hand and a long saber knife tired around his leg all the way to his knee as the top was hooked on his belt around his waist. He talked for a while then he began to curse as he talked about Jesus. I politely said, "Don't curse." "Oh, I'm sorry my queen." He was like the bumblebee thinking he was a misfit because society told him so.

He looked across my yard and said a few more things I didn't understand just before left talking again to an invisible man. Darkness filled a place in his mind where light should be. Rejection has become his companion, as he felt grace and mercy has no place in his heart. As the cloud passed over and the sunshine is dancing and comforting the ground, I'm praying a warm word from my heart spoken to this man will come a part of his memory as he goes through this day and the ones to come. Also, a pray is prayed for this hurting soul confused from war of mind raging in uncertainties to be renewed with a mind knowing Jesus loves him, not despising him because a war of darkness has been poured in this man.

When I think of Jesus' love, I hear His parable of the lost sheep and coin in Luke 15. No one is forgotten by God. He runs us down with His love and sing over us. The prodigal son's father ran to meet him, which usual for an elderly man in the Middle East. He kissed his son even with him selling like the pigpen. Physical filth doesn't matter to God, it's the spiritual filth God frowns on. This wondering soul isn't hopeless, nothing is hopeless with God. The bumblebee went into hiding in the holly bush, but it will return when it finishes its job. Sadly, a broken spirit and a hurting soul find rest in isolation and imaginary friends. Despair is a friend to the hurting. Weariness is a companion to the rejected. Wars always have casualties be it physical or spiritual lives are changed; God have the answer and He teaches out hand to war and our fingers to battle (Psalm 144) the only gear needed is trust partnering with faith.

Memories of Love
Where is your faith? Luke 8:25

꧁ The wind sings the memories of my walks with God. My mind is reminiscing the Wednesday, December 14, 2011, the sixty-third year of my birth...I allowed the Holy Spirit to take me on a quiet walk with Him. However, there were communications between He and nature relayed to me. He showed me clearly there will be storms in this life...however; it is up to each of us how we will carry/walk through each. Nevertheless, we will surely go through them...but how will we go is the question:

Standing in faith that God's Word is true...He will never leave me...or forsake me, or bend over in doubts and fears...that God's promises are not true? Nevertheless, rest assure, the storm will not fade until it is over. On this walk, the Holy Spirit took me to the pond...the water was clear, and the sun rays were dancing on the windy waves. The ducks were floating freely and lovely on ripple...so it seemed. Wherever the waves moved... the duck flowed with them...the beauty of obedience was amazing and peaceful to look upon. The ducks were submitting themselves to the will of their Creator. They were trusting Him on the windy waves...they were trusting Him to be their Guide and Provider...they were trusting in Him because He was their compass in the wind...as He is also ours.

Then, I heard once again, this sweet whisper of reassurance. "No matter the battle, no matter the struggle, no matter the pain, no matter the many disappointments, no matter the storm you are in I Am the Compass which guides you in each storm." So, on this sixty-third year of my birth. I allowed God to carry me on the windy waves of this day because I know my arms are too weak although, God is not too short to go against the wind. Moreover, God's arms can calm each ripple. How will I go through the storms of life? I choose to go standing in faith because bending over in the battles of life causes pain to the back. Happy sixty-third Birthday to me and thank You God My Father for keeping and holding me these many years as you calmed each ripple in the storms!

Songs of the Night

In the night His song will be with me. Psalm 42:8

Good morning, this amazingly beautiful day the birds are singing from the south, the crows hollering from the north, the geese flying over squawking from the east, the Cardinal perched on the tip of the windmill (I'm grateful it doesn't have vertigo), the sun light pointing finger like rays to the west, and as usual my disobedient dog, Sugar is running in all directions of the yard. This is a wonderful day I was awaken with the morning songs of the flying birds and fowls of the air. The morning amazements are a welcoming of Jesus to a new day. The birds of night sang as I sought a good night sleep, but sometimes my Heavenly Father wants a one-on-one-time with me since my days are filled with the business of the day. "Yet the LORD will command His lovingkindness in the daytime, and in the night His song will be with me, a prayer to the God of my life" (Psalm 42: 8).

My Father keeps me with His song during the night and wakes me with His beauty of the new day. I'm always amazed in the early mornings of Spring and Summer to see God's designs new every morning. Even if it's cloudy or rainy His love pushes away all doubts and fears the enemy wants to feed as our morning meal. The meal of God's early morning wonders takes my heart to a level only the deep calling to the deep (Psalm 42:7) can understand. God is desiring my presence as I desire His. He's seeking to speak to me as I desire to hear Him. He feeds me with His care, He caresses me with His love, He baths me in His promises to never leave me, He touches me with His gifts of assurance that He is near. The bird songs are gifts of Him speaking to me because they sing in the beauty of the morning, they seek the light of the morning sun and follow where it leads them through the day. I never noticed until Thursday how the birds are in my front yard early in the morning and during the day, but as the sun goes over the horizon toward the west the birds of the morning follow the sun. After the sunset they cease to sing until the next morning. Yes, Lord I see the birds following Your light, and I'm willing to do the same.

Hello Morning

Weeping may spend the night, but there is joy in the morning. Psalm 30:5b

Good morning, the birds woke me with song at the opening of the dawn. The sweet aroma of the bacon from the oven and perking coffee reminds me of the days when I caught lightning bugs and closed them up in a jar... Grass at the bottom and holes in the top didn't keep the lightning bugs from losing their glow, it made them weak. Captioning beautiful things to use for your own pleasures isn't God's way. God gives us freedom to run the race of life. As He gave lightning the beauty to light up a spark in the darkness of night. God calls each of us to peace with the many things He created. I don't understand why God created a snake, but He does.

So, sit back and hear the voices of the Lord. He speaks yet we ignore His voice for the sounds of the world. Relax and see the beauty of the Lord, yet the TV, phone, social media speak the sounds we want to hear. Recline and feel the joy of a newborn baby given to lonely parents who waited years to receive the gift of new life in their arms. Smell the newness of the early morning mowed grass. Caress the aroma of the opened rose. God is speaking. Don't you hear Him? Don't you see Him? Don't you feel Him? He's longing to be asked to fill your house not as a guest, but to order your steps. Sitting in the sunlight of the day, God is holding me with His love. I'm not the only house He fills but He treats me and holds me as if I'm His one and only child. Cleansed from the crimes of yesterday with Jesus' blood when I said yes to God's commands and rejected men. I'm victim no more of faults and failures because Jesus won victory for me at the Cross.

The wasp flies by in search of a place to land so it can make plans for a family keeping God's plans. The Rose of Sharon are beautiful as they sway in the afternoon breeze, but the enemy planted a seed of a wild bush so the Sharon bush can't breathe in the space of its own. Life apart from God brings the seed of the enemy to steal joy, to smother out hope, and to drown the promises in bitter tainted waters of stressful thoughts. Which feed the roots that moves the sweet from the water to fade away with drought of hope deferred.

God is speaking. Can't you hear His in the sounds of the wind? Can't you see His heavenly glow resting on the top of the trees? Come Holy Spirit fill each seeking vessel with this hope today that hope is renewed each morning. God made me to be me, and you to be you with His desire to be sought after while He can be found. How desperate are you for a new touch of grace each? A new hope and love that never wastes away or fade in the age of time. I'm excited to be called God's own. I am a lightning bug out of a jar to shine because Jesus shines in me.

LORD, I seek refuge in You; let me never be disgraced. Save me by Your righteousness. Psalm 31:1

Words Make a Difference

Heart be acceptable to You, LORD, my rock and my Redeemer. Psalm 19:14

Good morning, Holy Spirit! Are my first words each morning. Good morning, this sunny day the birds are singing in all directions around me. The sun rays are resting beautifully on the leaves of the trees and the grass, and as I see rats playing in the grass I frown with hatred. I hate rats, but why? They are God's creation too! It's amazing that I have never seen a rat playing in the grass until now, but I realize God is showing me this for a reason. I have no rights to hate anything God have made. I don't want rats in my house, so I watch from a distance because God is showing me something (He will explain it to me later).

God has spoken, despising rats is easy because it's a rat. Same with heartaches, we want to stop loving period because of disappointments and hurts. C. S. Lewis wrote "To love at all is to be vulnerable. Love anything and your heart will be wrung and possibly be broken. If you want to make sure of keeping it intact, you must give your heart to no one, not even an animal. Wrap it carefully around with hobbies and little luxuries; avoid all entanglements; lock it up safe in the casket or coffin of your selfishness...The only place outside heaven where you can be perfectly safe from all the dangers...of love is hell."

"God has spoken once, twice have I heard this: that power belongs to God" (Psalm 62:11). When God speaks listen! A rat can teach us a lesson of love. Good morning, this lovely cool sunless morning the mourning doves wings sing as they fly to the light lines, the woodpeckers are singing as they fly to a new tree for food, the crows' choir is singing in the distance, the blue jays are perched lovely on the tree limbs, the whippoorwills are silent from their night lullaby, and I'm calling in my disobedient dog, Sugar, and I don't see a rat.

God knows each of His creation voices as He knows each of ours. God knows our cry for help and our songs of joy, so today use the grain of mustard seed, that little faith entitles us to the promises that the mountain will move.

Ifs, buts, and perhaps are sure murderers of peace and comfort. Know in times of trouble as Job did, "For I know that my Redeemer lives, and He will stand at last on the earth" (Job 19:25). But you must say in your heart and mouth, I Know, not I think, or hope, but I Know my Redeemer lives, and all my needs are met! Thank You, Father in heaven.

Laughter
The One enthroned in heaven laughs. Psalm 2:4

Good morning, this cool sunny day the woodpeckers are pecking tunes in the tree limbs looking for their morning meal. God makes me laugh in joy each morning as He greets me with His lovely sights of His many creations celebrating Him through their morning prayers of trusting... The birds sing, the trees sway with the wind, the dogs barks, the crows holler, the geese swim, the grass shines with the dew, the clouds move, and I wonder why I even trouble over the burdens of life when Revelation 3:14 says "Amen." The word Amen solemnly confirms that which went before; and Jesus is the great Confirmer; immutable, forever is "the Amen" in all his promises. (Charles Spurgeon).

Jesus is Yea and Amen in all His promises. Trust Jesus above your doubts and fears. Once again, good morning, this cool windy gloomy day the geese are still making ripples on the water, the crows and birds are singing with the wind, the trees are still receiving their many colors of green, and I'm still rejoicing from the Resurrection service from yesterday. The presence of the Lord makes a difference in every life seeking to be changed from misery to joy, sorrows to peace, from slavery to freedom. Yesterday, I saw something so amazing that I'm still bathing in the Spirit of the Lord.

A five-month-old beautiful baby parents brought her to be dedicated to the Lord. The father called me when he and his wife first got pregnant and asked me to dedicate the child to Christ Jesus when she was born. Also, they came by during the pregnancy and I prayed a blessing over this child in the womb. Yesterday, as the Scriptures were read and the Word preached, this child would lean her body toward the person preaching the Word, her eyes never moved from the preacher until the Word given was over.

Matter of fact, another five-month-old baby came on Good Friday with the same spirit of God. Each one I prayed a blessing over in the womb. Children anointed by God are His storehouse of blessings to the world to make a difference. Parents, put Jesus first in your child's life and everything else will be added to it. I laugh because I am happy to see the hand of the Lord on the children when the world is trying to kill them in the womb, and harm the ones alive. I laugh because God laughs in heaven knowing the end of the ones harming His little ones.

The Spirit of the Lord

Isaiah 61:1 "The Spirit of the Lord GOD is on Me, because the LORD has anointed Me to preach good news to the poor. He has sent Me to bind up the brokenhearted, to proclaim liberty to the captives and freedom to the prisoners."

Good morning, this cloudy rainy morning the birds still sing with the wind welcoming the new day. As I hear God singing through the wind, trees, birds... etc. and they are honoring His majesty I rejoice.

I bow in thankfulness and weeping with a heart of joy, gladness, and sorrow because Jesus suffered an unfathomable crucifixion for souls of mankind. As the devil laughed over the sight of his winning lost soul, but his silliness of inciting man to crucified Jesus was his failure as mankind won the victory because of Jesus' suffering on the cross. I rejoice! The cross dropped into the hole of the ground dislocated Jesus' shoulders and brought unimaginable pain to his nailed hands as hideous taunts were hurled at him... "All they that see me laugh me to scorn: they shoot out the lip, they shake the head" (Psalm 22:7).

Because of love, Jesus stayed on the cross and I am free of condemnation. Because of Jesus coming and dying for the lost sheep He never said a word so my sins wouldn't be poured back of me or you. Because of His heart that holds the hurting souls, Jesus allowed piercing in His side. Because of peace for the seeking souls Jesus endured the ridiculed of his royalty. Because of love, He stayed on the cruel cross despised and rejected of man for man's soul and peace, He stayed. If you don't mind me sharing my heart, thank you for receiving these messages as I weep in love because of the Cross.

God Hears
The LORD took notice and listened. Malachi 3:16

Good morning, this lovely sunny day the birds are singing, the sun rays dancing through the leaves of the trees, the windmills obeying the wind, but most of all, the geese squawking as they make beautiful ripples on the water as they glide gracefully on it. Looking at the lovely designs the geese make as they glide on the cool early morning water outweighs their squawking sounds. The design on the water reminds me of the opinions of man to tell us what is beautiful and is not, what we should follow and what we should not, what we should think and what we should not. But what God designed each of us to look like, to be, and make our own decisions to follow Him is what makes each of us beautiful and unique. We are fearfully and wonderfully made as each of God's creative designs is. Food for today: When we live as lives pleasing to God, we make beautiful designs that many desire. God listens to our conversation (Malachi 3:16) because we are His ripple on the water...

Each new morning creation speaks and rejoice with a morning praise to its Creator. This cool day the birds and geese are flying two by two in the sky. Have you really watched the birds and their many ways? As the geese flew low over my house this morning, I could hear them coming before I saw them. Two by two they flew over me as they sang their squawking song. Then it came to mind how geese fly together not one but two. When they pair together, they stay together until one die. If one of the mates is hurt and can't fly, the other mate stays with it until it can fly or die. It never leaves its side. Think of this, "The Son of Man came to seek and to save the lost" (Luke 19:10). And Jesus left a command for each of us, "My command is this: Love each other as I have loved you" (John 15:12). We, each can take a love lesson and marriage class from the geese of the air. The birds that fly high with the sharpest eye, the smallest Martin can put a hawk to flight.

For many years I have watched the lovely things of the morning, and I even watch as many of the things change at noonday. The flowers standing gracefully in the early morning dew but bow in weakness as the heat of the sun bear down on them. However, they rise again as the sun moves to the west and the coolness of the evening rest upon each one. Amazingly the squirrels follow the sun to the west as it moves toward the western sky, and the birds do the same. Seeking the light is the desire of many flowers and other creature of the day. But there are many flowers only blossom at night when the sun goes down, and many flowers that seek only water to grow and blossom. Some birds sing at night a beautiful song as the day is over. And some birds hide in the bushes until night comes. God speaks to us through His creations, yet we fail to see and listen Jesus is speaking. When the lightning bug light up the dark night, God is speaking to the night sky to light up with the stars that speaks but we cannot hear them. Through each part of the day God is in control and made beautiful things to grace the darkness where the seed burst open in the darken soil. God never said the night was evil, darkness of the soul refusing to seek the light is evil.

The heavens declare the glory of God, and the sky proclaims the work of His hands. Day after day they pour out speech; night after night they communicate knowledge. There is no speech; there are no words; their voice is not heard. Their message has gone out to all the earth, and their words to the ends of the world. Psalm 19:1-4

God speaks through His creations when we choose to stop and listen to what He is saying. Trusting God in the midst of the storm is my lesson from the birds.

Awaken

I pray that the eyes of your heart may be enlightened in order that you may know the hope to which he has called you, the riches of his glorious inheritance in his holy people. Ephesian 1:18

Good morning, this warm misty day the birds are singing a new song with the crows and gliding geese upon the water. The dandelions are receiving the night dew as the yellow martins drink from their blooms. This is a beautiful day the Lord awaken me to see and hear its beauty. I cut my hand yesterday putting together a windmill in the soft rain. I couldn't finish writing my weekly cards and letters to the sick, inmates, elderly, and many others I write. But texts and call came in offering help to do the writing, even a lady from her hospital bed with oxygen wanted to help. I smiled with thankfulness and tears as I look saw God's servants seeking to be hand and feet in God's service. Food for today: God's grace is like a gentle voice that says, "Here is the world. Terrible and beautiful things will happen. Don't be afraid. I am with you." Frederick Buechner

God will not let His kingdom business go lacking because He has servants waiting to be used. "Awake, my soul! Awake, harp and lyre! I will awaken the dawn" (Psalm 57:8).

Good morning, this sunless gentle windy morning God is speaking through the thunder and raindrops. A new Corinthian bell tuned to the G tone went up yesterday, and now my porch houses the musical scale...the melody God is singing through to quieten me with His love. Amazingly, the world wants to give you peace with medication, but Isaiah 46:2 says, "They (Idols) stoop, they bow down together; they could not deliver the burden, but themselves have gone into captivity." But God's reassurance to His people: "Even to your old age... I am he who will sustain you. I have made you and I will carry you" (Isaiah 46:4). Food for today: I am thankful I decided to follow Jesus, my Keeper through my old age and hereafter. Listen, listen, see, see, hear, hear, feel, feel Jesus is all around His creations receive Him this day.

We, each was born on Main Street of salvation until we

detoured into the world of many streets of desires and dark alleys of forbidden fruits. Good morning, this is the word given to me this day by the Holy Spirit as the birds of many kinds sang in the background and the sun rays danced in time with praise. God is speaking through the wind and His creations, listen, listen, and as Job 12:7 says, "Ask the animals, and they will teach you, or the birds in the sky, and they will tell you." Food for today: Jesus loves and cares for you and me, even when we don't understand our circumstances. Look around and learn of Him.

Journey to Freedom

My angel will go ahead of you and bring you into the land of the Amorites, Hittites, Perizzites, Canaanites, Hivites and Jebusites, and I will wipe them out. Exodus 23:23

I sometimes laugh at myself because when I say I'm going to rest, I find myself praying. Well, I can say I'm resting in the Lord. I see this time here as a work shift and my time off will be in heaven. We are entering the Passover Season when Jesus became the Ultimate Passover Lamb sparing each of us from the sting of death.

Passover is the time death passed over the ones under the blood of the lamb in Egypt, and even now the Blood still works. Even with things seeming so bad with sickness and a weak economy, the ones under the blood of Jesus are spared the plans of the enemy even if the natural eye can't see it. In Egypt the plagues only touched the ones in Egypt, not the ones in Goshen because they were protected by God (read Exodus). During this Passover season many are in the hospital, and many sick from different ailments. During this Passover, Jesus is still the Lamb of God who took away all our sickness, diseases, and sins of the world. And Jesus is still telling us to come before Him with a Passover offering. In Exodus 23:15 God commanded us, as we observe the holy days, not to stand before Him empty-handed. When we observe the holy days and obey with an offering...God promises seven Passover blessings:

1. God will assign an Angel to you, Exodus 23:23
2. God will be an enemy to your enemy, Exodus 23:22
3. God will give you prosperity, Exodus 23:25
4. God will take sickness away from you, Exodus 23:25
5. God will give you long life, Exodus 23:26
6. God will bring increase and inheritance, Exodus 23:30
7. God will give a special year of blessing, Exodus 23:29

The Passover and other holy days were so important that God told us to observe them forever (Exodus 12:14; Leviticus 23:14). During this Passover I am so stirred with the useless deaths of the unborn, and the sex trafficking of babies and children, I'm planting my offering for LIFE and FREEDOM!

Testimonies: The seven blessings of Passover have been

fulfilled in my life and so many others. One lady began observing the holy day with offerings after she heard the teaching on it. Each promised blessing was fulfilled in her life. Her daughter was saved from death, her health restored, her inheritance was so great, that she is helping to build a young lady's house, and she has given 41 acres of land away. Sold one of the homes left to her and uses the other home for guest.

A second lady's bank note was paid in full. When she went to the bank to pay a note the whole loan was marked paid on a Sunday. The amount of the loan was the total amount she paid for her mother's burial. Another couple was given money to get a car. You don't observe to get something in return, you observe because God say to do so, and He gives the return. Night Watch was down to the bare minimal 2020, a ring of my phone and a ring of my doorbell brought a young lady who gave me a brown paper bag with thousands of dollars inside. She knew it would go toward God's kingdom business. Trust God with everything you have because you are only giving back what God have given you to give.

Written Pages

God has come to test you, so that you will fear Him and will not sin. Exodus 20:20b

Good morning, this windy morning after the storms of the night passed over, God sheltered me. The birds are rejoicing with the wind in a musical chorus this cloudy morning as God directs their praises, "Jesus Is Alive!" I am rejoicing! Each new day, hour, minutes, second, moment is a new page in my book written of what Jesus have done for me. No wondered John said the things Jesus did, "not even the world itself could contain the books that would be written" (John 21:25b).

Life is a book filled with ups and downs, blessings and tears, joy and sorrow. How can your life write a book of Jesus' love and grace? But more so, who needs to hear what Jesus has done for you? Let me tell you what God has done for me. When I was webbed in the web of sin, Jesus recused me. When I sing of His mercy He gives me each day, my voice echo through space and time the wondrous unexplainable love of Jesus. Each note writes a book of my love for Him. Each line I walk straight each day tells of Jesus' saving grace because He allows me to sing a victory song of heavenly bliss.

Line upon line records the moment I was saved, and I am not ashamed to tell of the pit of despair God's pulled me from. Every smile writes a line that sadness can turn into grace which bring joy unmeasurable. Each pain turned into healing speaks another chapter of dry bone can live again. Write steps in the sand, write up stretched hands, write bowed knees giving thanks for victory won. "I will sing of the mercies of the LORD forever; with my mouth I will make known Your faithfulness to all generations" (Psalm 89:1). My worm of a life unfolding into a butterfly of God's amazing grace is my arms once bound now soaring through the clouds. Life, live to write of the victory of Jesus because I am one of them.

Thank You Father for this life You have given me a voice to sing of Your limitless love. Amen.

Feeding Fear

Do not have other gods besides Me. Deuteronomy 5:7

How do we feed Fear? While in prayer this message came," Stop feeding Fear." First, I must ask God for forgiveness for even being afraid in my spirit. I want no part of fear in me. Fear is like a magnet; it draws all the family and friends of fear, and it becomes a neighborhood of undesirable residents. I realized fear can exhibit itself, yes, itself because it is a spirit in ways that many accept as the norm. Years ago, I walked in fear of what the tomorrows held, I slept in fear with a sleeping pill, I whined in fear with a prayer covering of words alone. Then God rescued me from myself...and gave me boldness so I can tell you who are in fear that there is no fear in love. Jesus is love. After I finished breakfast, I still was pondering over the word the Holy Spirit spoke "Stop feeding fear." How was I feeding fear that I knew not of? One thing without me realizing it, I never look at the news, but during these last two weeks I have been watching it. I never check my Facebook before I pray and have my one-on-one time with God and do all the other things I have to do in the morning, but for the last two weeks I have been checking my Facebook to see the lastly opinions and or updates. So, I was feeding fear of the unknown by seeking what others were saying about the virus; even though, I knew what the Holy Spirit had already said.

Only God knows what is ahead and fear will keep me and you from hearing and seeing what God is saying to the Church. So, as I ventured out to one of my favorite places(porch) I began cleaning my chairs, tables and rails...my hands were covered with yellow fuzzy pollen afterward. Danger is all around us, but God has His angel encamped about us. Invisible danger lurks in places we can't imagine, but God is the Shield of protection. With the pollen falling even in our house when the windows are up, God protects us. We run from one danger but there are troubles all around we do not see, but we are safe in the shadow of the Almighty, my Shelter (Psalm 91). Today, I took pictures of the unseen pollen on my porch rails, and God allowed me to see it on my hands. Yet He showed me the beauty of His creation all around us...to show He surrounds each of us with unfailing protection. God made the clouds, He made the sun, He made the trees, He made you and me, so you know if He takes care of the trees, He will take care of me.

Morning Paradise

God is not a man who lies, or a son of man who changes His mind. Does He speak and not act, or promise and not fulfill? Numbers 23:19

Good morning, windy day the wind of God singing through the Corinthian bells woke me with this message and to pray.

Is the world your keeper?
Your deliverer?
Your savior?
Your guide?
Your provider?

Some will say no. Some will say yes. The Word says the world loves its own, but it hates the ones who follow Jesus. The Word says to teach your child in the way he should go. So, who comes first in your life Jesus your Redeemer, or the world that brings the sins and the enemy of your soul? Who or what is influencing and teaching your child? I hope not Mickey Mouse or Sesame Street that teaches it's alright to be a girl when God created you to be a boy, or a boy when God created you to be a girl! Many won't like these questions, but many didn't and don't like Jesus our Redeeming Savior. This is question and test day that answering, and actions will determine each of our eternal home. Jesus words are true and if He says what is right and what is wrong and we refuse to hear, is it Jesus fault that you stumbled into hell? No! Jesus is coming even if the world says He isn't real.

We are entering the Passover... During the Passover meal, Jesus and His friends sang a series of Psalms known as the Hallel, Psalms 113-118. He sang because heaven inhabit our praises. I sing because I am happy and thankful Jesus chose me.

So, good morning this semi-cloudy day the birds still serenade the new day's arrival with songs so we can rejoice and be glad in it! The birds were singing with the multitude praising Jesus' arrival as He rode into Jerusalem on a donkey a few days before His crucifixion. But I wonder if birds sang as Jesus' pass-through seas of his own blood to win the crown that blacken day He hung covered in darkness with our sins! But the days before, "the whole city was stirred and asked, 'Who is this?'" (Matthew 21:10). Still today, people are still curious about Jesus. The answer is the same as it was over 2000 years ago, Jesus is our Redeemer, He has redeemed us. But when He comes back, He will not be the suffering Lamb, He will be the Judging Loin of Judah.

We must be ready to answer as the curious onlooker who ask, "Who is Jesus?" The birds know. Do you?

Song of the Morning

Hallelujah! Give praise, servants of Yahweh; praise the name of Yahweh. Psalm 113:1

Good morning, this windy morning filled with the harmony of heaven harmonizing with the birds and wind as background singers as heaven's song welcome us into a new day. If you didn't know it, God wakes you each morning with a song of His love, "The LORD your God is with you, the Mighty Warrior who saves. He will take great delight in you; in his love he will...rejoice over you with singing" (Zephaniah 3:17).

God's blanket of love keeps the burglars of your soul away. Rejoice as the Father in heaven tenderly sings songs of love over you to show how He loves us and how he wants us to love ourselves and forgive ourselves from yesterday's wrongs. God's song sang over us brings a troubled heart to the throne of peace and grace of love overflowing.

So, this morning, I forgive myself...Herticine God forgives us for our transgressions as we forgive those who has trespassed against us, but we don't forgive ourselves. So, Lord, I forgive myself for hearing man's word of who I am rather than receiving Who You say I am, Herticine. I forgive myself for accepting man's insults over Your plans for me. I forgive myself for denying who I am according to who You say I am, Herticine. I forgive myself for holding back thinking I'm not worthy when You said I am fearfully and wonderfully made. I forgive myself for seeking man's approval over Your acceptance. I forgive myself for giving my ideas to someone else that You have given for me to do. I forgive myself for wanting to look like the world when You said I am chosen to speak to the world about You. I forgive myself for thinking I'm not good enough, but You show me diamonds from heaven. You have forgiven me when I confessed these sins to You. Now, right now, this moment, I forgive myself. Amen.

Forgiving ourselves give us peaceful rest and assurance in God's sanctuary of healing from the failures and pains of yesterday. Tears the heart only cries but never make it to the eyes is a hold from not forgiving yourself. Jesus knew what condemnation does to the heart, this is the reason He restored Peter after he denied Him three times. Forgive yourself so God can use you fully for His kingdom business. I did and I'm glad about it!

Welcome

Praise the LORD, all nations! Glorify Him, all people! For His faithful love to us is great; the LORD's faithfulness endures forever. Hallelujah! Psalm 117

Welcome, Herticine to your new day of adventures and wonders you have never seen before. This is a new day I have made! Rejoice, I chose to wake you to this day...times are in My hands. Now, webs of temptations, doubts, fears, worries, and webs that will cause you to stop and question which path to take are awaiting you. The webs are hidden from your sight, but not Mines, I will strengthen and guide you. This is a day of choices and decisions you must make as you do each day, I welcome you to.

Listen, no daily path is easy when you go ahead of Me. This day, as each day of adventures you take with Me will end in joy and fulfillment. Let your day begin with a renewed hope of wonders and miracles you haven't seen before because this is a new day I have made, and no day is the same!"

This is what I heard the Holy Spirit say as I saw the sun rays peeping through my windows shades and hearing the music of the Corinthians bells welcoming the morning.

As I woke at 6:00 this morning I began to pray. I was thankful for this day in a usual excitement. I began to realize that God welcomes us to the new day, so we must also welcome Him into our space. I prayed and smiled as I lingered in God's presence. When I pray most times, I smell a sweet, pleasant aroma of God's presence, but this morning I had two visions (only one I will discuss) rather than His fragrant.

First, God was giving me a message for me and maybe some of you too. In the first vision, the hand of God was writing out this Word as He spoke it to my mind also... And I was saying what He was writing. "But they that wait upon the LORD shall renew their strength; they shall mount up with wings as eagles; they shall run, and not be weary; and they shall walk, and not faint." Isaiah 40:31

Even more, God had shown me a spider web the day before with the spider hiding above the web out of sight. The web was beautifully webbed with the sunlight hitting each silky thread making it resemble the colors of a rainbow. I smiled with joy and gratitude knowing my Heavenly Father never let us go unaware. God had already shown me in the natural how the enemy hides his plans of destruction in the darkness to devour us when we are pulled by the false signs of hope. Each day we are faced with decisions, and we must choose wisely. Today, I must decide on cutting the weekly Revelation messages for the sick to hear, or study for the next messages. I decided to cut the messages because her spirit is crying out to hear the Word, she's too sick to come to hear each week. Waiting on the Lord to guide me to what is important to Him, I will always choose wisely. God sent this lady's sister by (who have never been to my house before) to let me know how her sister needs to hear the Word and message of God because she's trying to give up on life...and she's yearning for the messages of God for comfort.

Thank You Father for welcoming me to this day, which is Your day, hopefully You are pleased with my adventures today to see Your creations rejoicing in song, and Your Word was shared with a soul wanting to give up on life. Thank You for revealing the webs of choices to choose to share the Word rather than closing my door to a sick soul seeking a way to the light. Amen.

Walking with God

Enoch walked with God; then he was not there because God took him. Genesis 5:24

Each day is an adventure with God. My first book title was my 'Daily Adventures with God' my thirty-three days of healing walking with God through nature around me. God does speak! My adventures today started at 5:30am with my one-on-one with God. I want my walk with Go to be like Enoch, that God is pleased with me. This is my first revelation of the day God has opened my spiritual eyes to see, I love looking at trees and how each is so beautiful in its own way. They stand in the strongest wind and obey as the wind moves them. The wind makes the trees strong and looking at the twisted limbs tell the storms the tree being through. This is how our true walk with God is, we stand immovable when the winds of troubles come knowing God is fighting our battles. We may get bruised and, but bruises heal just the twisted limbs hold to each other in the windy storms.

Amazingly, the word 'true' comes from an old Indo-European word for tree. Trees do not move, and this is how truth is, it never moves. Lies fail and move like shoes in sinking sand, but truth stand like the trees each morning greeting the sunrise.

The second revelation this morning: when we were having breakfast the waitress came over to talk (she calls me sweet lady), and she told of an incident that happened Saturday. A father put his four-year-old son out of the car at the stoplight and left him. The little boy was running across the park lot screaming and crying trying to catch his father. She (waitress) was crying as she talked about the incident. The father came back and got his son and said, "No child is going to disobey me." God loves His children and abandonment is not His correction for a small child. However, the Holy Spirit will flee from us is disobedience, but in repentance He returns. Our True Heavenly Father runs us down to give us peace, when we run back to Him in humble submission, He caresses us with His grace and mercy.

The third revelation, as I walked into the grocery store to get dog food, I noticed the grill meat on the hot bar. I walked away but I came back to the bar and picked up two containers to carry to the sick. I called to let them know I was coming but no answer. As I was driving home, the Holy Spirit said, "Stop here. Give it to Helen." I stopped and obeyed like the trees. As I talked with her on the phone she said, "You don't know how much I needed this today! Thank you! I needed this to today!" Her husband was sick and so was she.

Fourth revelation, I went to another house to check on a neighbor with terminal cancer. She was in bed asleep, but her son came to the car to thank me for the things I have done for them. He said, "I'm looking for peace and now I found it. Thank you for everything." I smiled with gratefulness that God chose to plant me like a tree by the rivers of water to serve Him in spirit and in truth. So yes, having a true walk with God is like a tree, obeying and moving as the Wind of the Spirit directs. Today is a wonderful day to be a tree of truth with my walk with God, He never move without carrying us with Him.

Stillness

Why should I fear in times of troubles? Psalm 47:5a

Sunday afternoon of quiet peaceful time with God in the midst of His immeasurable wonders. Hawks flying heights above the trees as the sun fades in and out beneath the skippy clouds. Taking a rest after service and a simple yet delicious meal is my time with God today. I'm silent as God sings His songs of still peace through the Corinthian bells to caress me with the needed rest from a long week passed. I trust God as I see the trees trusting in the wind, and the clouds obeying the glow of the sunshine reflecting through them.

However, with my trusting the enemy desires to move my trust like the waving of the leaves on the trees and the moving of the cloud's formation. But the sounds of the bells as God direct them to sing pulls me back from my wondering. Service was wonderful as God breathed hidden manna of His love on each in attendance, I rejoiced, yet felt disappointed. Not of what God was doing, but how man/religion forgets about the one who have served faithfully from their childhood until their health no longer allow them to at this moment in time. I see my husband, a faithful servant of his church a lifetime, but now that his health doesn't allow him to go now, he has not received a phone call from the Shepherd of the house since he became ill, this sadden me and him.

Many pastors call to check on him from different churches he hadn't even served, but not from the one he has served faithfully. Then the Holy Spirit pulled my mind to Calvary with Jesus hanging and bleeding from the cross, He was rejected and forgotten by the ones He had healed, delivered, taught, and loved, but only the ones not afraid of death stood near the cross. Why am I discouraged when Jesus never forget, never leaves, never forsakes, never turn His love away? Because the enemy showed me disappointments, when Jesus shows me overcoming victory. He gives us the beauty of the noonday to give us peace; He place friends in our path we lease expect to give a helping hand; He shows beauty of a rainbow to show His promises; He reminds me through His Word of Abraham's faith. So, I will know God tests my faithfulness when disappointments come to see if I stand on the rock or the sinking sand. I sing because I'm happy in Christ Jesus, not man's song of how great I am because when I'm down Jesus sends the one, He trust to help me. What a lovely Sunday afternoon with God and I...my Savior.

Wanderer

Even when I go through the darkest valley, I fear no danger, for You are with me. Psalm 23:4a

I was an adventurous child and loved the wonderful creations of God in my surroundings. Pulling down icicles that hung on the house during the winter; skating, well sliding on the frozen water hole in the woods with silly child skills. I could have sunk in the freezing water, and my parents would have been absent of a child during my daily adventures. But God said differently, He was with me. As I said earlier, I loved the surrounding of God's creations: laying in the grass as I watched the bees circle the red cloves. Hearing the hens cackle as they laid their eggs, even me picking up the warm egg as soon as it was laid. Climbing trees to feel closer to the moon and stars. Watching the cows grazing on the noonday grass. Fishing on one of the fishing places we had. My mother would even allow me to pick blackberries from the huge patch to sell in town for .75 a pail.

I realize now that the Holy Spirit had anointed me then to be watchful of my surrounding, and not only watchful but to see the beauty of God through each thing. Everything around me as a child I saw beauty except the wet cow dungs. Laying in the hay in the barn carried me to places in my imagination I was dreaming to see, and God allowed me to see most of the places. But home on the farm is where I wanted to be. Knowing your neighbors, having room to play in my own yard without stepping on the neighbor's grass. Seeing the birds fly high without an airplane hitting them as it passed by. Letting my dog play in the yard without a latch. Growing the trees, I want and like, and as many as I like. Dreaming of bees in the grass and sap from the gum tree were my dreams rather than sugar plums dancing in my head.

I remember catching a wild goose in the hay that my brother let go of because its wings fluttered. I was saddened because I wanted to give the goose to my parents. Looking back on my childhood, the Holy Spirit was preparing me for this time in my life. I saw beauty even in a worm crawling on the limb of the cotton in the fields. The clouds floating over head as my air conditioner. I remember my first opened vision as a child, which I thought everyone had visions. My sister and I were walking to a neighbor's house to borrow milk pads for our parents, but before we could get to the house sheep after sheep crossed in front of us and disappeared into the pasture. No one in the neighborhood had sheep. No one told us our spiritual eyes were opened, I learned this year and years later.

We, each have a purpose/assignment here in this life to fulfill, but the enemy blinds too many with the troubles and worries of this life and the assignment is misplaced. Many in the scripture missed their full assignment, Samson for one. He only met half of his assignment because the enemy blinded him to his purpose and gave him visions of lustful desires. Today, at this moment is a good day to speak blessings over yourself and mainly your children because God created each beautiful in His sight with an appointed assignment, He want us to fulfill.

Humble

Clothe yourself with humility. 1 Peter 5:5

My day begins with prayer and praise and ends with praise and prayer because God brought me through another day minute by minute. I start with prayer because I know I can't get out of bed nor woke myself; it was God's living touch. Then I praise Him for another opportunity to do His will with His strength. I close my day with praise because God carried me through and did not let me fall into temptation, and He delivered from evil. I pray because I want my last act of the day to be prayer which is my one-on-one conversation with the Holy Spirit before I fall to sleep. And I still pray the prayer I was taught as a child and taught my children as babies, "If I should die before I wake, I pray to You Lord my soul to take." I'm in His presence before I go to sleep and definitely wants to be in His presence if He chooses to take me while I sleep. As I'm writing this my mind reflected back to my teaching and example before my children. It's too late to question if I set a good example before my children because they are adults now. But I can look at the Scriptures to see if I followed them as I raised my children. The Ten Commandments for Guiding Your Children according to the Word:

1. Teach them, using God's Word (Deuteronomy 6:4-9).
2. Tell them what's right and wrong (1Kings 1:6).
3. See them as gifts from God (Psalm 127:3).
4. Guide them in godly ways (Proverbs 22:6).
5. Discipline them (Proverbs 29:17).
6. Love them unconditionally (Luke 15:11-32)
7. Do not provoke them to wrath (Ephesians 6:4).
8. Earn their respect by example (1 Timothy 3:4).
9. Provide for their physical needs (1 Timothy 5:8).
10. Pass your faith along to them (2 Timothy 1:5).
11. In this life we do the best we can and thank God for not taking us in our foolishness. I have learned from my one-on-one time with God that spilled milk isn't useable. Meaning the mistakes, we have made in life, repent, confess, and erase that path from the

map that directs you.

I'm so thankful for God's unlimited grace and mercy that carry me through the valleys of uncertainties. This is the reason I pray and praise my Living Savior Jesus Christ... He's Awesome!

Testimonies

Bind the testimony. Seal up the instruction among my disciples. Isaiah 8:16

I love testimonies of love and encouragement. By the way, each of our life is a testimony of what we should not do or what we should do that others see and many follow. Think of how many tattoo bodies you see because Hollywood and professional athletes are doing it. Same with our daily walk, someone will pattern his or her walk from it.

I loved my childhood even though we had to work hard, but I look back on that time and smile. We didn't have much, but our parents made us feel rich with love, care, and protection. They would not let us work in anyone fields, homes or babysit. All of our friends wanted to come home with us on Sundays when I wanted to stay in town with them, which never happened. I realized over the years that our friends wanted to come home with us because we had the best of food, and plenty of it because my parents were farmers. My mother was raised by railroad parents. She had the best. She lived in a house with upstairs and streets with lights. When she married my father, she walked into another world and way of living. She brought with the marriage Crystals, porcelain lamps, beautiful mahogany dining room furniture, and other lovely things. She loved and took special care of these precious things. Well, one night while my parents were at the PTA meeting, my sister and I were running in the living room (which was forbidden) and we broke one of the lamps. My sister and I tried to put it back together, it didn't work! We got in trouble!!! After that night my mother never mentioned the lamp being broken, she fixed it with homemade glue. As I think of this, we (her children) were more important to her than the lamp.

As my sister pass my house today, I began to think how I always kept her in trouble, yet she would still try to take care of me. When we were in college, we moved more than we stayed in the rented rooms we must live in because I would always speak the truth to the point of getting in trouble. When the landlords would put me out, they would put my sister out too because they knew she wasn't staying if I didn't!

Reflecting back over the broken lamp, I realized honesty and truth have always been a part of my life. However, being earnest have always gotten me in trouble, I have loss jobs because it. But God always gave me better because I always stood on right and truth. I tell people when they meet me for the first time, what you see is what you get. I'm this way all the time to the point, truthful but kind.

Many today are being forced into taking something they don't want for job's sake. But more are refusing than giving in because God honor truth and He never impose on our will. Truth is a rock that never sink, the waves of the stormy sea can't wash it away. Truth stands like a rock when the sand all around it is washed away. The sinking sand is like the lies and threats of the enemy they are washed away by each wave of the evening tide. This day I rejoice because God created in me what I would be before the beginning of time, He knew me. He knows you too. I'm thankful God builds the house we are walking in... Psalm 127

Guidance

A man's heart plans his way, but the LORD determines his step. Proverbs 16:9

A father puts his four-year-old son out of the truck and drove off as the boy runs screaming and crying trying to catch him. Drug addicted son praying for the healing of his sick parents. Mentally abused son broken but seeking God. Estranged daughter now preparing meals for her mother. Childhood Disappointments in life cause many to put their eyes and hope on idols things which leads to destruction and bitterness. Spirit of abandonment becomes a house guess that soon becomes a resident. Spirit of rejection become ruler over faith of a better day coming. Drugs become ruler over the emotions of love and trust of God's faithfulness. Too many people use the excuse of outburst, anger, disrespect, name calling because of what happened years and years ago as bitterness sours the taste for renewed love and forgiveness. Many are member of a church congregation, read their Bible, yet forgets the Word when anger presents itself. And rejects that the Word is Jesus made flesh. His Word is a two-edge sword... as Hebrews 4:12 says "For the word of God is living and active. Sharper than any double-edged sword, it pierces even to dividing soul and spirit, joints, and marrow. It judges the thoughts and intentions of the heart."

Excuses to not honor father and mother leads to missed promises...as written in Ephesians 6:2 "Honor your father and mother" (which is the first commandment with a promise)." No one's childhood was alike, but the majority of the parents did the best they knew how to nurture their children. My saying is, as a mother I had a permit. As a grandmother I have driver's license, learning from my mistakes as each of us should. For the four-year-old boy, Jesus will be his source of strength if he chooses Him as his Savior. For the drug addicted son becoming free from drug, God knew the time He would wash him clean. The mentally abused son, Jesus bled from the head for his deliverance. For the daughter God washed her eyes with His cleansing blood so she can see her mother the way He does. There is nothing in this life that we can't overcome when we walk with Jesus and trust Him with our needs.

Everything is easy for Jesus. In conclusion, when you hear the voice that says you will never be free of yesterday's pain, know it's the liar because this is the only power the devil have is to lie and make you feel guilty. Failure is not in Jesus' Dictionary for any of us only miracles the in Book of Remembrance that contains our daily walk in this life.

Student

But the Counselor, the Holy Spirit...the Father will send Him in my name...will teach you all things and remind you of everything I have told you. John 14:26

God is teaching me daily that there's a reason to smile. He is with us and shows Himself in ways we can't even imagine. He reveals Himself in simple yet profound ways that He's in the boat with us on the raging waves. He cares so much for us that He has an obedient hand of His servant doing His will. We are never alone or forgotten when the dark cloud rolls in. He is the soft voice of comfort and reassurance we hear. How do I know? I'm a living witness of His outstretched arm of comfort and protection. I received a call from my doctor's office with an appointment that I hadn't made, but I accepted because I knew why? My doctor knew John had been in rehab and was now home. She wanted to make sure that I was alright, and to make sure my pressure was under control.

I smiled with tears thinking of the love shown toward me, and the care given because God was making sure I knew I'm not forgotten nor alone. When I walked in the office this morning the receptionist already had me checked in. The nurse came and put me in a room so I would not have to stay in the waiting room. I waited about thirty minutes before the doctor came in. As she walked through the door, she greeted me with a hug and smile. I told her I knew she made the appointment herself to make sure I was alright. She laughed and said, "You are important to me. Whenever I see your name on my roster I laugh because I enjoy when you come." I felt so honored and humbled to know I'm never off of God's mind, and He puts me on the mind and hearts of others. God speaks to His servants in ways we can't fathom. He speaks through His creations.

God speaks through the sun rays dancing through the trees. He shows Himself in the formation of the sun rays on the grass. I hear Him with the tone of the Corinthian bells. God is not dead as so many treats Him. He is alive and sees all our needs. Yesterday afternoon, I walked out on my porch (since the phone calls would not allow me to sleep) and as I sat and looked at the sunlight dancing through the tree's footprints were on the grass. I saw God dancing with the sun on my grass, which brought me joy. I could hear and see I am not forgotten and never alone, and neither are you!

Tears In a Bottle

Put my tears in Your bottle. Are they not in Your records. Psalm 56:8b

I'm crying because so many don't know how beautiful Jesus is. He is so compassionate, but yet rejected still by the ones who once said they accepted Him as their Savior. I'm crying because I feel Him in my heart, a heart that was once hard with fear, doubts, bitterness, and unforgiveness, and yet Jesus still chose to come into it to use me. He chose to forgive and warm my cold heart with His warm love and compassion for the hurting and lost too. I'm crying because I was once a filthy worm, He chose to turn into a butterfly to lead others to the flower of His amazing beauty and love.

Yes, I need Jesus' touch of forgiveness daily because sometimes I want to complain, I want to say I'm tired let someone else do this. But Jesus touches me and refreshes me with hope of another person giving his or her life to Him each new day. Jesus dances with me as I put my feet on the floor each morning, He sings over me as I open the doors to greet the morning. He kisses me with the cool breeze caressing my skin with the early morning misty dew. Yes, I'm crying but now each tear drop is fading because I feel the touch of Jesus' love wiping away each teardrop as He puts each tear in a bottle (Psalm 56:8). I'm crying because as I finished reading Revelation 22, I know Jesus is coming with a reward. And what I'm doing here is worth it all when I stand before the 'Reward Station' and a reward is next to my name for each soul I have led to Jesus because I chose not to complain but asked Jesus to hold me when tiredness and despair tried to overtake me.

I cried yesterday as I watched my neighbor mow my lawn when his needed it too. I cried even more as I watched another neighbor come to help him mow his lawn to beat the fallen rain. So why was I crying this morning? Because I'm not forgotten when I see the grass growing high, God sees it too and sends a helping hand. So how do I say thanks? By passing it on one day at a time.

Rooted

He is like a tree planted beside streams of water that bears its fruit in season and whose leaf does not wither. Psalm 1:3

We as followers of Christ Jesus are planted like trees in the forest of the world. Some may waver in doubts, worries, and fears, and follow the roots which mislead. But some are rooted in faith, trust and truth because their seed chose the right soil to be nourished from.

There's a stream of clear water during the forest awaiting the roots of the trees to drink from its clear living water. The invitation is opened to each tree. However, some of the trees seek to drink while some are too afraid to let their roots go deeper because seeds of the 'lie tree' has been planted in the midst of the forest by a bird of prey. Some of the trees whose leaves once trusted God are fading because their roots chose to seek their drank from the lie tree that creeped in and is spread among the forest. "There's a better life for you than this. Try this water from the lake of fun." The lying tree speaks, and many of the trees' roots followed.

Following the lie that there's a better life apart from the root of their Creator, more leaves fade and the limbs become runner of lies like vines and vines of an unruly bush without a purpose or harvest. Many trees believed the liar over the Creator of the forest. When the storm came and the wind blew against the trees, the leaves blew off, the bark peeled, the vines sought a place to anchor roots, but there were none! They had chosen their master without power to save only to destroy. The trees bent and fell under the pressure of every lie they had believed and received as truth. Wonderfully, the trees of faith and truth rooted and drinking from the clear living water stood unmoved in the wind. Their leaves still hanging on, bark still intact, and roots deeper as each held to the promises of their Creator to be their shelter in the storms. But, having the love of the Creator feeding them, when the trees of doubts and fears cried out for help and needed a friend to help them through the storm, each tree drinking from the clear living water gave a helping limb and helped to repair their broken limb and shattered leaves.

As I awoke this morning the Holy Spirit poured in my spirit how Christians are the helping hands, He uses to repair the broken. We are each a tree in the Forest of God's kingdom business. Jeremiah 17:7-8 reminds us of who we are in the kingdom of God. "But blessed is the man who trusts in the LORD, whose confidence is in Him. He is like a tree planted by the waters that sends out its roots toward the stream. It does not fear when the heat comes, and its leaves are always green. It does not worry in a year of drought, nor does it cease to produce fruit." Which fruit are you bearing?

Shelter

"Whoever dwells in the shelter of the Most High will rest in the shadow of the Almighty." Psalm 91:1

I almost wanted to complain as I was driving early this morning. But I was reminded of the one-on-one time I had with the Holy Spirit as I woke at 5:00am.

"Good morning Holy Spirit, I won't even ask You what's on Your heart for me today. All I want to say is, 'Thank You for this day. Thank You for showing me Your vast, unlimited, immeasurable, unimaginable wonders. No matter where I am, you are giving breath to me and the whole, entire world at the same time. If I'm in the sky flying above the clouds, you give me breath as You give the fish of the sea, the birds of the air, the worm in the cocoon the same breath to live. You love each of Your creations. Father, I'm not worried about this day because You rule over the heavens above, the seas below, the land between with Your immense power. You tell the sun to rise and the waves to come, so I trust You.

My Teacher, I'm not troubled about tomorrow because You have already written out the plans for my life each day. I'm not afraid when the enemy attacks because You guard me in the front and back. You are the God of Israel! You have gone before me, and You are my rear guard. I won't run in fear as if I have no hope because Your faithfulness is my wall and shield of protection. So, Father, since You chose me, I know I'm in the hand of security, love, grace, shelter from the storms of life, and victory in the battle. Father, You didn't say it wouldn't be storms, You invite us to the shelter of Your comfort and safety. I know it's left up to me to accept the invitation, and I thank You for welcoming me into Your fortress where the falcon's eye has never seen, the bird of prey is afraid to enter, and the loin's feet have never trotted. Thank You, Father for being my 911 when emergency arises. Psalm 91:1 "Whoever dwells in the shelter of the Most High will rest in the shadow of the Almighty." Amen. Your humbled and honored servant, Herticine.

Words
Missing scripture

We can harm ourselves and others by the words we speak. What we speak will live...be it good or bad, and words spoken can't be retrieved from the atmosphere, hearts, or soul of a person. I came across this information while reading, "Communications experts tell us that the average person speaks enough to fill twenty single-spaced, typewritten pages every day. This means our mouths crank out enough words to fill two books of three hundred pages each month, twenty/four books each year, and twelve hundred books in fifty years of speaking." So, our mouths write many books over our lifetime. So, the question is, what is in your book that will touch a person's life? And yes, our words touch lives to give hope or dig a pit of despair. And remember your words speak what's in the heart. Psalm 126:2-4 says, "Then our mouth was filled with laughter, and our tongue with shouts of joy; then they said among the nations, "The LORD has done great thing for them." The LORD has done great things for us; we are glad." Our words write the directions of the path we follow each day... Examples:

Good morning Holy Spirit, welcome! Be my guide this beautiful day (even if it's cloudy) You have awaken me to see! Tell me what's on Your heart for me this day!

Or do you awake with, "I will be glad when this day is over! I'm sick of this job and the crazy people I'm working with each day! They drive me crazy, and I'm tired of seeing them each day!"

You just wrote six different books that will live because you gave the devil permission to ruin your day with five of them, and you only gave the Holy Spirit control of your day one time. You wrote one book of joy and hope for a bright day. However, you wrote a book of sickness over yourself. One of giving away your time to misery. One of confusion of the mind. One of no hope of a better day, and one of sorrow and hopelessness for yourselves and other people.

Words show our walk with God and His faithfulness toward us as Psalm 126:2 days nations saw God's goodness for His people. So today, is a good day to give each of your words careful thought because you are writing a book of your hope or no hope in Christ Jesus. Bless yourself with the words you speak rather than cursing who God ordained you to be...fearfully and wonderfully made.

Conjugal

And the LORD said, "That's right, and it means that I am watching, and I will certainly carry out all my plans." Jeremiah 1:12

I was getting ready for bed last night, but I kept hearing this in my spirit: there are some things I refuse to do. So, I stopped what I was doing and began writing. One, I refuse to interfere in my children's marriages, because while I'm still angry over something my son-in-law or daughter-in-law have done, they (husband and wife) are in bed making babies while I'm angry.

Two, hold grudges over the things from yesterday and what someone's gossip have done. Three, repeat someone's secret he or she has trusted me with. Four, gossip about someone's failures. Five, kick a person when they are down even if he or she have kicked me with words. Six, don't become angry when someone uses racial slurs. Seven, tell a lie to make myself look good. Eight, not go along with a person's anger against someone else. Nine, tell a person the truth when he wants a lie. Ten, looking at someone who needs help and not have compassion to do my part. Eleven, vote for someone who comes against the Word of God. Twelve, know my loneliness is God exclusiveness to use me.

Why did the Holy Spirit keep me up to writing? Because He showed me how people are going into bad health because they refuse to confess their sins and repent. They are holding the pain of darkness done years and years ago and this chosen path is destroying so many minds and bodies. They call it dementia when it's the black secrets syndrome the worms of destruction are hatching despair and memory loss. Jesus told us to confess our sins one to the other. He told us to forgive too. I mentioned forgiveness to a lady some years ago and she replied with this statement, "I may forgive but I will never forget, because when you forget what the person have done you have amnesia." I stood there and wept for her soul. Hopefully, before she stepped into eternal life she forgave and forgot the deed she thought was so bad. I saw the suffering of sickness before she left this side of life, and her memory was confused and bitterness.

I don't know who needs this, but God does! If you are constantly attacked in your body, check your spirit and ask the Holy Spirit to reveal your secret sins and purge you before the worms of hidden despairs and buried burdens eat away what Jesus died on the cross to preserve for each of us. Did Jesus pour back on us the wrongs and sins we have done, so what rights do we have? Life is too precious to allow invaders of destruction to live inside of us...choose to do it God's way.

Enemy Is Loud

Our enemy rushes down on us like storm clouds! Jeremiah 4:13a

In this life dark clouds will roll in and we can rest assured of this. However, each dark cloud isn't the same and doesn't pour out rain it just huffs and puff and threatened with thunder and lightning. This is the way of the enemy, his shadow is larger than his mouth, and his mouth dangerous than his actions. He is like the threatening thunder clouds without rain. It's important for each of us if we have prepared for the storm with an Umbrella of faith. Matthew 7:24-27 Jesus told His disciples to build their faith on the rock because the winds and waves can't wash the rock away, same with faith when it's anchored in Jesus. Some will ask where is your faith since you walk with God, He will take care of you? Yes, He will! Timothy got sick, Paul told him what to do to get well, this is the reason we prepare with faith. We prepare with car insurance. Are you planning on having a wreck? We prepare with house insurance. Are you planning on your house burning down or blowing away? You prepare with health insurance. Are you planning on getting sick?

So, preparing the umbrella of faith when the dark clouds come is wisdom from God. The dark clouds will come in life more so than us using our car, house, or health insurance. How do we prepare for the dark clouds rolling in? By feeding on the Word of God which is like a fiery hammer which break the rocks into. You can speak and rebuke the dark clouds of trouble if you have filled yourself with the Living and Active Word. Tears won't make demons flee, shouting hallelujah won't make them run, running to the Bible to lookup a Scripture will allow them to invite other friends to rain on your flicker of faith. So yes, prepare and dress yourself daily with the Word of God, and saturate yourself in the fragrance of His presence so your umbrella won't have holes in it when the dark clouds come with rain. Jesus is our umbrella of faith and protection in the storm.

Times of Troubles

"I have not departed from the commands of his lips; I have treasured the words of his mouth more than my daily bread." Job 23:12

During David's troubles: from his brother fussing at him, to Saul praising him one day and trying to kill him the next, to his son, Absalom taking his kingship, David's mind stayed on God, and he never stop trusting Him. Yet, I see too many today turning to despair when trouble arises. When the mind is attacked God is forgotten, secular music is played, and praise and worship are forgotten until the Sunday gathering. What's up with this? 'It's a me, me, me moment of comforting things not familiar to me. God, you know what's best for me-moment of listening. It has to be what I want with a mouth wide opened and the two ears closed drama which leads to unrepairable failures.'

Then, I was reading, and this question was asked, "What would you think of a person who possessed a priceless treasure but treated it as something of little value. Well, we could be guilty of that if we were to neglect the Bible. In this book The Wonder of the Word of God." As I kept reading a true story appeared about a man that suffered through an explosion, and his face was badly disfigured. He lost his eyesight as well as both hands. He was just a new Christian, and one of the greatest disappointments was he could no longer read the Bible. He heard about a woman in England who read Braille with her lips. He sent for some books of the Bible in Braille. But to his dismay, he discovered that the nerve endings in his lips had been destroyed by the explosion too.

One day, he brought the Braille pages to his lips, and his tongue happened to touch a few of the raised characters, and he could feel them. He thought with excitement, I can read the Bible using my tongue. He read the Bible through four times before his story was written about by Robert Summer. This man made no excuses to unwrap the gifts of God's wonders of His Word. We, each have the answers to all our needs when we open the priceless treasure of the Bible. I'm made ashamed, so Lord help me to treasure You like this! "I have not departed from the commands of his lips; I have treasured the words of his mouth more than my daily bread." Job 23:12

Fishing

Bring some of the fish you've just caught. John 21:10

Jesus said He didn't come to judge the world, but to save it. There was 153 people Jesus led to the Kingdom with the Gospel, and 153 big fish in the net when He told Peter where to cast it. The meaning of one hundred fifty-three "The Sons of God". If the 153 people would have refused Jesus' call, Jesus would not have forced them to come. If Peter would have refused to cast his net on the right side, Jesus would not have forced him. Jesus wept because the people in Jerusalem refused to let Him carry them under His wings like a mother hen, He wept but He didn't force them to come. We are running to and fro with no resting place when we put the things of the world first while leaving Jesus on the back burner until we need Him. In so many ways we are like the gazelle running for its life, and the lion chasing after it in Africa when we make Jesus last in our day.

An article in The San Francisco Chronicle said, "Every morning in Africa, a gazelle wakes up. It knows it must run faster than the fastest lion or it will be killed. Every morning a loin wakes up. It knows it must outrun the slowest gazelle or it will starve to death." When the sun comes up the lion and gazelle know they better run to survive the day or die or stave. It is a stressful day knowing you must constantly run to live. Charles Spurgeon wrote, "If you are not seeking the Lord, the devil is seeking you." David in Psalm 5 came to God early in the morning asking for His protection. Early in the morning when the dew is still falling on the grass seek God. Matter of fact, seek God when He wakes you in the midnight hours because "the devil prowls around like a roaring lion looking for someone to devour" (1Peter 5:8).

We are like gazelles running for our lives when we serve self rather than God. And like the lion starving to death when we don't seek God as our Source. Jesus is our daily bread and the Holy Spirit our living water... Without God we run blindly when troubles come by the mouth of the enemy. And like the leaf falling from the tree, trust God as the leaf trust the wind to carry it to a safe landing...

Jesus is our food when we are hungry, our peace in the storms, our protection in trouble waters, our strength in weakness, our Light in the darkness, our hope in weariness, our victory in the fight, our never-ending Redeemer! Need I say more!

Kind Words

A word spoken at the right time is like gold apples on a silver tray. Psalm 25:11

How often have someone thanked you for asking "how are you doing?" Yesterday, as I passed by a man in Kroger, he spoke and I spoke and said, "How are you doing today?" He turned to me and said, "Thank you for asking how I'm doing!" We laughed and said a few words and walked away in different directions. Then I read this, "Which of the 31,173 verses in the Bible is your favorite?" I thought for a moment, then said, "I am Yours; deliver me, for I have sought Your precepts." Psalm 119:94 Since I gave myself to Jesus, I'm His to use as He pleases.

But still I wasn't satisfied so I began thinking "Know that the LORD set apart the faithful for Himself; the LORD hears when I call to Him." Psalm 4:3 God is my Protector, but still this one didn't fill that hunger completely. So, I began to think "For we must all appear before the judgement seat of Messiah, that each one May receive his recompense in the body, whether it was good or bad." 2 Corinthians 5:10

I gave myself to Jesus, I'm His and He protects me, and since I know I'm His and He protects me, it's time for me to stop trying to please people thinking it will make them happy, it's time for me to let each bucket sit on its own bottom. I can't right someone else's stumbling, I'm only responsible that I'm not the one who made them stumble. So, now my favorite verse is 2 Corinthians 5:10

I can only stand before Jesus for myself no one else. Once again, the Holy Spirit have shown me that I must be about His business not what man tells me I should be doing. This is the reason I smile because I gave myself away to Jesus to be used as He directs.

What is your favorite verse?

Fear Fades with Praise

I am like a solitary bird on a roof. Psalm 102:7b

Why is it easier to lose faith rather than fear? Proverbs 9:10 says, "The fear of the LORD is the beginning of wisdom, and knowledge of the Holy One is understanding." I hear daily people talking about their fear of the virus and the world's conditions. And they have put themselves in a 'fear prison' without a key. Over the weekend a young lady called overwhelmed with so much fear she was about to pass out. As I talked to her the fear began to lift and the sickness left. She said, "I can't carry you in my hip pocket." I said, no, you can't. You are not supposed to carry me, but you are to carry the Holy Spirit. Also, as I sat in the dentist office a neighbor walked in and he saw me and took the chair next to me. He said, "Did you take the shot? When my two friends died, I ran and got mines. You know the church leaders are weak now and so few are coming to church. My wife is afraid to go, and I don't want to go and carry something back to her." My reply, "It amazes me how people are afraid to go to church, but they eat out and don't know whose cooking their food." "You know that's right!" Faith is rejected and fear received. Why?

The Holy Spirit showed me something simple yet amazing and profound this morning, be blessed from this revelation: I'm watching a bird sitting on my porch rail facing East singing a lovely song as if it's hearing music as it sang. It wouldn't move when I told it to, and it never stop singing as I was shooing at it. When it finished one tune it flew away singing and still sang as it perched on the tree limb under the leaves. It wasn't afraid of me, and it didn't stop singing the praises of the morning. Psalm 104:12 says, "The birds of the air nest beside the springs; they sing among the branches." Yes, the birds were singing in the air, not one but many were singing. Later in the morning I went to my prayer room, and as soon as I sat on the couch, I heard something on my roof. As I looked up through my skylight, I saw birds on it... birds flew to my door, birds were around the steps, birds were flying to the top of my shortage house singing a beautiful tune.

What is the Holy Spirit saying this lovely day? Each of us should be singing because there is victory in praise, there is peace in the storm, the battle is not our but His. Fear stops man from singing and steals the song heaven inhabits our praises and makes fear fade.

This day is another day God has shown Himself as the Joy of my salvation and my Peace in the winds through the birds singing all around me. Psalm 104 says God's messengers are like the wind... Thank You, Holy Spirit for Your message to not fear because You are running me down to sing over me and quite me with Your love (Zephaniah 3:17). Amen.

Judge Ye Not

Be careful not to practice your righteousness. Matthew 6:1

I am guilty this morning of seeing with the natural judgmental eye. Matthew 5 tells us not to swear by heaven because it's God's throne; nor by earth it's His footstool; nor by Jerusalem the great king lives there; nor by the head can't make one hair white. Then Jesus tells us in chapter 6 when darkness is inside us, we only see darkness. I realize a former mindset of criticism will try to take up the light of seeing people through the eyes of God. Darkness is a trap of promises like a spider web hides in the sunlight.

We are all filthy rags, but God sees us fearfully and wonderfully made as He created each of us. God sees our filthy through the blood of Jesus which cleanses us through confession and repentance.

This morning I looked at a young man with long hair, baggy clothes, and a cigarette in his mouth as someone I didn't want to be around. I didn't see him through God's eyes, I looked at him through my judging eyes. As I walked out the door, I begin seeing him as an employee at the restaurant I had breakfast. As we passed each other in the parking lot I was ashamed of the thoughts I just had twenty minutes earlier. Then we met each other as I was going to my car, and he is coming toward the door, he said, "Have a good day and be careful." These are the words I always say when I'm leaving a place. God brought my pride to its knees, and how thankful He did. I'm thinking about Peter and his pride and shunning the Gentiles he was eating with when his Jewish friends came into the restaurant. He was ashamed to be with them in the presence of other Jewish friends he felt was above the Gentiles in honor. But praise God, Paul corrected him and pulled him from the path of pride and judgmental attitude to seeing each person created in God's image. The Holy Spirit pulled me back to the humble path and corrected me also. I don't know why I thought the way I did this morning, but it shows how easily we can step from the narrow path. I looked at a spider web webbed across the full space between the light poles and how it will trap things blind or unaware it's there. Many things were caught in it, and the only way I knew it was there because the sunlight revealed it as the wind blow against it. The only way to stay free of the darkness is to seek the Light more...and do it God's way.

Then, I was reminded of a story I read about a young Korean Christian. He was so excited about his walk with Jesus that he walked hundreds of miles to recite Scriptures he had memorized to the missionary who led him to Christ. He quoted the entire Sermon on the Mount perfectly. The missionary said, "This is great, but you must not only memorize the Scriptures but also live what they say." The young man said, "I do. This is how I learned them. When I tried to remember them, I couldn't. So, I began practicing what the verse said on a neighbor who was not a Christian. After that I remembered each one." When my neighbor mistreats me, do I do what the scripture says? This young Christian did.

This testimony touched me deeply, and it revealed the condition of my heart. Can I say, "I have hidden your word in my heart that I might not sin against you." Psalm 119:11 Forgive me Lord!

I know the Word, but I must be a 'doer of the Word'. The missionary was a quoter of the Word, but he judged before he asked if the young man was doing what he quoted. I'm guilty of speaking before I know the truth. I see why God gave us two ears rather than two mouths. Oh my, God would have to have earplugs if we had two mouths. We need to listen more than we talk. So, I'm sitting on the porch in the sun confessing my faults and failures as I see the beauty of Jesus' holiness all around me. I bow before Him as one of His many servants seeking to have a guilt free day surrounded by God's glory of forgiveness. Do you have until tomorrow to surrender your all to God? This is a question only God can answer for us... But I tell you, I would not wait on tomorrow because it may not come in your lifetime.

Servant's Heart

Whenever you pray, you must not be like the hypocrites. Matthew 6:5a

There are certain people I don't like and don't like to be around the spirit they carry: A liar, a gossiper and murderer (gossiping murder a person's character), an accuser, a thief, a complainer, a selfish and ungrateful never enough person, and non-repentant person. As I think about it, God don't like these spirits in people neither because they will be casted into hell.

Life is so brief...we were once the youngest babies in the nursery, now many readings this are now senior citizens. There is no time to waste doing the things not pleasing to God because times are in His hand, and we don't know when the hands on the clock will stop turning on this side of life.

An ex-prisoner stopped by my house this morning and he reminded me of the conversations we had about Jesus the times he came to my house when he worked on the ministry with the company he worked with. He said, "You are still teaching, and you have to know the Word and have a heart of compassion to still be writing the inmates. Most pastors don't know how to communicate with the ones in prison. Jesus forgave the sinners." It has been over ten years since this man have been to house, but he remembered my teaching, prayers for lost souls, love for Jesus, and walk of faith. I thanked him for the reminder.

I'm reminded of Dr. Virginia Connally's saying, "Every day for me is a gift. As you live a life of faith, you're not looking for the results. I was just doing the things that God planted in my life and heart." So as my day became fuller and fuller with its commands I remembered her words, and Psalm 118:24...This is the day the Lord has made; we will rejoice and be glad in it."

So, this is one of the reasons I don't want to be around liars, gossips, or accusers because they are killers and blockers of the path of righteousness and lost souls are too important to God let liars take up room in my day.

Rewards

No one can be a slave of two masters, since either he will hate one and Leo the other or be devoted to one and despise the other. You cannot be slave of God and of money. Matthew 6:24

Another revelation today...God have always been with me and you. God knew me before I was woven in my mother's womb. He knows and is with me here, and He will be with me after I die. So, once again God's promise is proven true. "I will never leave you or forsake you." So, "Praise the LORD, all you nations; extol him, all you people. For great is his love toward us, and the faithfulness of the LORD endures forever. Praise the LORD!" Psalm 117

God's love toward us is great. He loved each of us before we were born; He will love us after we die. Romans 8:39 informs us that, "Not one thing can separate us from the love of God that is in Jesus our Lord. In the twenty-nine words of Psalm 117 the writer reminds us of the many reasons why we should praise the Lord and not be worried over the natural things of this world. God's faithfulness is our wall and shield of protection.

God's love doesn't move from us, we move our faith from Him. His hand doesn't close from us, we step out of it. I'm reminded of a phone call earlier this morning from a friend who went to the doctor's office in hopes she could be worked in because she wasn't feeling like herself. The nurse checked her blood pressure, it was good! She waited and called me, and we prayed. The doctor sent a message to her by his nurse, "Go to bed before midnight, stay off Facebook, turn off the lights and go to sleep! You are too old to be up that late!" She called and told me what the doctor said and then made this statement, "I'm finding me another doctor, telling me to go to bed before midnight and stay off Facebook!" I laughed and said, "Send that doctor some roses, some red or yellow ones because he told you the truth!" I will send him some black ones(laughing). God is with us, and He tells us the same thing, "stay off Facebook and have that time with Me. You will never regret it." Thank You Father, I have not regretted one moment I spent with You.

No Retirement
The LORD is for me; I will not be afraid. What can man do to me? Psalm 118:6

I received a phone call Saturday from a dear, dear lady around eighty-five. She wanted to check on me after her daughter told her about John's illness. "I'm not able to go any place now, so all I can do is stay at home and pray all day." She said. Then, I mentioned about Anna staying in the temple day and night fasting and praying after her husband died in Luke 2:36. Her prayers were answered, and she saw Jesus. How often do we make people in their older years feel helpless? Many time their children want to think for them even when their minds are sharp. Just because the legs don't work doesn't mean the mind and thinking have stopped working.

There was a woman named Margaret more than ninety years old who wasn't ready to surrender to old age, she was called a 'battler'. She was too weak to walk anymore, but she wasn't done with her ministry. Margaret was almost deaf and couldn't hardly move around. But in the four walls of her nursing home room where she lived, her ministry reached beyond the four walls. For hours every day she sat in her chair with a stack of prayer cards and prayed diligently for missionaries. "And sometimes, when she could push her frail body to do so, she would kneel beside her bed on creakily knees to talk with God. Margaret didn't have much more than prayer to offer her Lord." The report stated. She was the essence of the answer to the question in Psalm 116:12, "What shall I return to the LORD for all his goodness toward me?" An answer is found in verse 13, "I will...call on the name of the LORD."

Too many see the older ones useless to the world, God see each of us no matter the age vessels for the kingdom. Margaret is a Modern-Day example of Anna. She (Margaret) didn't allow weak knees and deaf ears to keep her from doing the ministry God chose her to do. Times are in God's hands and until that time is over there is still a need for our services in God's kingdom. Read Psalm 116, it will encourage you to stay the path you were choosing to walk. God sees beyond the wrinkles and weak knees; He sees the heart rooted in faith not willing to surrender until He says it's finished.

Too Often

Don't worry about anything, but in everything, through prayer and petition with thanksgiving, let your requests be made know to God. Philippians 4:6

Today, God showed me my many blessings, and to be truthful I'm ashamed knowing I have been selfish with the lack of thankfulness I give to Him. We, too often whine when we should be rejoicing. Complaining when we should be praising. Whoa me, when we should be, "Jesus, You kept me and my family from the hands of the Fowler."

God allows us to see misery firsthand so we can be a ray of light in a dark dreary place for the weary. I was asked this morning if there was a family reunion at my house because so many cars and trucks were at my house a few weeks ago. I said, "No, these were people coming to help with the things needed around the house." She said, "There are people at your house all the time." These comments came from a woman who has terminal cancer. She and her husband are giving up hope of living and wants to go to a nursing home to die. After service today a few of us went to their home to pray with them, but more so to be the hands and feet of Jesus. We made sure they had food and arranged for their home to be clean because neither (wife nor husband) of them is able.

Most times people think just because you have children close by they help with the things needed, but this isn't true of this couple. No helping hand comes from their children, but we must remember Jesus said, "Who is My brother? Who is My mother? Those who do the will of the Lord." We are the brothers and sisters of this couple now because they need help. Then, I looked at John helping to pray for this couple, and I bowed in thankfulness and thanked God for keeping him and sending people to help me during his illness. After we left this couple's house, we received a message of a neighbor dying from a stroke this morning. I looked at John again and thanked God for another day to help someone else.

Times are in God's hand (Psalm 31), and as long as He gives each of us another day let it be doing His will. I received a call yesterday checking to see if I was ok, and she said, "All I can do now is pray because I'm not able to leave home." My reply, "You are an Anna, she never left the temple because she prayed day and night after her husband's death. And she was one of the only two who saw Jesus' face to face when he was eight days old." God knows how He will use us, when He will use us, how He will use us, and how long He will use us because times are in His hands. All He needs from us are willing vessels to be used.

Are you willing to go where God sends you?

Home

You who fear the LORD, trust in the LORD! He is their help and shield. Psalm 115:11

One day at a time is all I can say about our walk in this life. But now I say one breath at a time. Also, if you do something for twenty-one days it becomes a habit. Wow, I'm rambling all over the place! But I'm saying all of this to say life is precious and we need to cherish each moment of it. Some didn't make it from yesterday to today, but the most important thing about life is, are you living a life pleasing to God? If Jesus chooses right now to bring you to your final destination, will you be prepared to journey there? Does your suitcase have the right garment for this trip into eternity?

Each of us have a spiritual suitcase packed with things outdated like bitterness, anger, hatred, jealousy, and the many things that take us to a tropical hell. However, when we walk close with God, we repack our suitcase with lovely things fit for the banquet table...love, forgiveness, a helping hand, and the outfits God smiles about as we unpack and wear each one.

Today, John left rehab and hugs and thank you were shared, he misses leaving the one who have been so kind to him, but he rejoiced as he walked through the door to feel the warm heat of the noonday sun on his face. I think about Psalm 114:3 "The sea looked and fled." Then verse 5 he asked, "Why was it, sea, that you fled?" The answer is implied: The seas were obeying the command of God. When the sea of adversity is threading, we only need to remember the awesome power of God in the storms. The sea fled before God, so when the obstacles that seem overwhelming to us come, they have no resistance to God's power than the waves of the sea. The obstacles of sickness fled from John by the prayers of many. So, as he walked through the door at home he said, "I feel home! I feel home!" The atmosphere and fragrance of the presence of the Lord welcome him home, as the memory of rehab is a cherish memory of restoration, but home is where his heart long to be. And this is what we will do, "We will praise the praise the LORD, both now and forever. Hallelujah!" Psalm 115:18

Bowing Down

There is no fear involve; instead, perfect love drives out fear, because fear involves punishment. 1 John 4:18

A chapter in my first published book 'My Daily Adventures with God' was about fear of going to the dentist. I like pretty teeth but not the dentist's chair. As I watched the leaves fall to the ground yesterday, I was reminded how God delivered me of fear by revealing freedom by the falling of the Fall leaves in 2007. The tree didn't try to hold on to the leaves, it released each one and the weight of the leaves from the tree gave the tree a long-awaited winter's rest. Fear is the weight of heavy burdens and torment (1John 4:18).

Fear of the virus is weighting so many downs in uncertainties of tomorrow, and too many have made the virus a giant while making Jesus look like a flea. Jesus is still Jesus, the One who defeated Satan at the cross, and rose victoriously the third day to give each of us victory.

At sundown today is Yom Kippur, the closing of the gates. This is a time to dress ourselves in the garments of faith, strength, hope, repentance, forgiveness, victory because we are not victims but victors. Yes, we are in a storm with the many attacks against the church, but remember Jesus is in the boat with us. As we observe Yom Kippur with praise, thanksgiving, communion, come dressed in the aroma pleasing to God, not like the guest in Matthew 22:11-15 had to be thrown out for improper dress. Yom Kippur is not for the proud but humble, as Jesus humbled Himself. Fear is stripping too many of faith. Many are too afraid to assemble together to worship or visit the sick. This is where the enemy wants you, hiding rather than standing boldly in the face of fear and proclaim Jesus did it all at Calvary, and He sent the Holy Spirit to be our guide to victory when the enemy comes in like a flood. God is the standard of our protection. Repent and forgive others before the window of heaven closes at the closing of Yom Kippur... God desire our hearts to seeking Him rather than bow to the enemy which is fade from the light of Jesus' glory.

Kindness

Dear friends, let us love one another, because love is from God, and everyone who loves has been born of God and knows God. 1 John 4:7

Each second and fourth Monday of the month is grooming day for my puppy, Sugar. This is the first Monday I have taken her for her grooming since John being in rehab, because a sweet friend has been taking her. Well, this morning as I waited on her grooming I decided to go to Jack's for breakfast. At first, I thought about sitting in the car to eat, but when I drove into the parking lot I decided to go inside. As soon as I walked through the door this lady greeted me with the warmest welcome as if I was the most important person who walked through the door. As I walked to a table with tray in hand, I noticed table after table and booth after booth were filled with groups of older men and only one booth with a couple. As I began to eat, I heard different conversations, and this lady(waitress)was in each one of them. She walked from table to table talking to each group while serving them more coffee. The older men were talking about their health and what they were going to do the rest of the day...etc.

As each man would leave, she greeted each one with a word of safety as each walked through the door. Then only one man was left from one group. He wanted to stay longer but his friends were gone. She said to the man, "There's another man coming, stay and talk with him." 'No, I'm going to get some cat food. The others are gone so I will go to Walmart and get some cat food.' Ok, see you tomorrow.'" When she came to my table to fill my coffee cup, I told her how she reminded me of the waitress from the movie "Tuesday Morning Breakfast Club." The waitress in the movie befriended a group of old men who lived alone and gathered each Tuesday with their friends for breakfast. She would listen to all their stories of years passed. This lady, this morning listened to each of the men's stories because some were lonelier than the other.

The only thing one man had to look forward to for the rest of the day was getting cat food. One man comes in three times a day because his wife is in the nursing home, and he feels a touch of home through this lady. So, this morning the Holy Spirit showed me once again that He needs His servants beyond the four walls of the building, because people are looking for a light of God in their dark time of loneliness. As I was leaving, I thanked this lady for being a light for the kingdom of God and gave her a tip that matched the cost of my meal. People are in need of a kind word and gesture from God's servants. Just as my chicken stand waiting at my door each morning for their special treat, people are seeking a door(path) leading to God too. Be that light and fragrance God is using to bring many to Him. As I walked out of the door the lady said, "Thank you, and bless you sweet lady." I smiled inside and out because I saw a miracle this morning.

Hidden Gifts
Nothing hidden that won't be made known. Matthew 10:26b

I just woke from a short Sunday nap thinking of my mother. On Sunday afternoon, I would go to my mother's house and sit back on her couch and talk about 'this that and the other'! Thinking back over those days when my mother got older, she would always have the TV on the Christian network. I would walk in (as my children do me) and turned the channel to some worldly stuff. She(mother) never said a word, but as soon as I would leave, she turned it back to the Christian channel.

I smile now over her humbleness of not saying a word about me changing the channel, she took each moment to enjoy my presence. I think of how she blessed me with words of encouragement of who I didn't even know I was a few months before she passed, but she did. Her house carried an aroma that's still there now. Today, I realized the aroma is the fragrance of God's presence. Service is held in her house each Sunday and many lives have been changed there.

Today, as the shofar was blown the presence of the Lord filled the house. Some in service even heard the door opening and His footsteps. I saw angels on the walls as the dogs barked along with the shofar. Even the chicken came and stood on the walk. Within minutes another car pulls in the drive and a man comes in with a mask on his face. He said, "I was driving up and down this road and I needed some place to stop, and I stopped here." Within minutes he took off the mask and received what the Holy Spirit had for him. After everyone left, he stayed two to three hours just needing to talk. He left with books I gave him on fear and other things he needed, and a written copy of today's message on the hidden gifts inside.

My father and mother built a home for their seven children, but before my mother stepped into eternal life, she filled the house with the presence of God to be passed on to the next generation. Maybe God gave her a vision of souls being saved in this house, I don't know! But I do know she blessed me with a prophesy of going forward and she knew I could... I didn't, but God showed her that I could. My mother saw what was hidden in me as I was seeing myself broken and sick...She saw my today and the souls her house had prepared away to come in the presence of God's fragrance of love. Even a little boy told his grandmother as they drove pass the house that a light was glowing over it... God has prepared a place that even the chicken come in the presence.

Hope

For He causes His sun to rise on the evil and the good and sends rain on the righteous and unrighteous. Matthew 5:45b

I'm hearing the sounds of the early morning and seeing the movement of God's creation receiving the blessings of this new day. The coolness of the breeze is almost too cool on my bears arms, but I'm enjoying it. The chicken again this morning pecks from the new overturned soil, but I gave them a little treat of sweet vegetables from last night's meal. The sun is a beautiful sight caressing the tops of the many trees surrounding me, so I can joyously say, I see God, I hear God, I feel God, and I'm alive this day to tell someone who needs a word of hope...our Savior lives and is able to supply all our needs.

If, yes if, we would just take a moment to stop with the hustle and bustle of the day we, each can see God and His goodness. I'm here to tell the ones who will listen that God never, never leaves us. I'm not ashamed to tell of God's never-ending blessings and how He puts people in our path to show kindness to along the path of time. Now, this is a fact, in this journey of life we need more than family, and we need to show kindness to more than family. Family isn't always near when we need help, but someone God has put in your path will be. I love Hebrews 13:2 "Do not neglect to show hospitality to strangers, for by so doing some people have entertained angels without knowing it."

A smelly, tattooed, and talking to himself man came to my porch years ago and asked my husband if he could see me. I went to the door and greeted him with a smile. He said, "I don't have any food to eat and I'm hungry. "I told him to wait a moment. I walked back into the house and filled bags and bags with the best food I had. It was so much John had to carry him home in the truck, and I fixed him a hot plate from the breakfast I was cooking. Each time he has no food he comes and ask because he knows I will not reject him. This man walks by each day wanting to know how John is doing and will help me with anything I need. My children and grandchildren are not near, but the ones I have treated with kindness comes when I call. But then Jesus said, "Who is My mother, who is My brother? Those who do the will of the Lord." Jesus lives because He never let the ones who have chosen Him go wanting.

Traps of the World
Woe to me for I am ruined... Isaiah 6:5

Birds singing before sunrise, dew watering the grass before dawn, wild geese flying in formation with a geese song, flowers blooming in the noonday sun, trees swaying with the breeze, warm summer wind blowing against a sweaty face, spider webs hanging from the tree limbs, morning walks with a love one, good cup of coffee on a cold winter's day, smell of Daffodils, and the touch of white cotton are a few of the many simple things taken for granted by many. When we take for granted the goodness of God, we are like the ants crawling inside the hummingbird feeder. They go in to drink from the sweet drink of the hummingbird's nectar and can't get out as they swim in the sweetness of their desire.

Then the sweetness becomes their enemy as breathing become miserable. They drown trying to get something only the hummingbirds can drink from. Watching in amazement I heard the Holy Spirit say this is the way the ways of the world traps you. We seek the forbidden things outreach and end up drowning in the world's desires. Drugs looks pretty when a friend you trust introduces them to you. Then the trap comes, and you began to drown in desires which should have been unreachable, but the enemy make sure you can reach them, and you drown in whoa-it-me.

Children rushing to grow up, the young rushing to retirement, the lazy not wanting to work and fake illness for a check, rushing time you can't get back, time is taken for granted, and many drown in sorrows afterward. Dreading job changes rather than rejoicing that you can work and have a job, taking blessings for granted. Time, times are in God's hand, but man wants to control it by looking at a clock. The simple things of life have no price tag, only what each of us makes out of it. There is no reason to rush time because time will pass. For example, I was the youngest baby in the nursery 73 years ago, but it only lasted a few very few minutes before the next baby was born.

Today, was such a clear reminder of man taking the simple

things for granted. The man across the hall from my husband was being put in the car with his wife as I was walking out the door at the rehab this afternoon. I said, "Are you trying to run away (with a smile). Are you going home?" He laughed and said, "No, I am going for a ride with my wife. I'm going to see the sceneries. You know, with all I have, it's the simple things I miss. The simple things should never be taken for granted." Seeing the flowers, brought him pleasure. Hearing the birds sing, brought him joy. Feeling the sun on his face refreshed his mind with thankfulness. The scent of the newness was still in the car as he let down the window, but the new car couldn't replace the simple things taken for granted. Being able to walk in the coolness of the day, but the wheelchair was and is his legs. Going to the bathroom by himself, now there is no privacy because extra hands are needed.

Have you given a thought of your blessings? Are you taking life for granted? The simple things you push aside with the hustle and bustle of business. Slow down, smell the coffee perking. Listen to the birds welcoming the morning with a song. Enjoy the sunset as it brings the night for rest. Feel the caress of the summer breeze on your skin, and remember, each moment is a miracle because you still can walk out and enjoy the simple things God have created for us to see and hear Him in the simple things of life.

Sweet Aroma

and Aaron's sons shall burn it on the altar upon the burnt sacrifice, which is on the wood that is on the fire, as an offering made by fire, a sweet aroma to the LORD. Leviticus 3:5

I just woke from a short Sunday nap thinking of my mother. On Sunday afternoon, I would go to my mother's house and sit back on her couch and talk about 'this that and the other'! Thinking back over those days when my mother got older, she would always have the TV on the Christian network. I would walk in (as my children do me) and turned the channel to some worldly stuff. She(mother) never said a word, but as soon as I would leave, she turned it back to the Christian channel. I smile now over her humbleness of not saying a word about me changing the channel, she took each moment to enjoy my presence. I think of how she blessed me with words of encouragement of who I didn't even know I was a few months before she passed, but she did. Her house carried an aroma that's still there now. Today, I realized the aroma is the fragrance of God's presence. Service is held in her house each Sunday and many up on many of lives have been changed there.

Today, as the shofar was blown the presence of the Lord filled the house. Some in service even heard the door opening and His footsteps. I saw angels on the walk as the dogs barked along with the shofar. Even the chicken came and stood on the walk. Within minutes another car pulls in the drive and a man comes in with a mask on his face. He said, "I was driving up and down this road and I needed some place to stop, and I stopped here." Within minutes he took off the mask and received what the Holy Spirit had for him. After everyone left, he stayed two to three hours just needing to talk. He left with books I gave him on fear and other things he needed, and a written copy of today's message on the hidden gifts inside.

My father and mother built a home for their seven children, but before my mother stepped into eternal life, she filled the house with the presence of God to be passed on to the next generation. Maybe God gave her a vision of souls being saved in this house, I don't know! But I do know she blessed me with a prophesy of going forward and she knew I could. I didn't, but God showed her that I could. My mother saw what was hidden in me as I was seeing myself broken and sick. She saw my today and the souls her house had prepared away to come in the presence of God's fragrance of love. Even a little boy told his grandmother as they drove pass the house that a light was glowing over it. God has prepared a place that even the chicken come in the presence.

Victory In Jesus
Sing to Him a new song; play skillfully with a shout of joy. Psalm 33:3

If God is dead...

Who tells the sun to shine...

The wind to blow...

The birds to sing...

My eyes to see His beauty...

My ears to hear His wonders...

And my heart to feel His love?

Jesus' suffering on the cross was not pretty as the cross He hung on wasn't beautiful like the crosses we wear around our necks. But Jesus hung naked on an old rugged cross to save us from ourselves and bearing the transgressions of us all. Torn from the Father and hanging helpless (Psalm 22:11) because of the blackness and filth of mines and your sins.

The Father would have no part of this blackness covering Jesus. However, this old rugged cross He hung on was beautiful to Satan because he thought he had won lost souls. He thought Jesus was dead. He thought there is no place for them to hide. He thought victory was his. He thought I deceived Adam now I can do the same now. He thought all hope lost and territory of the soul belonged to him. Each of us have thoughts, but as long as the blood dripped from the cross to be taken to heaven lost soul have victory because of the cross.

The Cross, which is Jesus, defeated Satan then and the victory from the cross is defeating him now. This is the reason we can pray for the lost, hurting, sick, the children because of the victory we have in Jesus. Because of the cross that bore sins of humanity I have victory. During the forty days leading to the cross we pray for the children as Jesus prayed a prayer for us the garden. There is nothing above the cross, Jesus did the finished work with victory. Jesus wants each of us to know, He is the Rock. Sometimes we act as if He is not. Sing in celebration because Jesus lives. Sing a song of joy because Jesus made the cross victorious because He is the Victory in the storms. He is the Victory in the valley. He is the Victory as we climb from the valley of despair to the mountain of victory.

Compassion

Whoever causeth the righteous to go astray in an evil way, he shall fall himself into his own pit: but the upright shall have good things in possession. Proverbs 28:10

Sometimes I think my heart is too compassionate. When I see the needy, I want to help them. When I see the hungry, I want to feed them. When I hear of the prisoners, I want to visit them through mail. When I see the sick, I care about them with food and cleansing of their surroundings. When I see children hurting, I want to protect them. When I hear of a mother wanting to abort her baby, I fight for this child's life through prayer.

As I was pondering these things over in my mind, I began hearing what the world says about helping others and giving of yourself and finances, remember, you haven't truly given if it didn't cost you something. Each time I go to the nail shop, I buy this special meal from the restaurant next door that I love, and I buy a plate for each person in my neighborhood who can't cook for themselves now. The world tells me I shouldn't do this, because my money may become low, and I need to keep it for the days ahead. But I pondered these things in my heart and the Holy Spirit brought this to my remembrance, as followers of Christ, we must do as He did when He walked the earth. Jesus stored nothing up for Himself of earthly and material things that will fade. Then I began thinking about the trees and how they warn each other when an attack is coming against them, and even the vultures share.

Contemplating these things in my heart, I do even more now. And the beauty of feeding the ones who can't cook for themselves and have no one to come with a hot meal, I rejoice because my manicurist and his wife places each order each time for me, and the restaurant gives even more on the plates because of them. It's always enough for two people for two meals. Each one in Nail Theology knows the reason for each bag I walk out with each time I'm there. They even help to get the bags in the car. When I told them that one of the ones, I carried a hot plate to died, they were saddened also, even though they didn't even know her. But they knew how they have helped with the plates these many months that she needed help... So, I rather have Jesus and His approval than silver or gold. But the great news about it is, I never go lacking for anything...God blesses me with overflow. I saw the overflow when John was in rehab.

Memories

Tell ye your children of it, and let your children tell their children, and their children another generation. Joel 1:3

When I see certain things in nature, they carry me back to the memories of my childhood. This time of year, all the harvests of the year were stored and began to be used for a long cold winter. I loved when the potatoes would rest in the hot ashes in the fireplace with the aroma filling the senses of our nostrils. As the peanuts would roast in the oven anxiousness awaited the handful each child would get as our parents talked, with me next to my mother's hip, as Uncle Remus fables played on the radio. But the popcorn on the cob was my favorite. I would carry my greasy bag of popcorn to school and trade it for pecans. Strange what was plentiful for me was scarce for others, and vice a versa. My trading partner had trees of pecan that I loved, and my parents had rooms of popcorn in the barn, all the children had to do were walk to the barn and get armloads of popcorn.

Thinking about it now, as I watch the leaves fall from the trees and see the hawk flying low to catch its prey, I realize I have always seen God through nature and didn't realize it. I never ever imagine how God would use the things that always got my attention as a child, that He would use to heal my years of insecurities. And to write about it today to bring encouragement to others that each person is fearfully and wonderfully made. As I looked at the steam coming from my rooster pitcher this morning, I smiled as my mind rushed back to the times God was preparing me as a child.

During my childhood I would walk the yard and pasture enjoying the beauty of my surrounding, and hearing and seeing God, but I didn't even know it. I have all way sang as I walked in the pasture and barnyard, and one sunny late afternoon a fisherman (our pastor) on the pond heard me singing in praise with my surrounding. When he finished fishing, he walked to my grandparents' porch where my parents were sitting and told them of the gift of their fifth child. I was called from my wandering to the porch and told, (not asked) that I would be singing in church on that

Sunday. A fisherman caught me, and he would take me to all the youth gathering to sing. Singing the joy and goodness of the Lord because He created me to be who I am, and I am still searching to see more of His beauty surrounding me.

Lemon Day

Believe ye that I am able to do this? Matthew 9:28b

Life gives each of us 'lemon days. Days when you wake up, you are already tired; your spirit is worn from praying against the enemy taking a life of a person God have shown you in a vision/dream; your feet are achy as you make the bed; the phone is ringing; the dog is whining; but you know, God has given man a plan for lemons, and each is good...

Everyday has its challenges, and everyday has its blessings. Matter of fact, I wanted to sleep later this morning, but the sun was peeping through my blinds as to say, "Get up and give thanks to our Creator for this new day." I covered my head, but that didn't work because the Holy Spirit reminded me of the name in my dream, and who this person was! I instantly pushed my 'lemon day' aside and took up prayer. I realized the reason for my lemon day, it was for me to put my mind on my 'whoa it me' and forget about praying for the protection of this person God is using for His kingdom business. Lemon days come to steal what God has ordained for the day. God wakes us to pray, because the devil never takes a vacation day or a holiday break. Furthermore, there are no record in the Scripture which tells us that Jesus took a holiday from praying on the Fourth Watch of the night. Jesus even saw the storm on the sea as He was praying coming against the disciples, and He walked on the water to calm the storm. Matthew 14

So, I'm asking as His disciples asked, "Teacher, don't pass us by." God made all fruits to be helpful and useful for man in its own way. Some are sweet, some bitter, some sour and tangy, but there's one thing about it, God knows/knew the enemy would distort the beauty of His fruits, as he tries to misuse the fruits of the spirit Galatians 5:22-23. To give hate for love, bitterness for joy, sourness for kindness, tanginess for peace, and the list goes on. So today, I decided to have lemonade, my daughter left in my refrigerator.

Taking A Break
They are not of the world, even as I am not of the world. John 17:16

Phones in each hand and silent in the midst of the room. Chargers sought for the dying phones as the TV plays lowly unnoticed by many. Microwaves going as leftovers are warmed for a second and third meal. These are a few of the things taking place in the gathering of the family. After a while God touched the heart of the one, He has called to proclaim His word to step up and turn off the TV, call the gathering together, as the phones are turned off to gain the attention of all in the house.

God is too often forgotten and something not of Him takes residence in the heart during the gathering. "Sorry, Father for making it seem easy for Christians to look like atheist when the atheists supposed to see You shine brighter than the pretty and tasty meal during every gathering."

So, last night from the young to the old were called into a gathering in the family room to give thanks to God for all His blessings and faithfulness. If I fail to proclaim God as my Savior to my household, I have failed. My children and grandchildren know my walk with God, but the mother and grandmother they know as the caretaker, hugger, giver, and preparer of all the special meals they want, had to become the 'feeder of the Word'. Prayer was placed over each one differently from the usual. The usual has changed to the unusual because my desires have changed from the mother, they knew six months ago to the mother having a deeper love affair with my Savior. I pour Him on them through my praise.
My third grandson was introduced to the rising sun praising God as the sun rays danced on each leaf of the trees. As he looked through the window at the sun peeping through, he saw the sun as alive for the first time. I had him turn to Psalm 148 to read the 29 categories of creatures that praise God. He saw the sun differently, as he had that experiential touch of God. My granddaughter, saw prophecy fulfilled when she learned the Holy Spirit told of her birth two years and two days from the date she was born. Down to her name and Hebrew meaning. Sometimes we must see the blessings in order to

truly appreciate God's blessings and favor. My children and grandchildren saw in real time the blessings God brings to this household, because of my love affair with my Savior. The TV and phones stayed off the rest of the night, and conversations and laughter replaced each because God was chosen over the worldly things at the gathering.

No More Putting Jesus in a Box

The fool hath said in his heart, there is no God. Corrupt are they, and have done abominable iniquity: there is none that doeth good. Psalm 53:1

Have you ever really given a thought to the blessings God have given each of us? Or are you taking each one for granted? It's easy to do, which is pride because it's Jesus' stripes which heals us and His blood which keeps us sealed from the enemy's attacks, not we ourselves.

I'm sitting in the doctor office with my husband, and I'm seeing the crippled from some type of illness. Part of arms missing but the person is still concerned for the needs of others. I'm hearing laughter and conversations about children and cats, I'm hearing about the death of a friend, and the one wanting to go to the funeral is worried about having enough gas in the car to go. I'm hearing about a lady who can't stay awake, and the doctors don't know why. As I sit listening and looking, I'm thankful for the blessings of God. I still hear the comments from one of my classmates who never ate anything she thought wasn't healthy, "I woke up one morning and couldn't move. I was in rehab a month which started my other problems."

She said with band-Aid on her face. I thanked God for giving me strength. I know the next day isn't promised, and I'm in God's hand for my protection. I don't know about tomorrow, but I know who's in my tomorrow preparing the way and clearing the path for me to walk in tomorrow. I'm reminded of Exodus 23, God promised when we come before Him at His appointed time, and not to come empty handed He has seven blessings He will give us. He promised the angel will go before us clearing and paving a way through the enemy's blockage. And He promised He will be an enemy to my enemy.

Sickness is an enemy and this is the reason Jesus took 39 stripes for our healing, and He nailed each to the tree. Why do we pass by the healing touch of Jesus to go to man's plan and medicines? I don't know why because I'm guilty of these many times. But I do know Jesus is the Healer. I'm ashamed of hearing man over Him. Each day is a reason to celebrate life, and I'm celebrating today and each day because Jesus lives. I have a friend, Raleigh who celebrates life each day through his paralysis from a stroke, and I have learned from his example to live beyond each day's circumstances.

Praise Songs

"Praise the LORD. Sing to the LORD a new song, his praise in the assembly of his faithful people "Psalm 149:1.

An old Jewish legend says that after God had created the world, He called the angels to himself and asked them what they thought of it. One of them said, "The only thing lacking is the sound of praise to the Creator." So, God created music, and it was heard in the whisper of the wind and in the song of the birds. He also gave man the gift of song. And throughout all the ages, music had blessed multitudes of people."'

I praise God because His creations are rejoicing this beautiful day: The wind is directing the colorful leaves on the many trees in rhythmic movement with the echoing of bells in their heavenly glorious melody. The musical movement of the leaves twirl in dance gracefully in praise with the sounds of heaven. I see Jesus this morning as the beauty of His creations pay reverence to Him in movable praise. The trees are bowing in ballerina movement of grace. The wind is whistling tunes of heaven the ears have never heard yet rejoicing because God has taken time to sing over His creation with heavenly grace, and sweet tones from His heart of love.

The crows' songs of praise rings in the air as they fly high in the sky. The blood moon fades in the distances as it waves hello and goodbye to the sun as it sings its lullaby to sleep until it's time for it to shine again. I feel the song of comfort and joy as the colored leaves flicker in the sun. As the warmth of the sun kisses my face, I feel love caressing me, and I hear Jesus saying, "look, can't you see Me in the trees with their graceful waltz before Me in the musical wind? Oh, can't you hear me in the midst of My creations surrounding you with unfailing love? Love that will never leave you. Love which holds you. Love that guides you. Love which never fades, but grows brighter and mightier the more you receive My touch which calms you? Let your heart long for more of Me. I'm waiting and willing to give you more of Me."

Oh, the love I feel this day of miracle. During the night the

Blood Moon obeyed the commands of God to shine. The lunar eclipse stayed a little longer since its stay about 600 years ago, but it obeyed the movement of God's commands. Can't you feel Him in the sunlight this day? Can't you hear Him singing over you and calming you with His love? Look closely and hear thoroughly the beauty of God's creations all around you, because He is comforting you and speaking to you through each one...

God is Love!

Call Unto Me

Call unto me, and I will answer thee and shew thee great and mighty things, which thou knowest not. Jeremiah 33:3

Too often too many children hear, "You are just like your mama and your no-good daddy! You will never amount to anything!" Each word takes life in the child's spirit as soon as he or she hears man's thoughts of them, rather than the thoughts God thinks of them. (Jeremiah 29:11)

The gifts God created in us are stalled until deliverance comes. Being good enough is a faded hope and an incomplete dream. Too many use their faded hopes to always give even when they really don't want too. Seeking approval sets in and unnatural giving to be seen different from what others see in them becomes a habit of being taken advantage of.

I too have seen myself different from who God created me to be. I have too often worn powered covered glasses of insecurity, when God chose me to be a vessel, He can use for Kingdom business. A few years ago, around ten or so, God sent me and another person to the hospital room of a dying man. He felt he wasn't good enough to come to God and be forgiven. I sang a song "I dreamed of a City Called Glory" and the prayer of salvation was prayed. This man accepted Jesus as his Savior on his dying bed. He died a week later. I was asked to sing this same song at his funeral. I sang the same song in another man's hospital room before he passed, and the man's room next door family heard the song and met me in the room to tell me how it brought comfort to him and the whole family.

Today, was another opportunity to be one of the voices for God here on earth to bring comfort to a lady on her sick bed. She hadn't said much to anyone, she was just lying there looking around when we walked in. We sat a moment without words, then I pulled my chair up next to her and began singing the same song. She looked and then closed her eyes. Then she said, "Everyone has a crown. Sing two more." I did, as she laid there with her eyes closed mouthing the songs. Then a hug and kiss from one of the others with me, she smiled and thanked her for the kiss. A prayer of peace was prayed for her and the home. As I was leaving, her daughter thanked me, but I was thanking God for giving me the gift of song that was taken for granted for too long because of negative comments years before I knew Jesus as the Giver of good things. Every gift is for His kingdom business. Never ever think of God's gifts in you as being Insignificant. Every good and precious gift comes from above, where each of us who follow Christ is seeking to be one day. I'm thankful God took the lock and key from the closet door of my insecurities. I cannot longer hide away from using what God created in me... Are you hiding?

Friendship

Don't you know that friendship with the world is hostility toward God? So, whoever wants to be the world's friend becomes God's enemy. James 4:4

What is true friendship, a smile on your face, a pat on the back, a call every day, a I love you? These are outer actions and mere words. True friendship tells a friend the truth rather than a lie to make them feel better. Friendship cares more about the soul of man than a pat on the back or people's applauses.

Friendship hurts when the friend hurts, cry when the friend cries over the loss of a loved one, pray for him or her as you pray for yourself, wanting the best for them as you want for yourself. Carrying a special dish from your oven rather than buying it from the store when a friend is too weak to do for him or herself.

So, friendship is doing it God's way. To love the unlovable, to pray for the lost, to forgive the so-call unforgivable, to give your best to the unappreciative, to go the extra mile for the hateful, to pray for the ones who dislikes you, to hate what is evil, to confront the liar with the truth, so I'm patterning friendship as I'm following Jesus' example of unwavering friendship.

Jesus looked through the cosmos and billions of galaxies and saw my need for His friendship. He didn't hesitate to come and fellowship with me, I hesitated by choosing to do it my way for too many years, yet He waited on me to maneuver through the thicket I allowed Satan to put there... The key word to this statement is, "I allowed, not him making me, because the only thing the devil can do is to lie to you and make you feel guilty. Today, I'm glad I have a friendship in Jesus. He loved me so much that He looked through the Galaxies and saw that I needed a friend Who knows me by name. Jesus knows each star by name, which are uncountable for us, and I'm thankful He knows me and all my needs. These are the closing thoughts for today that a friend will tell a friend. I found this list of the "Ten Ruled for Happier Living" that friendship offer:

1. Give something away (no strings attached).
2. Do a kindness (and forget it).

3. Spend time with the aged (experience is priceless).
4. Look intently into the face of a baby (and marvel).
5. Laugh often (it is life lubricant).
6. Give thanks (a thousand times a day is not enough.
7. Pray (or you will lose the way).
8. Work (with vim and vigor).
9. Plan as though you will live forever (you will).
10. Live as though you will die tomorrow (because you will die on some tomorrow).

Staying with the Familiar

A man's enemies are the men of his own household. Micah 7:6b

The familiar holds us in the place of God's "No" and let us accept the enemy's "yes, this is the safety thing for you." Accepting the enemy's yes, over God's 'no' is familiar for many of us, and we are putting doubts where faith should be. I'm not excusing myself, because we too often believe more in what we see than what is invisible. The strange thing about it is, we trust the debit card to have money on it, this is invisible. We trust the air that it will fill the lung so we can breathe, it's invisible. So, what do you do when you are facing the difficult decision of putting food on the table, or trusting God's plans and His provisions for you? When you are force to take something harmful in your body, or being threatened with unemployment, do you trust the invisible Savior or a visible foe? Do you walk away from the familiar of depending on man to sign your paycheck, or take the mandatory jab not ordained by God?

It seems easier to take the forced so-called vaccine, but anything forced isn't from God. God doesn't impose on our will; He lets us decide for ourselves. I was saddened by the news that I may be losing my doctor because she's going to refuse taking the so-called covid vaccine forced on her by the government. She's walking away from something she loves and prepared many years to do. I almost cried, but I refused to because I know God provides and this is how it will be for the ones left behind during the rapture. If you don't take the mark, there will be no job or buying food. I was asked to pray for God to turn this attack against the people around. Some can't see beyond the need to pay the house note and putting food on the table, but the Word says, "Blessed is the one who trusts in the LORD" (Proverbs 16:20). I can't see through a wall, I can't see into tomorrow, I can't see how God can take care of paying the house note or feeding me until I was reminded by the Holy Spirit that Jesus sent Peter fishing, and Jesus chose the fish with the golden coin to jump into Peter's net. Peter's bill was paid.

God knows the name of each one calling for His guidance... "He brings out the starry host one by one and call forth each of them by name," (Isaiah 40:26).

So, when we are troubled with decisions of the unseen tomorrow, trust God, because He is able to carry us with all our burdens. He knows each of our needs. So, remember God is the sovereign of the stars, and knows each one by name as He knows our needs. We need to remember also that God prepared a table for us in the presence of our enemy. Not me preparing it! Not the enemy preparing it! But God preparing it because He knows how to shame the enemy's plans against us. So, are the decisions to choose between the familiar or the invisible which feeds me easy? No! No battle is easy when we fight it under our own strength...and no war was won without a fight! But, in each battle there are more on our side than the enemy. We are David against Goliath, Esther against Haman, Moses against the Red Sea, Paul against the snake.

Rainbow Promises

I have placed My bow in the clouds, and it will be a sign of the covenant between Me and the earth. Genesis 9:13

 While in prayer, God gave me this message below.

My life is a rainbow
Filled with God's promises
He remembers each one because
He is the Creator of the raindrops
And Director of each ray of the sunlight
In the Ballroom of many colorful lights
Which dances with each drop of rain as its companion
As God's presence gives harmony to the dance
He is peace dropping beautiful raindrops of His love
As the birds sing His romantic song of His wondrous love
He's the reminder what He made is good
Every time He sees the rainbow of unspeakable colors
He remembers His rainbow promises
His promises flowing over unmeasurable distance
Just as His love and protection have no boundaries
He still remembers from the distance
He will not destroy us by water again
But we destroy ourselves through sins
And fire will be home in the final end
When the rain of troubles come in life
They will not destroy the promise
God made the rainbow as His reminder
And He's reminding Satan too that he doesn't control the rain
Or can stop the rainbow
With the rainbow of God's promises
Rejoicing is due to our Savior for His love
He sees us through the rainbow of His love ... Amen

He Is Mine

My beloved is mine and I am his; he browses among the lilies. Song of Solomon 2:16

"Used toos" are gone. I used to be the youngest baby in the nursery and written in the book of life until I was touched by the lies of the world of who I am and was created to be. I was born free of love and made in God's image with beauty and gifts, until someone told me I was not like the pretty baby born of light skin and curly hair.

I used to be the carefree child with gifts God created in me, until someone told me my gifts weren't good enough; the child next door down talked better, the child down the street spell better, the child on the bus read better.

What about me? I can read, I can spell, my voice is different because I pronounce my words differently.

Can't someone help me to speak better, can't someone help me to spell better? Won't someone say a kind word about me?

I used to be the child who ran free like the wind, until someone told me the wind isn't real, the moon has a man in it, the nights have danger lurking in it.

Then the use to be freedom to play at night turned into fear of the night, and blindness to the wind of God's Breath... Fear grabbed my carefreeness and locked it away from me.

The sun shining in the rain was Satan whipping his wife, but he had no wife, but I believe he did because the world told me so...

I used to have spiritual eyes, until someone told me only the ghost from the dead appears.

I used to be speaker of the truth until someone told me a white lie was alright. My use to led to hope deferred until someone told me who I am. This happened when the Holy Spirit took me by the hand and walked me to Jesus so He could fill my heart with His love, and now I am His, and He is mines. I was a child lost in time but now a child of the Great I AM where use to died.

The liar in this life will make you feel hopeless when you feel down. He reminds you of your failures, and your stumbling from years gone by, but we must realize this is the only thing he can do is lie and place guilts on us. The strange thing about it is, we too often listen to lies when we feel weary, and we overlook what God says in Word. Why? Because the enemy imposes his will on us through condemnation and half trues. He hits us in places of weakness and insecurities to try to get you to turn to something that will give "red eyes" rather than the Word and promises of God. Jesus is interceding in heaven for us now with a 'rainbow' around His head. When Jesus stands in the gap for each of our mistakes, the Father sees the 'rainbow' and remember His promises.

However, this is the good news, the enemy only knows your weary feelings when you speak to them, he doesn't know your heart or thoughts. The second good news is, God will always put the least likely person in your path to bring a word and ray of hope when you feel all hope is gone. I become weary with the lack of care and love for the hurting from the Christians occupying the pews in the wooden and clay churches. Jesus said to pray for our enemy, He prayed for each of us before He went to heaven. We were Jesus' enemy because of our sinful ways. But, as usual when my weariness comes because of a rejected hurting soul, the Holy Spirit always speaks to me through my surrounding. This morning, as I was seeking Him for the needs of a hopeless child, He showed me a limb on the tree with green leaves on it among all the fading and dying ones. I smiled because God has spoken..." There's hope in the midst of hopeless when you keep Me first." With Christ Jesus hope for a brighter day never fades, because He wears the 'rainbow' around His head to remind the Father of our needs.

In God's Presence

Where can I go to escape Your Spirit? Where can I flee from Your presence?
Psalm 139:7

In the stillness of God's presence, you can hear the leaves falling orchestrated by the breath of God through the wind. The wind moves the many Instruments in God's Orchestra of His Creation in unusual and marvelous ways. Can't you hear Him singing a lullaby for your rest and peace in the beauty of the day. The sun warms up each instrument of creation to be in harmony with the dancing of the leaves in twirling movement of the wind. I can't see the wind, but I feel it. The instruments of God's creation bow and obey where the wind leads them. The Holy Spirit is the wind beneath my wings. He comes with the wind of peace to calm me in the storms. The wind which blows upon me when the waves of life are raging.

Are you in the storms? Ask the Holy Spirit to breath upon you as you set in His presence. You don't need to sit in the wind, He is the wind. You don't need to hear the music of the falling leaves; He is the music. You don't need to beg Him to come, just welcome Him, and He will come. You don't need to let the sunshine on your face, He is the Sunlight in your day. Spider webs obey His touch as they float in the wind. The leaves obey Him as they change to fall colors man can't paint. The vastness of His creation and the coloring of each flower and leaf on the trees are too vast for man, and no factory can make enough paint. As John said of Jesus, "every book in the whole world could not contain what Jesus did while He walked the earth." Why let your heart be troubled when God is the only One who gives a spider web a womb of His beautiful-one-of-a-kind creation. I sing because I'm happy and blessed to be one of God's one-of-a-kind creations. You are one of them too!

Love Affair

How lovely is Your dwelling place, LORD of Hosts. Psalm 84:1

The sun is shining, and the breeze is cool, what a beautiful day to praise the Lord. The frost covered the housetops, and the chill of the wind caressed my skin with a cold chill this morning, but I saw and felt God giving life to the morning and welcomed His creation to for-take of His breath of life. Oh, how thankful I am to be awaken by the kiss of life from the Lover of my soul. I find myself falling deeper and deeper in love with Jesus, and the deeper in love with Him I become the more I desire to serve Him. Falling in love with Jesus is the only falling I will not try to keep myself from doing. The more I fall in love the more I forgive my enemy. The more I fall in love the more I let God guard my mouth and watch over the door of my lips so I will not speak words to harm someone. The more I be quiet from the enemy's rebuked. The more I fall in love, and the more I'm willing not to say anything to make someone stumble.

Each day I'm awakened with a kiss of life from my Savior, so I dress myself to indulge in another day of a love affair with Jesus. I awaken each day as if it's my first date with God, because there's something brand new to taste and see with Him. I smell His one of a kind fragrant, I feel the kiss of love on my face, I hear His song of the morning to arise, I dance with Him as soon as my feet touch the floor. Oh, I'm in love with Love and want Him never to leave me.

Since love have swept me off my feet each time we meet, I long never to be apart from Him. The deeper my love, the less I fear tomorrow. The sweeter His touch, the less I depend on man for my needs. The tenderer His arms of love around me, the less I doubt who I am in His sight. I'm His humble servant seeking a deeper love affair with my Savior so one day I will be wearing the wedding dress made from my obedient and righteous walk with Him. I am in love with the One who will never disappoint me or reject for another. This is my song of praise this new day of a many of days love affair.

Guard My Lips

"Set a guard, O LORD, over my mouth; keep watching over the door of my lips."
Psalm 141:3

David thanked God for putting a guard over his mouth and kept watch over on his lips in Psalm 141:3. Wow, is my only word for this! David was allowing God to have His way and control over his words, because he had given all his needs to Him. Thinking about this, I'm having a renewed heart, and my thoughts go to the uniqueness of our bodies made by God. He has everything in perfect order, and all man can do is be at awe of God's amazing wonders in each of us. No matter how smart man is he can't make a world or human with feelings of love over hate, care over hurt, peace over despair, heart of passion over weariness. I was told today by a caring friend that God has given me a heart of caring and compassion as a gift. So, I see we give gifts of God's love when we show compassion to the downtrodden and the ones feeling forgotten by society. When you just think of God's love, we can see it so clearly when we think of the human body composed of more than one hundred trillion cells. Only God can do this.

While water penetrates the skin outwardly, it cannot penetrate it inwardly. The bones are capable of carrying a load thirty times greater than bricks will support. The liver breaks up old blood cells into bile and neutralizes poisonous substances. The blood ten or twelve pints of a syrupy substances that distributes oxygen and carried away waste from tissue and organs and regulates the body's temperature. The heart weighing less than a pound, it's a real workhorse. On the average, it pumps 100,000 times every day, circulating 2,000 gallons of blood through 60,000 miles of arteries, capillaries, and veins. So, Lord, "I praise you because I am fearfully and wonderfully made" (Psalm 139:14). God made us beautiful and unique by His hands, so Lord guard my mouth and keep watch over the door of my lips so I can praise and thank You for Your amazing creation You created in me, rather than complaining. Why should my heart me weary when Your hands made me not man? Thank You Lord!

Word Fulfilled

When I became embittered and my innermost being was wounded, I was stupid and didn't understand; I was an unthinking animal toward You. Psalm 73:22

I've seeing more and more how The Word of God is being fulfilled. The wicked will come to their knees and God hears the cries of the righteous. I'm seeing the ones who have abused the ones who loved them are alone now and under the hand of the one once rejected. I'm seeing the one who used a loved one like a maid now wanting to die because the maid is not able any longer and gone from home. I'm seeing the one who looked at pornography and rejected prayer now wanting a touch from God just to breath. I'm seeing the abuser now lacking the abused.

I'm seeing the one who used racial slurs now hope the one called names will bring a meal. I'm seeing the one without compassion needing compassion. I'm seeing the ones who cherished and worshiped material things finding each as a burden to use. God opens the pages of life to show us His Word in action, but more so, His Word as true. His heart pours out for each soul because Jesus died for each of us. God knows how to soften each heart to save the one's thinking life is in their hand and Jesus is forgotten and rejected as the Giver of each breath. In lowness, looking up is the only answer to our needs and God will put someone in our path to lead us to Him. Life is precious and short and there is no time to waste on wickedness, and thinking you need no one. Even if you have riches, riches can't buy a loving hand to wipe away the tears of pain.

Riches only buys a hand that only last until the money runs out. God smiles when we follow Him, because when this life ends on this side, I want my step into eternity to be sweet in God's sight "Precious in the sight of the LORD is the death of His godly ones." Psalm 116:15. So when you think the wicked is having their way, God is laughing because He knows their end.

Planted in God's Soil

And if a righteous person is saved with difficulty, what will become of the ungodly and the sinner? 1 Peter 4:18

We, as followers of Christ Jesus are planted like trees in the forest of the world. Some may waver in doubts, worries and fears, and follow the roots which mislead. But some are rooted in faith, trust and truth because their seed chose the right soil to be nourished from.

There's a stream of clear water in the midst of the forest awaiting the roots of the trees to drink from its clear living water. The invitation is opened to each tree. However, some of the trees seek to drink while some are too afraid to let their roots go deeper because seeds of the 'lie tree' has been planted in the midst of the forest by a bird of prey. Some of the trees who leaves once trusted God are fading because their roots chose to seek them drank from the lie tree that is spread among the forest once of truth only. "There's a better life for you than this. Try this water from the lake of fun." They say, and many roots followed. Following the lie that there's a better life apart from the root of their Creator, many believed. More leaves faded and the limbs become runner of lies like vines and vines of an unruly bush without a purpose or harvest. Many trees believed the liar over the Creator of the forest and losing their roots to drying rot fitted for the fire.

When the storm came and the wind blew against the trees, the leaves blew off, the bark peeled, the vines sought a place to anchor but there were none! They had chosen their master without power to save only to destroy. The trees bent and fell under the pressure of every lie they had believed and received as truth. Wonderfully, the trees of faith and truth rooted and drinking from the clear living water stood unmoved in the wind, leaves still hanging on, bark still intact, and roots deeper as each held to the promises of their Creator to be their shelter in the storms. But, having the love of the Creator feeding them, when the trees of doubts and fears cried out for help and needed a friend to help them through the storm, each tree drinking from the clear living water gave a helping limb and helped to repair their broken limb and shattered leaves.

As I awoke this morning the Holy Spirit poured in my spirit how Christians are the helping hands, He uses to repair the broken believer. We are each a tree in the Forest of God's kingdom business. Jeremiah 17:7-8 reminds us of who we are in the kingdom of God. "But blessed is the man who trusts in the LORD, whose confidence is in Him. He is like a tree planted by the waters that sends out its roots toward the stream. It does not fear when the heat comes, and its leaves are always green. It does not worry in a year of drought, nor does it cease to produce fruit." Which fruit are you bearing, because times will end when God remove our vine from the Root to be planted in the River of Living Water in eternity?

Listening

Speak, for your servant is listening. 1Samuel 3:10b

Listening to other people's opinion when you have already asked the Holy Spirit is like putting ice cream between a hot hamburger. The ice cream melts before you can taste the smoothness of its creamy goodness. It's amazing how we allow our ears to hear the enemy's voice over God's after we pray. What's up with this lack of faith? We just prayed wasted words watered down by a flash flood of disbeliefs. It's also amazing how we think our visible hands can do more than the invisible hands of God's. This is the reason I try to walk a repentant life, so I can ask for forgiveness when I get in God's way.

I think about Peter wanting to please Jesus his way, but Peter's way wasn't Jesus' way. Jesus knew what was in Peter's heart, and He knew Peter had a heart of obedience and service to Him. But first, Peter had to move self out of the way and put Jesus at the center of his decisions. Yes, we stumble but God catches us before we fall and break. God in His amazing way will allow us to be burdened with only what we can bear but will not let us break because of His promises. "Come to Me, all you who are weary and burdened, and I will give you rest. "Matthew 11:28

Psalm 31:15 tells us that times are in God's hands, so He knows how long it will take for us to walk through the valley of burdens. God knows when we are able to stand in times of chaos and when we can't. So, either we trust Him or ourselves, and rest assure, when we trust ourselves over God we will crumble like dry bread and fail. Under our own strength tiredness, stress, weariness, blindness to God's plans become house guests rather than the presence of the Lord. Trusting God with my tomorrows gives me time to enjoy today. Closing out the voice of the enemy gives me peace that tomorrow is already taken care of. Closing my eyes to rest in God's presence lifts the blinders of hope deferred. So right now, is the time to say yes once more to God's plans for tomorrow since He's already there preparing the way and blocking the enemy from putting immovable mountains of despair in my way.

Winds of the Morning

The wind blows where it pleases, and you hear its sound, but you don't know where it comes from or where it is going. So, it is with everyone born of the Spirit.
John 3:8

The wind is blowing, the Corinthian bells are singing, the clouds are hovering in still grayness, the birds are silent, the chicken pecking in the wet mowed grass, and I'm watching as God directs His creation as each obeys. Sitting at my table in stillness with my cup of coffee watching the lower limbs on my huge oak tree bow to the ground under the command of the wind. This still day, I'm pulling closer and closer to Jesus' breast to hear His heartbeat beat with my heartbeat.

All I want is more of Jesus and to see Him rather than the troubles of the world or hear the cries of the hurting especially the children. I'm seeking to move to the time when Jesus matters more than anything else. I think of Stephen in Acts 6&7, he put his walk with Christ first, and heaven opened for him to see Jesus standing next to the Father. Now, I'm reflecting on the true story of Josepf, one of the heroes of faith during the Communist reign in Romania. The secret police interrogated and intimidated him to the point he fell on his face and cried out to God, "God, they are destroying me. I cannot take any more." Josepf said, "I think I heard the voice of God saying to me, 'Josepf, Get up!'" Who are the secret police compared to the One who sits on the throne of the universe?"

He got up from the interrogation with a new sense of fear, not man's fear, but a reverence and holy fear for God himself. Too often, people will call us stupid as the secret police did Josepf when he chose Jesus over fear. Same when we choose God's way over what seems right to man. Yesterday, was a new revelation for me to choose a reverence of holy fear of God by allowing Him to hold John in His hand because my hands are too small and arms too short to reach him from home. When Jesus matter more than any other thing, my life isn't my own but God's. I'm free, truly free to walk without chains of worries and doubts, fears of what if, blindness to God's plan, I'm free to choose according to God's will not mines. I can hear Jesus say, "Not My will, but Your will be done." Walking in freedom from man's opinions I can truly say, Father, let Your will be done. I'm willing to give what and whom I love to You!" The truth is, I'm giving to God what wasn't mines anyway.

So, freedom opens the eyes to see that nothing belongs to me, not even my life because it's God's breath which breathes through me as the wind brings songs of heavenly joy of the gifts of love from above.

Only God's Way

For I, Yahweh your God, hold your right hand and say to you: Do not fear, I will help you. Isaiah 41:13

My way is not God's way. But His way should be my desire. Too often we quote the Scripture from Psalm 37 "When we delight in the Lord, He will give us the desires of our hearts." How often we abuse this Scripture thinking the human way rather than God's way. Think about this, what if I desire the winning of a billion-dollar lottery ticket. I should win it, right? This is the fact; God isn't into gambling so it's not His will. Gambling depends on luck which is a lazy man's religion. God wants us to delight in Him so He can delight in us. Each day is a new challenge, but God promised to go before me and be my rear guard.

So, I ask God to go before each day, because the visits are getting harder for John because he wants to come home so badly, but just because he wants to come so badly doesn't mean it's time for him to come. God is using people to pull out of him the things he wasn't doing before rehab, so God is speaking if I listen! As we sat in his room doing devotion today, I could see even clearer that it's not God's desire for him to be home yet. So, I sat in my chair and prayed aloud, "Father, I don't understand the things you put on us. Then I repented and said, "No, you are not the giver of sickness, you are the giver of healing. So, you hadn't put anything on me, You are strengthening me as I walk through the fire. Be my shield and wall of faith as Psalm 91 tells me. Amen.'"

Each day I write what the Holy Spirit speaks to me. Hopefully, this healing journey with John will help others when faced with trusting God when it seems as if the fire is hotter than the day before, or the storms are raging when you are seeking sunshine. I do know this one thing, trusting in God can't be washed away, burned away, drown away, or pushed away when we stand on the Rock. Remember you can't sink through a rock, only sinking sand. So today, I decided to take my faith from sinking sand and put it back on the rock where waves only can cleanse it with each tide, not wash it away. I'm cleansed of 'what if' of tomorrow...to proclaiming I know who hold tomorrow, and it's definitely not doubts and fears.

Sounds of Trouble

I will act for My own sake, indeed, my own, for how can I be defiled? I will not give My glory to another. Isaiah 48:11

Troubles sound like horseflies, they are loud, sneaky, and painful when they sting, but there's a solution to the attack. Flyswatters, newspapers, and medication for the sting. However, even with the solutions other horseflies will come to attack, same with troubles, but it's how we handle each problem. Now, when I knock down a horsefly from the ceiling, I stump on it until it's dead. You can't leave a horsefly half alive because it will sting again...same with a half-corrected problem. Now, my porch is my favorite place to write because I hear and see God in His creations. Also, I have had Bible study, baby showers, salvation meeting, weekly services...etc. on this porch. But today with all the phone calls coming in for prayers from children running away from home, marriages breaking up, parents devastated over a child's suicide, to seeking counseling, and prayers were needed to cover each.

As I stood looking at the porch from the mailbox, my thoughts began to run with this question: am I doing enough? Where is the Church for the broken spirit people to run to for help. People are screaming..." Help me! I need someone to listen and hear! Where are You God? I can't seem to see Your light in the people I meet! Shine on Me God, I need to see how You look! Help!" This is the reason I welcome the ones who come to this porch with a smile. One young man said this morning, "I need to come by your house for some of that holy wine(communion) and oil. I haven't eaten in days!" "Come on and get some, you are welcome to it!" was my reply.

My heart was saddening with the phone calls of many needs. And then I realized that my mind and time have been spent on thinking about John's needs and how he feels, rather than allowing God to do what He does best, take care of us when we allow Him to do so. Did God tell me to stop doing what He called me to do because John is in rehab? No! This is the reason it's called rehab so we can get better, and God have added others to my daily devotionals since I decided to do it His way...Putting John on the altar because Jesus was the 'Ram in the Bush.' All we need to do is just trust God's plan. Pray for the children, many see no hope of a better day ahead.

Also, I asked God for forgiveness again when I asked where are You God? He is at the same place when I received Him as my Savior. In heaven watching over me and interceding for me.

Blot Them Out Lord

Turn Your face away from my sins and blot out all my guilt. Psalm 51:9

Lord blot out all my transgressions is part of my prayer for this day. Thinking you can and will get away with sin is like 'Blindness in a sawmill' you are in constant danger. Isn't dying before you confess your sin dangerous? The crimes and sins we are caught doing in the natural we go to court and sentenced to prison. The debt is paid, and we are not held accountable for it any longer. But the debt isn't paid in the heavenly realm if we haven't confessed our sins to God and asked for forgiveness. Each of our unconfessed sins are still new in the Book of Remembrance.

God knows our sins because He was seeing our lying, adultery, stealing, murdering with gossip, etc....as we did them. Many people rage in anger before they die, many can't find peace when their minds get older, some cry out in their sleep and are afraid to go back to sleep.

I remember in 2004 the Holy Spirit brought to my remembrance every lie I had told, every person I owed, every sin I needed repentance, every person I disliked, matter of fact, everyone I hated. So, for almost a year and maybe a few years I confronted the ones I had lied to and asked for forgiveness. I called the ones I literally hated and confessed, and love poured from my heart with each call. I wrote cards of confession to the ones I owed money and paid back the loan with interest. I wrote cards to the ones who owed me and forgave their debts. I asked forgiveness of the ones I had talked about. Each person the Holy Spirit brought to my remembrance I did what He directed me to do. I realized God had me to blot out my sins/transgressions with confession, restoration, and forgiveness.

Afterward, I was delivered of fear, and I no longer had to take a sleeping pill to sleep. I no longer was afraid to ride or drive at night, I no longer checked my doors during the night, I no longer needed a night light. I was free! Then I began having open vision, hearing voices from heaven, seeing the glory of the Lord and a glimpse of heaven. March 2007, God called me to preach His Word, and I didn't hesitate but a moment because I was familiar with the Father's voice. Now I see God purged me through the confession of my sins so my path would be clean, and the enemy would have no hold on me. I have seen too many sick because they refuse to confess their sins even if they were yesterday or years ago, they are still new before the heavenly throne today. Are your hidden sins worth your health and salvation?

Plans For My Life

For I know the plans I have for you "this is the LORD's declaration" plans for your welfare, not for disaster, to give you a future and a hope. Jeremiah 29:11

Everything I planned on the hoe in the fields as a child, God have blessed me with...and I humbly thank Him. I visualized a white house with picket fence and a beautiful yard. Traveling wherever I wanted to go, and God have blessed me to go to places I desired to go and many more I didn't dream about. I wanted an open house with many windows because I like the sunlight to fill each room. God blessed me with this also. I like the simple things like walking in the meadow with wildflowers covering my feet. Watching the cows graze in the grass while sitting on the hillside in the warmth of a noon day. Writing what I hear in my spirit and sharing it with others. Watching children play freely in a yard surrounded by angels. Yes, God have blessed me with so much that I don't have room to store them. My house and shortage houses are running over. I'm blessed beyond what I ever could imagine. I think of kings who want more and more, the rich who seek more richest, but how much can you use that you buy? Does it make you happier? You can only drive one car at a time; sleep in one bed at a time; eat one meal at a time.

As I sat thanking the Lord for His many blessings, I began to see also there's only so much you can do at one time. I'm guilty of working until I'm extremely tired. God can't use me torn-out and broken down, so I decided this is a day I'm going into the tabernacle just God and I. I was up most of the night praying for my dear friend who is weak from the flu... And even after being up most of the night I got up at the same time of 6:00am tired and all. Jesus pulled away to rest, so this is a message to me more than anyone else... It's time for a nap on this sunshiny day... and when I awake, I will be rested and happier.

The Holy Spirit is never wrong. He is our Teacher, Comforter, Guide, Wisdom, Strength. He speaks, and we call 'it thunders. Something told me'. He isn't a something, He is the Voice I hear when I need direction. He is the Strength I get when I'm weak. He is the Song I hear when I'm weary. He is the Arm I need when I'm too far away from my loved ones and my arm is too short to reach them with a hug of comfort. He is my Comforter in sadness. But more so, He is the voice I obey even when things sound strange and seem weird. Sunday, three of us stayed after service to write cards to the staff and residents at the rehab. And boy it was a full, full day. We were hungry because we had only had a small breakfast, and each person we called to bring us food was still in church or someplace else. Finally, we got some food, and stopped a few minutes from writing to eat. Eighty-two cards were written and each one of us was 'fit to be tired'!

As I walked in the rehab on Monday one of the nurses met me at the door with a good report. I walked down the hall with all the cards in the suitcase happy to share each one. The staff got their box, and the other boxes went to each resident. Why did I mention the Holy Spirit? Because He is the One who directed us to do the cards and write personal notes in each one. No card had the same note, because the Holy Spirit gave a different message for each individual. Also, earrings of the Tree of Life were added to the therapist's cards. Jamie, one of the therapists held my hand and said, "You don't know how much your note means to me (she didn't read what the card said just the note), it helps me so much going through this hard time. Last year was so hard with the virus that I told my husband if it happens again like last year I'm going to resign. But your cards and words make such a difference and encourages me to go on. I will always remember the Goree's and your time here every time I wear these earrings. You have been put in my path for a reason. Thank you."

How often we forget the pressure of the ones working in the hospital and other rehab centers during this time. Many of the ones in rehab can't see their family because of the virus, and they feel forgotten and abandoned, the staff must comfort them. Many go into depression because their family can't come in to visit, the staff must be the family with a word of kindness. Many become hopeless and stop trying to improve, the staff has to encourage each one. So yes, cards of thanks and gratitude were given to each staff because they are taking on the role of family when the family is not allowed to come. The Holy Spirit used the three of us and Jennifer to give a lovely card with a personal note of encouragement and thankfulness to staff showing love and kindness to the vulnerable. So yes, God knew the plans He had for my life as I stood on the hoe in the fields planning my life, and one part of my life have all ways been showing compassion to the hurting.

Not

He came near Jesus to kiss Him, but Jesus said to him, "Judas, are you betraying the Son of Man with a kiss?" Luke 22:47b-48

There are some things I try not to do: follow up gossip; refuse to hear 'he said, and she said'; pretend to be a friend; say I'm going to pray for someone and don't; put down someone's child; give and then talk about it later; talk about a person when he or she walks out the door; give a Judas hug and kiss. I never want to be like a Judas horse to lead other astray. Everyone who truly knows me knows what you see is what you get. I'm the same each time you meet me, and I don't 'put on airs' as the old saying goes!

Why am I saying these things? Because my prayer life is important to me, and when I pray, I don't just call out words, I seek the ears and heart of God to move on the behalf of the ones I'm praying for. Answered prayers from heaven are more important than my hurt and bruised feelings. Just because someone says something against me or misuses me, I will not run it down, God fights my enemies. You know what? It's their problem not mine. I'm praying for the children on drugs, the children on the street, the children sold and stolen from their home, the child in the womb (the silent voice), the children with wayward parents, the children in the classroom, the children who have never heard the name Jesus. Yes, my prayers are above what someone thinks of me, it's what God thinks of me that moves me!

This is why I ponder the words spoken to me in my heart like Mary. The ones who want to be my friend just to take advantage of the resources God have put in my path God cuts away. If I talk to others about what someone have done to me, I'm allowing Satan to have his feet in my door. If I don't forgive, I'm allowing Satan to have his hands in my door. If I cause someone to dislike the ones who have come against me, I'm allowing Satan to put his whole body in my door and enter the room of my heart. It's not worth my peace and walk with God.

Yesterday, as I was going to the rehab to visit my husband, my cell phone rang, and it was the manager from the radio station. She asked how I was doing and my husband. I told her and thanked her for calling. She said, "This is another reason I called. People are calling in to the station with all the things happening now to the children requesting the recording of your prayer for the children to be played. One lady said, "That lady's prayer for the children is played at the right time." Oh, how tears came in my eyes knowing God is still using a recording I did about three years ago "Praying for the children" and the radio station is still using it as a message to pray for the children safety. Too often we are waiting for God to use us when God is waiting for our willingness to be used. So, I give myself away so God can use me and hear and answer my prayers for the children.

Remembering

Whatever you do in word and deed, do everything in the name of the Lord Jesus, giving thanks to God the Father through Him. Colossians 3:17

Sitting on the porch reminiscing over the times God put people in my path. This morning as the bugs are singing and chimes ringing my mind went back to 1974 when I lived in a small military town in Havelock, NC. God put a lady in my path who treated me kindly. She was a beautician who greased my hair so...that it wouldn't stand up under the pressure of the oil. She invited me to church and me and my family went, and afterward she cooked dinner for the pastor and my family. Saulsberry steak from the frozen pan and heated in the oven was so good. Dessert was a cake from a box I was thankful to have. After dinner in a dark dining room, this lady packed bags of groceries for me to carry home. I was more than thankful, a family of three living off a PFC Marines' salary was needed.

Afterward, this lady offered a plot of land for my husband and I to grow a garden. My husband worked in the garden after work, and it was a beautiful abundant garden. Bearing more than we could eat. I remember the week my daughter and I came home on the bus for a visit. When I was picked up from the bus station by my family, I was carrying three suitcases rather than two because the largest one was filled with tomatoes and cabbage so my mother could make cha-cha. After I returned to Havelock we only picked from the garden once or twice more because this lady's neighbors were invited to share in the harvest. I didn't know anything about canning, but I froze what was gathered. Then winter came and pecan was invading my yard by the hundreds. Each day pecans were picked by my year-old daughter and myself. Pecans were shared and thousands were left on the ground when we moved away. Reminiscing over this time warms my heart because I realized even deeper that God have never left me alone and always have put someone in my path to show His love. Thinking about the lady who fed me when groceries were low, she was old enough for my grandmother because I was only twenty-five, but never offered me anything to drink because she drank heavily, and she trusted me with her secrets. God knew my walk of faith then because He knew the plans He had for my life. After we moved, I never heard from this lady again, but I have never forgotten her kindness when I needed it the most. Today, I find myself extending a kind hand.

So, my morning begins with gladness of God's goodness and mercy. His goodness supplies my needs, and His mercy blots out my sin. So, good morning Holy Spirit...
The sun didn't refuse to shine this cool morning. The trees didn't refuse to hold on to their leaves as the cool breeze blew against them. The birds didn't refuse to sing their morning songs with the rising of the sun. The geese didn't refuse to thank You with their goose song as they flew overhead this clear almost cold morning. The chimes didn't refuse to chime in harmony with the wind. Father, even the weeds didn't refuse to sway when You commanded the wind to touch them.

So, Father, I'm ashamed to say I didn't want to walk out in the coldness of the morning to see Your creations giving you praise this morning, but I'm thankful I did because I don't want the trees to out praise me. Good morning Holy Spirit. Thank you for this glorious day to give You my praise of thankfulness, and the remembers of kindness years past but not forgotten and taken for grant.

Surrounded By Love

Whoever heeds life-giving correction will be at home among the wise. Proverbs 15:31

Standing in my kitchen window enjoying the lovely sights of my yard and flowers...someone fought for my freedom to stand here. A thought of my children danced in my head; their father served in the Marines during the Vietnam war so they could have the best this country could give them. I took my overly warm bath in the bubble bath of my choice. Someone is standing guard against the enemy so I could enjoy it. My grandchildren live in larger homes than I someone, some soldier left his or her home to stand against the enemy so they can live where they want to live. Every freedom, every luxury, education, every going out and coming in, someone, some soldier stood in blood, slept in coldness, ate can food, saw things no one should see for my freedom and yours.

Yet the flag is not respected, the National Anthem is rejected, men rejecting who they are walking in women's dressing room before little girls half erected because someone died for this freedom taken for granted and misused! As I look at the raindrops falling on the grass and the flower's blossoms pointing upward, I'm thankful yet sadden by the many who take their freedom lightly. People are going to jail and losing their jobs because they are exposing the lies for the truth of the many things going on behind closed doors. David Johnson became a whistleblower to expose Critical Race Theory of the Toy Giant Hasbro. He was more concerned about the welfare of the children than getting fired from his job. He was fired because he exposed the attacks coming against the children! The vaccine adverse event reporting system (VAERS), there have been over 400,000 adverse reactions reported to the COVID vaccine. Last week there were 1,918 total COVID-19 deaths in the United States. Last week also there were 2,092 deaths from the COVID vaccines-according to the CDC-linked VAERS website. In California transgender males are allowed to use the same dressing room as the women. They are walking around naked half erected in front of little girls. China buying up American farms.

French police lay down shields join 100,000 protesters marching against vaccine passport. School can require Christian teacher to use transgender pronouns and names. At least 45 Christian Churches set on fire in Canada as attacks escalate.

Yes, I stood looking out my window this morning in thankfulness... No matter how bad things seem we live in the Good News neighborhood of Jesus' love and protection of Psalm 91. Let not your heart be trouble, just stand in truth and refuse the enemy's lies.

I'm learning not to try to prove or apologize about the revelations the Holy Spirit gives me anymore. Over the past year the enemy thought he would gain more Territory and mind of the people, but when evil increases grace abounds. I'm thankful for the time God isolated me (I don't know about you) because He taught me to step out and do more for the kingdom. When I was asked to do the daily devotionals, I almost allowed self-worth to block me because I didn't like the way I looked on camera or my voice. But I knew I had to obey the voice of the Holy Spirit because He had told me to do more, and so I stepped out of my comfort zone. By during so lives have been changed, loneliness turned into seeking to hear what the Lord was saying. Marriages saved, souls coming to Christ, and scales removed from many eyes. The daily devotionals have had thousands of views from someone God trusted to step out because He said so. A smile what I have taken for granted all my life touched someone's pain.

A voice of pronunciation of words different from many got the attention of many across the world...not because of Herticine, but the Holy Spirit shining and speaking through me. Prisoners are writing, sex trafficking victims have been put in my path because I obeyed the voice of the Lord. The prayer list for the children is so large it takes hours to hear what God is saying for each one... Many wants the Bible study materials because they are hungry for the revelations. Then friends have been added because God used the isolation for His glory.

Time is accelerating as Matthew 24 tells us. Come wanting to be fed and learn what is going on during this time because many lives are hanging in the balance and it's each of our responsibility as servants of God to be prepared to warn the ones we meet that Jesus is coming. And I can show you this through Revelation 4 with the sounds in the air.

    This was a word of encouragement from a lady this week I have never met...she heard God in me, not me... "Beautiful I love all of your videos that I have heard wonderful stories thanks for being my friend. May God bless you all in his glory keep telling the world of the God and his blessing. God bless you and all you speak to of God words that is what we all need to hear more than anything this world needs Jesus. Herticine Goree The pleasure was all mine... I have several friends that I want to listen to your messages. I know the Lord is pleased with you."

Unfailing Promises

All these blessings will come and overtake you because you obey the LORD your God. You will be blessed in the city and blessed in the country. Deuteronomy 28:2-3

Are you so focused on what you don't have that you are blind to what you do have?

You have a ticket to heaven no thief can take,

an eternal home no divorce can break.

Every sin of your life has been cast to the sea.

Every mistake you've made is nailed to the tree.

You're blood-bought and heaven-made.

A child of God...forever saved.

So, be grateful, joyful...for isn't it true?

What you don't have is much less than what you do.

A LOVE WORTH GIVING

Feeling overwhelmed? Troubled over a wayward child? Troubled because each day seems dark and gloomy? Troubled over bad reports about your health? Don't be discouraged because God's Word is alive and active and, when it seems as if all have failed, remind the enemy of the Word of God because it never returns void. "Do not rejoice over me, my enemy! Although I have fallen, I will rise; although I dwell in darkness, the LORD is my light." "For no good thing will God withhold from the one who walks uprightly. Blessed is the man who trusts in God." Can't you hear the enemy running because you trust God over troubles?

So, when you pray remember, 'There is no ifs in God's plan'...the devil uses ifs to discourage you from the answers. God moves by faithful prayer. Micah 7:8; Psalm 84:11b

Look Lord

God do not keep silent. Do not be deaf, God; do not be idle. See how Your enemies make and uproar those who hate You have acted arrogantly. Psalm 83:1-2

My friends, do you realize that God is watching us from His throne room? Job says God test us each moment. How are you standing in faith during this moment in time? Which side of the fence are you standing on? You know it's only one side that God approves of, and that's the right side where He stands. Do you know there's no excuses for siding with wrongs no matter who it is you are standing with if it's against the Word of God. Snatch yourself from the fire if you are siding with wrongs. God is watching from heaven to see whose standing for Him. I'm crying because I want to be found worthy of my calling. Worthy to be called a child of the King. Worthy to be a voice God can use to cry out for others in the wilderness of despair. God is watching! Remember this, God is watching even if you think you can hide, God sees everything hidden and revealed!

Know what's ironic? When a person has been diagnosed with a terminal illness people will say, "Well, he has time to get himself together before he leaves here!" Guess what, in that case, we all have terminal illnesses called "sin and death", and each of us has time to get ourselves together before death comes, because each of us will die! We know not the time, repent because death will come if we are ready or not to gather us home...be it heaven or hell!

Foolishness Blinds

I will listen to what God will say, surely the LORD will declare peace to His people, His godly ones, and not let them go back to foolish ways. Psalm 85:8

This Christmas Day of December 25, 2020 is a day of God seeking me as I arose from a warm and safe night's sleep. The children and grands calling to wish me a Merry Christmas, as the sunlight shines through the windowpane as the shadows of the wheel of the windmill dances on the wall directed by the Christmas morning breeze. "Merry Christmas, Jesus! No, Happy Birthday. No, still not the right phrase. Thank You Jesus for coming!" Were the words from my mouth, and love from my heart. The sun pushing the blinds open, so it seemed with its brightness, beckoning me to see its presence this Christmas morn to proclaim our Savior was born and lives, and wanting to be welcome in my heart... Then to my amazing surprise as I opened the blinds, the sun proclaimed in many rays of colors Jesus is not in the manger but lives in heaven and still gives gifts to man.

The sun from my bedroom window this Christmas Morn was beauty of love from above... The sun was telling of Jesus' love this Christmas Day. I have never been more honored to give a testimony of God's goodness than right now. A new friend came by my home the week of Thanksgiving to sit on my porch to listen to the many Corinthian Bells hanging on each corner of my it. I then realized that God was using the bells/chimes and the porch to give hope to many in this time of uncertainties. Many have come to the porch since the virus just to sit. That week I hung two more bells/chimes with the musical note of E and Eb. That afternoon, I received a phone call from a young lady crying because she was so sick from stress, and she couldn't find sleep or peace. I walked out to the porch as the wind was blowing through the bells/chimes, and I asked her to listen and tell me what she heard. She began with, "I hear music. I hear soft music." Then I moved to another part of the porch and asked her what she heard... "I hear music. You are playing music." I moved to another part of the porch and asked her to listen again. She made the same statement but added, "The music is putting me to sleep." I came into the house as she talked in a soft sleepy voice.

Then I told her that I was not playing any music what she heard was God singing through the wind that moved the chimes. Then I told her how much she was loved because Zephaniah 3:17 tells us that God runs us down with His love to sing over us. She was so amazed over hearing God singing through the bells/chimes over her to give her peace she said, "Wow! Wow!" She heard God's voice, and she knew then how much she is loved from above. She went to sleep with the song of the Lord blowing sweet music in her ears. Oh, what a wonderful Savior to look down from heaven and send the wind of His voice to sing through the chimes of His love to the ones needing to hear Peace in the wind... Investing in the Corinthian Bells is one of the best investments I could have made. Souls have come back to Christ by hearing God sing through the chimes. Healing have taken place by the sick and weary hearing the bells/chimes sing the heavenly praises. Even some who crossed over into never ending time heard God's sing through the chimes. Yes, this is an eternal investment with everlasting returns...Thank You, Father for using my porch which sings Your heavenly songs day and night. And Merry Christmas Jesus this beautiful morning You allowed me to see Your love through the sunlight and heard You sing Your love song through the bells which rings of Your unfailing love.

No Other God

I sing about the LORD's faithful love forever; I will proclaim Your faithfulness to all generations with my mouth. Psalm 89:1

There is always a reason why God does things the way He does. The Word tells in Obadiah 15, "For the day of the LORD is near upon all the nations; as you have done, it shall be done to you; your deeds shall return on your own head." Why did the Egyptian throw the Hebrews boys in the Nile River to kill them? Hopi the god of the flooding water of the Nile...was one of Egyptian's gods served. The Nile is known as the water of death. Pharaoh wanted the Hebrew boys killed to keep the promised child from being born. Without a boy, the girls couldn't have a baby of Hebrew blood. The boys were thrown into the Nile as a sacrifice to Hopi the water god of Egypt.

But the Word says in Obadiah 15 that "your deeds shall return on your own head." The way Egypt killed the Hebrew boys by water which came from the water in the womb...the Egyptian soldiers were drowned in the Red Sea...by water, and Hopi couldn't save them. Also, remember the first of the ten plagues was turning the water into blood. Exodus 14:28 says "The waters returned and covered the chariots, and the horsemen, and all the host of Pharaoh that came into the sea after them. There remained not so much as one of them." The Egyptians died by the means as they killed the Hebrew children...by water.

Matthew 7:2 "For with the same judgment you pronounce, you will be judged; and with the measure you use, it will be measured to you." Be careful of your deeds. The amazing thing about God, He has a reason for everything He does. Two in bed, one taken one not...two in the field one taken, one not. During this time the people didn't know there was other parts of the world. Matter of fact, they thought the earth was flat, and when the sun set there, it was someplace else...Jesus knew, so when He said two in bed, one taken one not. He was saying, I may be in bed here because it's night, and one in the field in Japan. When Jesus' returns this will happen at the same time here and Japan. day here, night there. One in bed at night there one working here Why did Jesus said in Matthew 26:53, "Do you think that I cannot now pray to My Father, and He will at once give Me more than twelve legions of angels?"

There was no human force on earth strong enough to take Jesus if He didn't allow Himself to be taken. This is why He later told Pilate... "Thou couldest have no power at all against Me, except it were given thee from above..." (John 19:11). A legion of angel is 6000 angels...12 legions equal to 72,00 angels. Isaiah 37:36 records that a single angel obliterated 185,000 men in one night... "Then the angel of the LORD went out and struck one hundred eighty-five thousand in the camp of the Assyrians. When others woke up early in the morning, these were all dead bodies." So, if a single angel had that kind of power, how much combined strength would there be in twelve legions of angels. Six thousand would be enough to destroy 1,110,000,000 people. Twelve legions were enough combined strength at Jesus' disposal to have annihilated at least 13,320,000,000 people. Thirteen billion which is more than twice the number of people on earth. Jesus didn't need Peter to cut off the servant's ear, He could have destroyed the whole human race...but He chose to die for man's sins.

Jesus told us not to worry. Why? Because God helps the ones the world rejects when He writes the plans for our lives...Leah was rejected by Jacob but chosen by God. The priests of God came from her womb, Levi which the priesthood of Israel came through. From Levi was born Moses, through Moses came the Passover, the Exodus, the Ten Commandments, the Law, the sacrifices, the Holy days, and the Tabernacle...the Promised Land. Through Judah came David. And from David came the royal house of Israel, and Jesus

God knows His plans for us... Why do you trust the world's thoughts of you? The servant of Abraham found the girl chosen by God, Rebekah, at the well where she drew water. God's written plan for her was to marry Isaac, the chosen seed. The servant said, "Please give me a little water from your pitcher to drink (Genesis 24:45-46)." Jesus went to Jacob's well in Samaria (John 4:6). There he saw a woman, and he said to her the same as Abraham's servant had said to Rebekah: "Give me a drink". The Bridal Church of Jesus draws water for Him from His well of salvation and receive from Him the living water of enteral life. Jesus is seeking 'a wife' believers who will respond to His call to leave behind their old life to follow and serve Him, to love and obey Him. Consider the necessary qualities to become the 'Bride of Messiah Yeshua.' Abraham was the father made righteous through faith, Isaac was the son born through the promise, and Jacob was the son chosen through Divine election. Each represents salvation through the Messiah, and through these three, God's covenant was fulfilled. Jesus became the 'ladder' to heaven. John 1:51 "Truly, truly I say to you, hereafter you shall see heaven opened and the angels of God ascending and descending upon the Son of Man." Jesus wants to reveal Himself to His Bride.

My Prayer

As father has compassion on his children, so the LORD has compassion on those who fear him. Psalm 103:13

I haven't written a daily post lately, but I feel the need to write one tonight because it may make a difference in someone's life. I'm writing with tears in my eyes. As I laid in prayer this lovely night, it's a dreary night for a grieving family. As I laid in prayer closing my eyes to sleep the phone rang. The voice on the other end said, "Hertic! What are you doing?" I replied, "Praying." "Good, pray for (she called the person's name) her granddaughter hung herself!"

With my head on my pillow, I wept. And I began to pray again. I asked the Lord to show me what to do to help the ones feeling hopeless. I asked Him to strengthen the hurting family. I wept again and said, "Lord covers the children. Put someone in their path to guide them to You."

The children are falling victim to the enemy. Cities are being burned down while the children are begging silently for help. Computers and cell phones are becoming their parents rather than mother and father having dinner around the table with their children. Hatred is taught rather than love. Jesus is only a Christmas tree ornament rather than the living Savior. Hope is waxing cold for the young…. because coronavirus is the name of the news and fear the anchorperson, the mask an idol god without eyes to see and ears to hear. Jesus is made to look helpless because the doctor tells you what tomorrow holds, and many believe it rather than Jesus' word that we know not about tomorrow.

Hold your children close in prayer because the enemy is waiting for an opportunity to steal them. Put your children in God's hand because He promised nothing can snatch them out of it. I love the Lord because He hears my cry…He answers my prayers because His ears are not too dull to hear my cry…His arms are not too short to reach me and pull me from despair…He is my protection… Psalm 91:4b "His faithfulness shall be your shield and wall." I love Him because He gives us all we need, yet He keeps it hidden until we are mature enough to be grateful for Who we have as our Savior….He calls us friends. God gives us what we need, but we must figure it out through the leading of the Holy Spirit. Prayer is what the children need and each believer being the light which leads them to the table of the healing bread. Jesus is the Bread of Life the children bread never forsaken of His love ye who are weary.

Feelings
Little children, let no one deceive you! 1 John 3:7

If you are feeling down during this pandemic, remember Jesus is with you in the good and bad times. The news gives the reports of the tragedies in the world, but the Good News gives you the reports of Jesus' sacrifice on the cross and defeating the enemy with His blood. The Special Report is, Jesus is interceding for each of us before the Father in heaven now...and His blood is still active and flowing over the ones calling out to Him now. The suicide rate is up 600 percent since the pandemic, so please tell the ones in weariness and fear "Jesus is able. His arm is not too short to reach them, or ears too dull to hear them." He is more than able! He is the Good News that the sickness bows at His name. Use Jesus' name rather than stressfulness.

Have Thine Own Way, Lord! "Lord, it doesn't matter what You bring into our lives, just have Your way with us." Anonymous. We are the clay in God's hands, and sometimes God's 'NO or Wait' are God's way of showing me a flaw in my life. God is the Potter, and He breaks a defective vessel, and then mold my life again in His own pattern. A word from Jeremiah 18:3-6 when he visited the potter's house. "I found the potter working at his wheel. But the jar he was making did not turn out as he had hoped, so he crushed it into a lump of clay again and started over. Then the LORD gave me this message. "O Israel, can I not do to you as this potter has done to his clay? As the clay is in the potter's hand, so are you in my hand."

During times of discouragement, turn to prayer to God so He can show you how He's breaking the defective parts in your life that need remolding, because you are in His hands. Also remember, when He breaks and remolds you, if you are an ex-convict, an ex-whiner, an ex-stealer, an ex-drug addict, an ex-nonbeliever, an ex-all the mistakes of the past. When God remold, you He has X out all the sins of your past. Have Thine own way, Lord! Have Thine own way!
Thou art the potter.
I am the clay.

Mold me and make me after
Thy will,
While I am waiting,
Yield and still.
Have Thine own way Lord...
Have Thine own way!

If you do not allow God to break and mold you, you are open game for the enemy who only breaks without mending.

So, we each, must know this truth from the Word of God, "Not a single person on earth is always good and never sins"(Ecclesiastes 7:20). But it's not an excuse to keep living in sin, since God so freely wants to remold you so you will become an EX-victim of your past... and a new reformed inmate with a testimony, "I once was lost but now I am found. Blind but now I see the bars of sin can hold you bound. Have Your own way Lord, have Your own way."

Lost

This is My beloved Son. I take delight in Him. Listen to Him Matthew 17:5b

I once was lost in sin, but Jesus took me in. Oh, what a Savior! Jesus loves me just as I am. Oh what endless love! Without Jesus I would be a leaf flowing uncontrollably in the invisible wind. My, my, my what deep love! These thoughts came to mind this morning when Jesus brought to my mind the conversation I had yesterday with a man sitting at my table. I met him with love, and I welcomed him to sit at my table with no judgmental thoughts or action. He came to my house two days back-to-back...so to speak. Yesterday, as he sat at my table, he looked at me and asked, "Were you told about my background and what I did?" I smiled and said yes, I was told. But I'm not allowed by God to go into the sea of forgiveness and pull up what you have confessed and repented of to God. God has forgiven you and now your mistakes of yesterday are sealed under Jesus' blood. We are in today so let's go forward.

Big teardrops were welled up in his eyes. Then he told me about his freedom from twelve years of another life of destruction...now ten years of freedom as a new man. Yet a bad day had him bound because he did not know how I would react by knowing about his yesterdays. Fifteen years ago, I asked Jesus to let me feel with His heart...not knowing feeling with His heart meant seeing a person's faults yet praying rather than accusing! Forgiving what I once would have cursed and held to in hatred. Seeing and hating the spirit rather than the person. Yes, feeling with the Father's heart causes you to be quiet rather than gossip... Pray rather than talk. Give rather than keep. Be uncomfortable rather than comfortable when others are suffering. I'm Sleeping while hugging Jesus' love rather than fearing. Awakening early and kissing Jesus with a good morning salutation rather picking up the remote to the TV.

Oh, I'm thankful God shared His heart of love with me...and knowing my mistakes are in the sea of forgiveness and anyone who thinks it's ok to dive in to get them...God sees. I'm free but whoa to them who seek after someone's forgiven sin because Jesus' blood sealed each mistake with forgiveness, and no one has the rights to retrieve not one. If God forgives and forgets our sins when confession and repentance are made who am I to do it my way!

The man left with a smile and wanted to hug me because he was shown God's Word in action... "Forgive other trespasses so we can be forgiven." this is not a request from Jesus...it's a step to the stairway of heaven. I rather do it God's way. Many days afterward he came almost daily and sat on my porch watching the birds feed and listening the song of heaven through the Corinthian Bells. This man became a friend, and he shared many stories of this past with me, and he wept because he was lonely for his family who had rejected him. Rejected because of the wrongful life be lived. No forgiveness from the family was ever given him. He died two months after we met, I wept over his passing, but I knew by a mutual friend that he saw Jesus through our short time as friends.

A Word of Encouragement in Times of Weariness

Trust in the LORD with all your heart and lean not on your own understanding. Proverbs 3:5

My air conditioner unit started malfunctioning during a hot summer week a few years ago. I noticed the house was warmer than usual and one part of the unit never shut off, and also there was a smell of something burning outside I thought. Now, this is how God works, He always have someone in place in your times of need. I called my son-in-law, told him what was taking place, and he told me what to do until he got here. He came in with all his tools, hooked up the unit to test the different levels. Everything seemed clear according to his equipment, but the house became warm again that Saturday night. I sweated through the night, but I made it through even though my pillow was wet with sweat! Some people said after they found my unit wasn't cooling correctly, "Oh, I can't take that!" But too many complain about an air conditioner not cooling on this side, but not living their lives right to keep from going to hell of everlasting thirst and a heatwave a million times hotter. I have ice water on this side.

However, my son-in-law had to come back a day afterward, because a part of the unit still would not shutoff, but it was cooling the house. He found the problems, thermostat and the board. Unfortunately, it was too late to get a thermostat, but God made away. My brother was in Home Depot at that time (5:44 p.m.) and the store closed at 6:00 p.m. He got the thermostat, but he had air conditioner's problems when he got home, so he could not come by my home. Then my unit stopped working completely, because it threw a breaker in the switch box. You know something was very wrong now! No air conditioner working at all. But this is the Good News, God's promise to keep us in the midst of any storms, and storms come in different packages. The home was 85* according to the thermostat, but during the night as I slept, I didn't sweat, I didn't get hot, there was a cool breeze over my bed all during the night. It was as if the air conditioner unit was on. Whenever I felt a little warm, a breeze would cover me. I had to sleep under the bedcovers.

God took care of the unseen dangers lurking in my house and cooled it too. The Board to the unit had burned out, but God made sure the Breaker to it shutoff so there would be any fire.

This is the miracle: God put two men in my path to find the problems; my son-in-law had to go back home, but he made sure my brother knew what to be watchful of before he left. My brother was at my door before I could walk that morning, to put in the thermostat. He found the Breaker had tripped so there would be no fire, and he found the Broad burned out. God protected us from a fire, and He still cooled my house while the unit was being repaired. I didn't know how long it would take, but I know I did not get hot, or I sweated during that time.

So, the next time before you become burdened down in worries, know God has taken care of the unseen things you know not of. Oh, missed picking my Blueberries and walking that morning, but I was too excited and thankful to God for His protection to complain. Tomorrow is another day to walk and someone else picked the Blueberries that afternoon...just saying! Also, the birds sing when the storm passes over, but they are still and know God is keeping them during the storms. How wonderful it is that God gives us examples how to rest in Him during the storms from the birds. Thank You Wonderful Savior.

Sadden

As a mother comforts her child, so will I comfort you; and you will be comforted over Jerusalem. Isaiah 66:13

Yesterday was a sad day for me. This morning feels empty of a passing of a loving friend. Right now, I'm looking at the birds still about their daily routines of flying about from feeder to feeder eating and singing their different bird songs. The sun came up this morning as usual without delay. The dew watered the grass, and the spiders still made their webs as the mosquitoes are doing their best to sting me. So once again, God has spoken soft and clear that He knows the beginning from the end, and He knows the time clock of each of our lives.

Time goes on...it's left up to each of us how we use it. Once again today, I'm observing two different mourning for a passing of a loved one: One mourns with sadness and tiredness because everything human's possible was done to care for a loved one. But there aren't any regrets. One mourns with regrets of not being there for a loved one during illness. I received a thank you card from a man whose mother passed in April thanking me for the card and gift I mailed to him. He had stop going to see his mother. Regrets of yesterday are the only thing he sees now! This is what he wrote in the card, "I didn't know what it means to lose a mother, but now I know. It's a weird feeling, which comes and goes." Condemnation is always weird because there is no condemnation for those in Christ. Don't waste time thinking only of yourself, because there will come a time when you will be by yourself and Satan reminding you what you didn't do when you had a chance. Try to live this life doing God's will so there will be no regrets.

Your Gifts

Everyone who hears these words of mine and puts them into practice is like a wise man who built his house on the rock. Matthew 7:24

No matter the size of the gifts God has given you, none are too small to make a difference in someone's life. Each thing we do under the guidance of the Holy Spirit lives will be changed, even the one He's using.

Over the years I have had the desire to mail cards to the ones sick, in prison, lost a loved one, or just needing a word of encouragement. I also love to take pictures of nature and unusual clouds. And I never knew what I was going to do with them until the Holy Spirit directed me to write a daily message on them. Well, sometimes when you seek praises of man, you will tend to stop doing God's will because you want to hear from man and if he likes what you have done. However, when God says to do something there should never be seeking man's approval.

Today, God showed me this clearly by two phone calls I received. The first call this morning came from a lady who drives trucks long distance, "I haven't received my daily devotional since June 11, 2017, and I forward those each Friday to others." she said. I apologized and sent her each one missed since that day.

The second call came in from a 91-year-old man, "I got my birthday card. I'm 91 and I cried because you never forget me. Your prayers are keeping me here, I will never forget what you do. Say what you say at the end of each card. Say Blessings! I want to hear you say it." Blessings were my reply. Then he said, "Thank you, Herticine! I love you!"

A simple card with 'Blessings' as a closing to a man I have never seen. And a morning devotional to one away from home made a difference in someone's life. Use what God have given you no matter how small, because He knows who needs it and why. If I can help somebody as I travel on...then my living will not be in vain, and neither will yours.

Who Am I

So, Moses said, "Please do not leave, inasmuch as you know how we are to camp in the wilderness, and you can be our eyes. Number 10:31

I'm a Jovial yet weepy person! I'm happy just watching the leaves moving in the breeze...as the sun rest on them. I'm jovial and weep with joy when a soul comes to Christ...I'm jovial when my financial seed/giving becomes a harvest of souls! But I weep when people keep their seeds in their pockets that will remain a seed that never will touch soil to become a harvest. I weep when people beg from someone's else harvest who released their seeds as God ordained. I weep when people resent someone's else abundant harvest. I weep when people don't seem to care about souls because their tongues won't be still with complaining.

This message is just a reminder that serving God is more than saying 'Amen'...serving God is doing all He ask of us including giving to the kingdom of God! I don't need to tell you what you need to confess and repent of because you know better than I do what you are holding inside. Many may say, "God knows my heart." You better believe God knows your heart better than you do, and He knows what you need to repent of too.

Father, go into the tiny corners of my heart and reveal what I don't even know is there. Wash my heart so I can feel with Your heart. And Father, each person who have read this word of the day feel Your touch and hear Your voice through each bird song of the day. Amen...

I am who God says I am.

Herticine Goree